Santa Fe to Taos
Thru-Hike
Pocket Guide

Edition 1.0, May 2025

132 miles from Santa Fe Plaza to Taos Plaza
Over New Mexico's Sangre de Cristo Mountains

Published by The Santa Fe to Taos Thru-Hike,
46 Old Pecos Lane, Santa Fe, NM 87508
SantaFeToTaos.org, contact@santafetotaos.org,
505-660-7072.

ISBN: 978-0-9898682-1-1 (paperback), ISBN: 978-0-9898682-2-8 (ebook)

If you find any errors or outdated information in this book, **please let me know**. I'll send you a small gift as thanks for your time.

Cover photo: Beatty's Trail approaching the Santa Barbara Divide in the Pecos Wilderness, Pam Neely, August 2024. All photographs and maps by Pam Neely.

MOUNTAIN BIKERS: The route described in this book is not intended or good for mountain bikes because 1) much of it goes through a wilderness area 2) at a pace of 14-16 miles per day, you would be doing 1,900-4,800 feet of elevation per day, all at over 9,000 feet elevation 3) the route goes through remote areas and on unmaintained trails that can have considerable blowdown. Go to SantaFeToTaos.org/mountainbikes for your recommended route.

WARNING: Considerable effort has been made to verify the information in this book, but mistakes can slip in. Conditions change. New information becomes available. How something appears on a map or is described in a guidebook can be very different than actually experiencing it in the field.

Hiking in mountainous areas is a high-risk activity. Weather can change quickly. Snow doesn't melt in the highest elevations for months after it has melted in town. Physical activity at high altitude can have medical and physical performance impacts. Trail conditions like blowdown or washouts may slow you down more than expected. Emergency services may not be able to get to you for days or more. This guidebook is no replacement for experience and common sense.

Anyone who uses this guidebook takes full responsibility for their actions and the outcomes of those actions.

TABLE OF CONTENTS

PREFACE

The backcountry described in this guidebook is in a fragile state. As average temperatures rise, forests and wildlife are under increasing stress. This is visible even in the map on the opposite page. The pink sections are burn scars. More than a quarter of the Pecos Wilderness has burned in the last twenty years.

Our presence has impacts. Every footstep, every campsite use adds up. I am keenly aware of this as I publish a guidebook designed to bring more people into the woods.

But our presence can have positive impacts. Every time we have a positive experience in nature, we care about it more. The more we care, the more likely we are to take meaningful actions to preserve it.

If we never see the backcountry, we won't know the experience of wholeness and vitality it can offer. We won't know how it can restore us. Without a direct experience of the wild, we may see it as nothing more than a resource to extract things from. And so, while publishing and promoting this guidebook will have its impacts, I believe it may help preserve these precious, sacred places.

Fortunately, there are things we can do to minimize the negative impacts of our time in the woods. The seven Leave No Trace principles are simple and effective. This is a distilled version of them. Learn more at LNT.org.

1. Plan Ahead and Prepare.
- Learn about where you're going.
- Be prepared for any conditions you might encounter.
- Visit in small groups and at times of lower usage.

2. Travel and Camp on Durable Surfaces.
- Camp at least 200 ft from water.
- Walk in the center of paths, even if they're muddy.
- Stay on existing trails and use existing campsites.

3. Dispose of Waste Properly.
- Pack it in; pack it out.
- Dig a cathole.
- Pack out or bury toilet paper.
- Pick up all trash.

4. Leave What You Find.
Take photos, do a drawing, but leave it so someone else can discover it.

5. Minimize Campfire Impacts.
- Consider not having a campfire.
- Pour two liters of water on a campfire, then stir the ashes.
- Keep fires small. Use wood you can break with your hands.

6. Respect Wildlife.
- Stay far enough away from wildlife that they look about the same size as your thumb.
- Do not feed wildlife.
- Control your dog at all times.

7. Be Considerate of Others.
- Yield to others, especially if they are climbing up a trail.
- Be quiet.
- Be friendly and courteous.
- Bikes yield to hikers and horses. Hikers yield to horses.

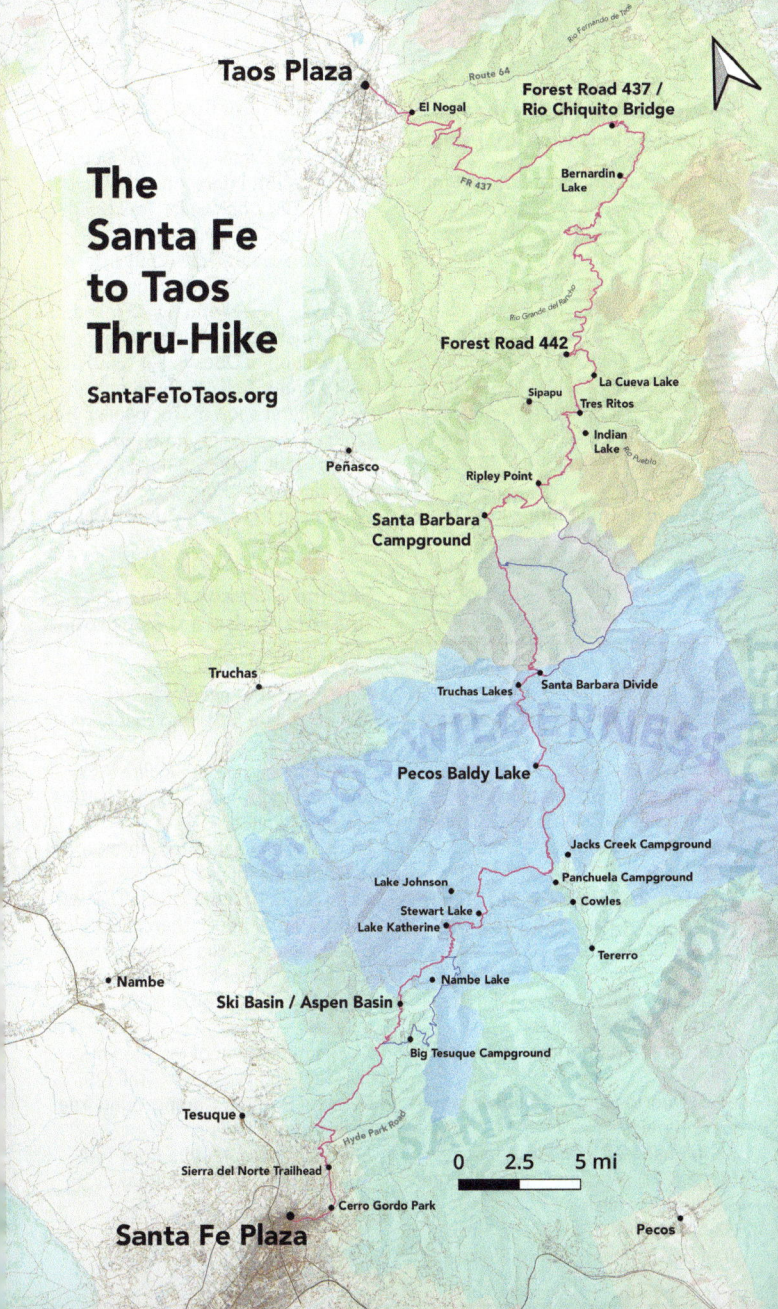

The
Santa Fe
to Taos
Thru-Hike

SantaFeToTaos.org

Taos Plaza

El Nogal

Route 64

**Forest Road 437 /
Rio Chiquito Bridge**

FR 437

Bernardin
Lake

Rio Grande del Rancho

Forest Road 442

Sipapu

La Cueva Lake

Tres Ritos

Indian
Lake

Rio Pueblo

Peñasco

Ripley Point

**Santa Barbara
Campground**

Truchas

Truchas Lakes

Santa Barbara Divide

Pecos Baldy Lake

Jacks Creek Campground

Lake Johnson

Panchuela Campground

Cowles

Stewart Lake

Lake Katherine

Tererro

Nambe

Nambe Lake

Ski Basin / Aspen Basin

Big Tesuque Campground

Tesuque

Hyde Park Road

Sierra del Norte Trailhead

Cerro Gordo Park

Santa Fe Plaza

Pecos

0   2.5   5 mi

ROUTE SUMMARY

Section 1: Santa Fe Plaza to Santa Fe Ski Basin (20.1 miles)

S1-1: Santa Fe Plaza to Patrick Smith Park. 1.4 miles.

S1-2: Patrick Smith Park to Arroyo Polay Trailhead via Cerro Gordo Park. 1.2 miles.

S1-3: Arroyo Polay Trailhead to Sierra del Norte Trailhead. 1.8 miles.

S1-4: Sierra del Norte Trailhead to Little Tesuque Creek / Juan Trail (Trail 399). 3.4 miles.

S1-5: Little Tesuque Creek / Juan Trail (399) to Winsor Trail (254). 1.8 miles.

S1-6: Winsor Trail (254) / Juan Trail (399) intersection to Winsor Trail (254) / Chamisa Trail (183) intersection. 3.25 miles.

S1-7: Winsor Trail (254) / Chamisa Trail (183) intersection to Winsor Trail (254) / Borrego Trail (150) intersection. 1.84 miles.

S1-8: Winsor Trail (254) / Borrego Trail (150) intersection to Forest Road 102. 1.9 miles.

S1-9: Forest Road 102 to Winsor Trailhead at the Ski Basin. 2.9 miles.

Alternate route: Tesuque Peak

Section 2: Santa Fe Ski Basin to Pecos Baldy Lake (26.2 miles)

S2-1: Ski Basin / Winsor (254) trailhead to the Y. 2.4 miles.

S2-2: The Y to Puerto Nambe. 2.2 miles.

S2-3: Puerto Nambe to Lake Katherine. 2.8 miles.

S2-4: Lake Katherine to Winsor Ridge (271) / Skyline Trail (251) intersection. 3.6 miles.

S2-5: Winsor Ridge (271) / Skyline Trail (251) intersection to Skyline Trail (251) / Cave Creek Trail (288) intersection. 2.9 miles.

S2-6: Cave Creek Trail (288) / Skyline Trail (251) intersection to Cave Creek (288) Dockweiler Trail (259) intersection. 3.3 miles.

S2-7: Dockweiler Trail (259) / Cave Creek Trail (288) intersection to Dockweiler Field and rill. 4.1 miles.

S2-8: Dockweiler Field and rill to intersection of Dockweiler (259) and Jack's Creek Trail (257). 2.5 miles.

S2-9: Intersection of Dockweiler Trail (259) / Jack's Creek Trail (257) to Pecos Baldy Lake. 2.6 miles.

Alternate route: Puerto Nambe to Spirit Lake to Winsor Creek / Winsor Trail

Section 3: Pecos Baldy Lake to Santa Barbara Campground (19.6 miles)

S3-1: Pecos Baldy Lake to Intersection of Skyline (251) and Jose Vigil Trail (351). 2.8 miles.

S3-2: Intersection of Skyline (251) and Jose Vigil Trail (351) to Truchas Lakes. 2.5 miles.

S3-3: Truchas Lakes to Santa Barbara Divide. 2.4 miles.

S3-4: Santa Barbara Divide to West Fork of Rio Santa Barbara. 5.4 miles.

S3-5: West Fork Rio Santa Barbara to intersection of Middle Fork Trail (24) and West Fork Trail (25). 3.6 miles.

S3-6: Intersection of Middle Fork Trail (24) and West Fork Trail (25) to Santa Barbara Campground free parking lot. 3.1 miles.

Alternate route: Middle Fork Trail

Alternate route: Jicarita Peak

Section 4: Santa Barbara Campground to Forest Road 442 (18.7 miles)

S4-1: Santa Barbara Campground free parking lot to intersection of Indian Creek Trail (27) and Bear Mountain Trail (28). 2.1 miles.

S4-2: Intersection of Indian Creek Trail (27) and Bear Mountain Trail (28) to intersection Indian Creek Trail (27) and Divide Trail (36). 2.6 miles.

S4-3: Intersection Indian Creek Trail (27) and Divide Trail (36) to Los Esteros. 1.5 miles.

S4-4: Los Esteros to intersection of Agua Piedra Creek, Trail 19A and Trail 22. 3.8 miles.

S4-5: Trail 19a/22/Agua Piedra Creek to Agua Piedra Campground entrance. 1.9 miles.

S4-6: Agua Piedra Campground bridge/entrance to La Cueva Canyon / Trail 492. 0.9 miles.

S4-7: La Cueva Canyon / La Cueva Trail (492) to intersection of La Cueva Trail (492) and Ojitos Maes Trail (182). 1.7 miles.

S4-8: Intersection of La Cueva Trail (492) and Ojitos Maes Trail (182) to intersection of Ojitos Maes Trail (182) and La Cueva 8. 1.4 miles.

S4-9: Intersection of La Cueva 8 and Ojitos Maes Trail (182) to Forest Road 442. 2.7 miles.

Section 5: Forest Road 442 to Rio Chiquito / Forest Road 437 (26.0 miles)

S5-1: FR 442 to the beginning of the Sardinas Canyon Fire burn. 4.73 miles.

S5-2: Beginning of the burn on FR 442 to Forest Road 439 / Rio Grande del Rancho. 4.2 miles.

S5-3: FR 439 / Rio Grande del Rancho to the beginning of the Connector. 4.0 miles.

S5-4: The beginning of the Connector to Forest Road 438. 4.0 miles.

S5-5: FR 438 / end of the Connector to Bernardin Lake. 2.4 miles.

S5-6: Bernardin Lake to Puertocito (intersection of FR 438 and FR 478). 2.3 miles.

S5-7: Puertocito to Rio Chiquito / Forest Road 437. 4.5 miles.

Section 6: Rio Chiquito / Forest Road 437 to Taos Plaza (20.0 miles)

S6-1: Rio Chiquito / FR 437 to Buena Suerte Canyon / FR 437. 2.3 miles.

S6-2: Buena Suerte Canyon to Manzanita Canyon on FR 437. 3.0 miles.

S6-3: S6-3 Manzanita Canyon to Drake Canyon Loop Trail (165) on FR 437. 2.2 miles.

S6-4: Intersection of FR 437 and Drake Canyon Loop Trail (165) to intersection of Drake Canyon Loop Trail (165) and unnamed trail. 3.4 miles.

S6-5: Intersection of Drake Canyon Loop Trail and unnamed trail to intersection of Ojitos Trail (166) and Talpa Ridge Trail. 1.5 miles.

S6-6: Ojitos Trail (166) from intersection with Talpa Ridge Trail to Ojitos Trail (166) and intersection with Ojitos shortcut. 4.1 miles

S6-7: Ojitos Trail (166) / Ojitos shortcut to El Nogal. 1.1 miles.

S6-8: El Nogal to Taos Cow. 1.7 miles.

S6-9: Taos Cow to Taos Plaza. 1.4 miles.

Get GPX files of the full route or of subsections at https://SantaFeToTaos.org/gpx-files/

Section 1: Santa Fe Plaza to Winsor Trailhead at the Santa Fe Ski Basin

20.1 miles

S1-1: Santa Fe Plaza to Patrick Smith Park. 1.4 miles.

S1-2: Patrick Smith Park to Arroyo Polay Trailhead. 1.3 miles.

S1-3: Arroyo Polay Trailhead to Sierra del Norte Trailhead. 1.8 miles.

S1-4: Sierra del Norte Trailhead to Little Tesuque Creek / Juan Trail. 3.6 miles.

S1-5: Little Tesuque Creek / Juan Trail (399) to Winsor Trail (254). 1.9 miles.

S1-6: Winsor Trail (254) / Juan Trail (399) intersection to Winsor Trail (254) / Chamisa Trail (183) intersection. 3.3 miles.

S1-7: Winsor Trail (254) / Chamisa Trail (183) intersection to Winsor Trail (254) / Borrego Trail (150) intersection. 1.9 miles.

S1-8: Winsor Trail (254) / Borrego Trail (150) intersection to Forest Road 102. 2.0 miles.

S1-9: Forest Road 102 to Winsor Trailhead at The Ski Basin. 3.1 miles.

Get a GPX file of Section 1 at https://SantaFeToTaos.org/gpx-files/

Unnamed trail that runs parallel to Camino Pequeno along the Santa Fe River. Section 1-2.

Pacheco Canyon Fire burn scar,
June, 2011

**Winsor Trailhead
Santa Fe Ski Basin**
end Section 1

Medio Fire burn scar,
August, 2020

Tesuque Peak Alt Route

Big Tesuque
Campground

Winsor Trail (254)
/ Borrego Trail (150)

Borrego
Trailhead

Hyde Park Road / Route 475

Winsor Trail (254)
/ Juan Trail (399)

Chamisa Trailhead

Sierra del Norte
Trailhead

Arroyo
Polay
Trailhead

**Santa Fe Plaza
granite marker**
begin Section 1

0   2   4 mi

S1-1: Santa Fe Plaza to Patrick Smith Park

1.4 miles. 126 feet ascent. 0 feet descent.

From the southeast corner of the Santa Fe Plaza, look for the granite end marker for the Old Santa Fe Trail. From the marker, walk south along Old Santa Fe Trail. You'll pass the La Fonda Hotel on your left.

Continue on Old Santa Fe Trail, cross the intersection with Water Street, and continue along Old Santa Fe Trail. You'll pass the Loretto Chapel (with the spiral staircase) on your left just after the intersection. Keep walking towards East Alameda and cross that intersection, to the river side, and take a left. You'll be on East Alameda, facing east. The Santa Fe River will be on your right.

Walk along the sidewalk and through the Santa Fe River Park, past the Archangels. Continue along Alameda for 1.4 miles, crossing Paseo de Peralta, Delgado Street, and East Palace Avenue. There are several little bridges along the way.

Consider crossing to the opposite side of the river at "Enchanted Small Falls," which is about 600 feet after you've crossed Delgado Street. Just know that you'll have to cross back to the other side of the Santa Fe River before you get to East Palace Avenue. There's another little bridge you can cross at about 600 feet before you reach East Palace.

Get back to the sidewalk along East Alameda by the time you reach the intersection with East Palace. This would be a good place to cross the street, too, so you're walking along East Alameda on the north side—the side opposite the river. A little bit further down East Alameda you'll cross Gonzales Road on your left.

Keep going another 750 feet or so and you'll see the access road to go into Patrick Smith Park on your right. You don't have to go into the park; we're just using the road to it as a marker. You have just completed Section 1-1.

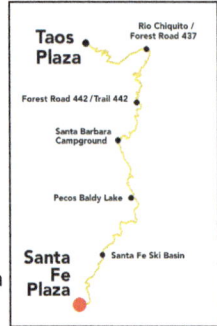

This granite marker in the southeast corner of the Santa Fe Plaza is the end of the Old Santa Fe Trail and the beginning of the Santa Fe to Taos Thru-Hike.

Taos Plaza
Rio Chiquito / Forest Road 437
Forest Road 442 / Trail 442
Santa Barbara Campground
Pecos Baldy Lake
Santa Fe Ski Basin
Santa Fe Plaza

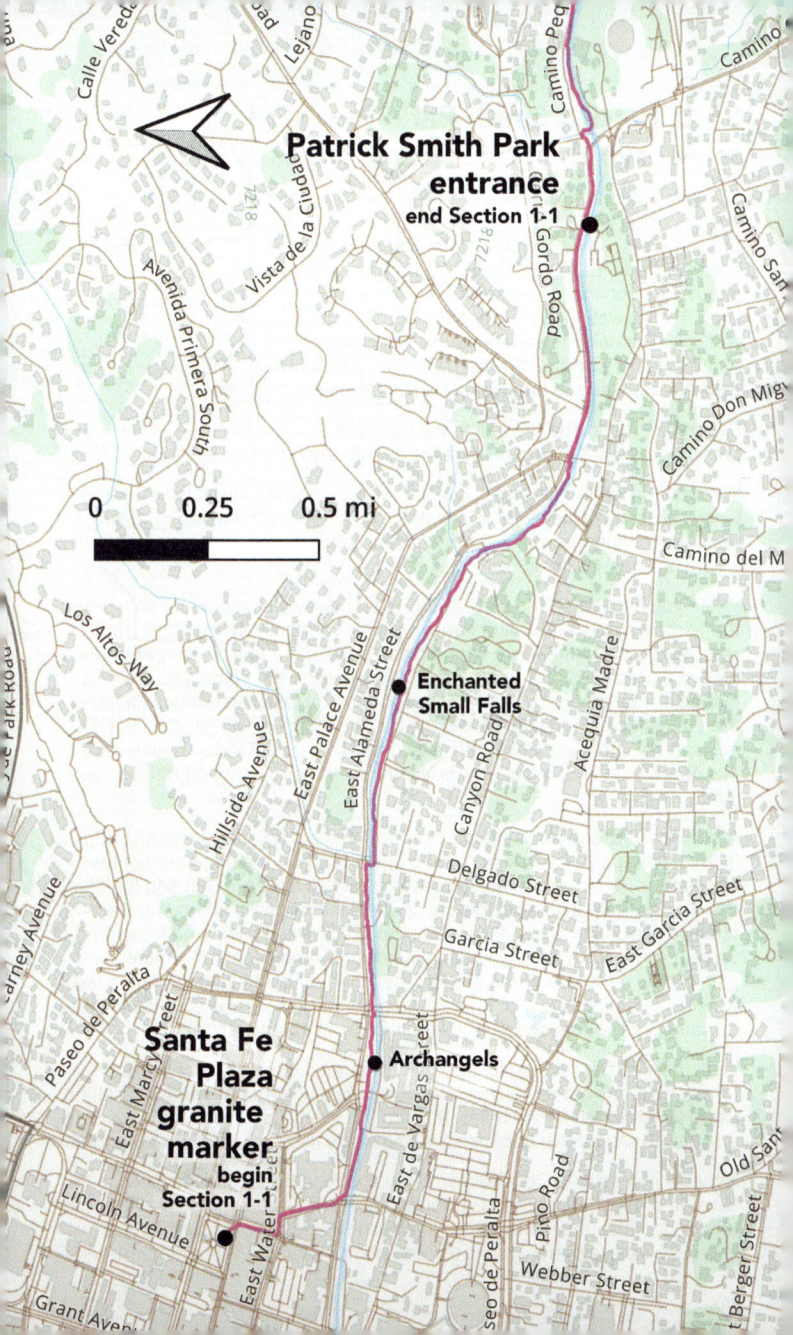

Patrick Smith Park
entrance
end Section 1-1

0   0.25   0.5 mi

Enchanted
Small Falls

Santa Fe
Plaza
granite
marker
begin
Section 1-1

Archangels

S1-2: Patrick Smith Park to Arroyo Polay Trailhead

1.3 miles. 193 feet ascent. 8 feet descent.

Stay on Alameda on the side of the road opposite the river. Alameda makes an almost 90-degree right turn about 300 feet after the entrance to Patrick Smith Park. As you walk up to the beginning of that turn, you'll see a small intersection with a dirt road just to the left. The primary dirt road that runs parallel to East Alameda and to the river is Camino Pequeno.

Camino Pequeno and the trail to the right of it are public access, but please respect the people who live here as you go through.

Walk along Camino Pequeno, heading upriver. About a third of a mile from where you left Alameda, look for a path on the right off Camino Pequeno. It's not marked, and the willows may conceal it, but the ground is well-worn. It is a hard, 90-degree right.

When you look down the path, about 15 feet away you should be able to see the Santa Fe river and a very narrow, simple "bridge," really a plank, that crosses the river here. It's a tight squeeze (and good reason to not bring a bike or a reactive dog through here). After walking the plank, you are now in the corridor along the Santa Fe River. The trail takes an immediate left in front of a stacked log pile. Follow the trail, heading upriver, for the next 0.4 miles or so. There are many little side paths that go out to the houses along this corridor; stay on what seems like the main trail. Do not go through any gates.

After 0.4 miles, and just a bit after you've walked over another small bridge by the tire swing, you'll see a sign and a fence marking the beginning of the Up-aya Nature Trail. If you're standing in front of this sign, turn left and look for a trail that goes up a small slope. Go up that slope. You'll come out at the edge of Cerro Gordo Park (aka "Adam Gabriel Armijo Park"), with the fenced Adam Gabriel Armijo Community Garden in front of you on your left. Follow the path on the right side of the garden, then over to the parking lot. There is a water fountain here, picnic tables, and a jungle gym. This is your last access to water until you reach Little Tesuque Creek in about an hour.

Walk through the parking lot and follow the road out and as it makes a sharp turn and comes out on Cerro Gordo Road. Take a hard right and walk along Cerro Gordo Road for 0.4 miles. Most of this road has decent shoulder. Drivers tend to slow down because it is frequently used by walkers and joggers.

After 0.4 miles along Cerro Gordo Road, the road turns right sharply. On the left side of the road, at the turn, you'll see a series of boulders spread out to block cars. Just beyond those boulders is the Arroyo Polay Trailhead of the Dale Ball Trails system. That is the end point of Section 1-2 of the thru-hike.

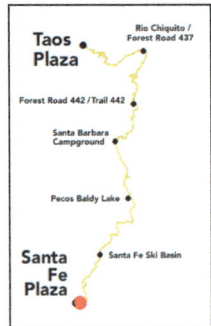

Chasing
Dreams

**Arroyo
Polay
Trailhead**
end Section 1-2

Cerro Gordo Road

der Ridge

7546

Armijo
Community
Garden

**Cerro
Gordo
Park**

Upper Canyon Road

Canyon Road

Calle Lejano

Lejano Lane

Cerro Gordo Road

7218

first bridge
along Santa Fe
River
corridor

Apodaca Hill Street

Water
History
Museum

Camino Cab

Gonzales Road

Camino Pequeno

Calle Vereda

Barranca de Oro

Vista de la Ciudad

7216

**Patrick Smith Park
entrance**
begin Section 1-2

Canyon Road

Camino San Acacio

Avenida Primera So

**Patrick Smith
Park**

East Alameda Street

Camino Don Miguel

Camino del Monte

Palace Avenue

Acequia Madre

0   0.25   0.5 mi

7546

S1-3: Arroyo Polay Trailhead to Sierra del Norte Trailhead

1.8 miles. 466 feet ascent. 171 feet descent.

Walk into the arroyo from the Arroyo Polay trailhead. Continue walking 0.84 miles north along the trail, through the arroyo. Along your way you will pass "Chasing Dreams" on your left, which is an abandoned convertible facing upstream in the arroyo.

After 0.84 miles you will reach marker #24 of the Dale Ball Trails. This marker includes a simple but useful map of the other trails and markers in the area. Keep walking forward/north on this trail.

0.24 miles after marker #24, you'll come to marker #20, where the trail splits. Keep going straight/rightish, continuing up the arroyo and heading north.

0.25 miles later you'll come to another marker, #18. Another trail will be crossing yours from right to left. Just like before, keep going straight ahead.

In another 0.34 miles you'll come to marker #12. There will be another trail on your left, breaking off a bit behind you on your left side. Again, don't take it. Continue on straight.

Chasing Dreams.

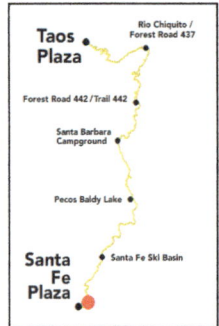

After another 0.45 miles heading north on this trail, you'll come up to marker #13. Route 475/Hyde Park Road will be on your left. Climb up the little slope and you'll see the Sierra del Norte trailhead parking lot on your left, across Hyde Park Road. There will also be a road into a housing development going off on your right. The arroyo will also be on your right.

Carefully cross Route 475. Just behind and to the right of the "Dale Ball Trails" sign is a little trail that will bring you up to the parking lot, with the lot on your left. Or you can just walk up the road and into the parking lot from Route 475.

The northeast corner of the Sierra del Norte parking lot is the end of Section 1-3.

**Dale Ball Trails
Sierra del Norte
Trailhead**
end Section 1-3

Hyde Park Road / Route 475

7546

**Dale Ball Trails
Arroyo Polay
Trailhead**
begin Section 1-3

Santa Fe River

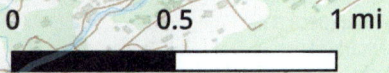

Cerro Gordo Road

Cerro Gordo
Park

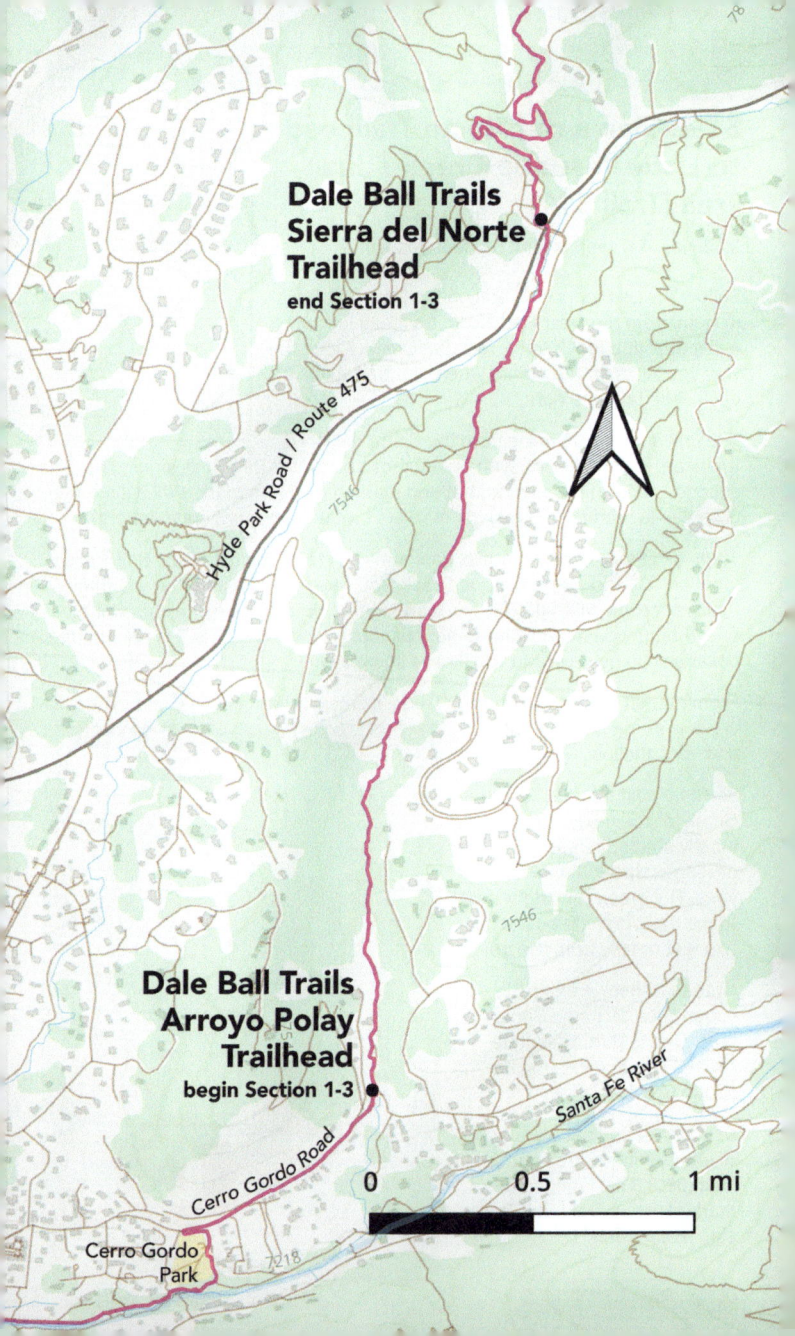

7218

7546

78

0   0.5   1 mi

S1-4: Sierra del Norte Trailhead to Little Tesuque Creek / Juan Trail (Trail 399)

3.6 miles. 447 feet ascent. 512 feet descent.

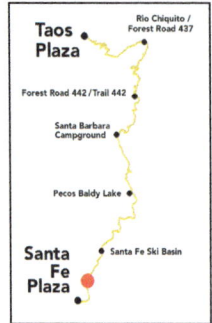

Follow the La Piedra trail, still on the Dale Ball Trails system, from the Sierra del Norte trailhead for 2.2 miles until you reach Little Tesuque Creek. Along the way you'll pass three points where the trail splits. At each split, take the right.

The first split is 0.05 miles from the Sierra del Norte trailhead. It is marker #1, with one of those nice Dale Ball Trails signs. The second is 0.27 miles beyond that and marked #2. From marker #2 it's another 0.7 miles to marker "A" (yes, the markers switch from numbers to letters).

Then it's 1.1 miles, mostly down, sometimes a steep down, to Dale Ball Trails junction "D" and Little Tesuque Creek. You'll see a sign along the way that this is a "technical trail." This is a warning to mountain bikers; hikers will be fine, though you might want to get out your hiking poles. There is decent tree cover as you go down, so you'll have some shade.

From marker D (aka "junction 'D'"), you'll cross Little Tesuque Creek. The creek is about five feet wide and very shallow.

You'll be next to Little Tesuque Creek for the next 0.7 miles, in mostly shaded forest with a few passages through mini canyons. The creek runs right next to the trail. At some points it is two feet or less from the trail.

Note that there are two "Tesuque Creek"s in the Santa Fe area. One is "Little Tesuque Creek." The other is "Big Tesuque Creek."

Section 1-4 ends at the junction of Little Tesuque Trail and Juan Trail (399). This junction is marked with a Dale Ball Trails sign as Junction "F."

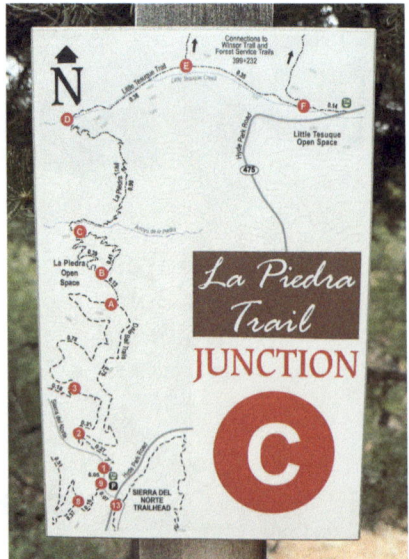

One of the Dale Ball Trails signs.

Carol Connector

Carol

Juan (399)

Hyde Park Road / Route 475

Little Tesuque Trail

Little Tesuque Creek

Dale Ball Trails System Junction "F"
end Section 1-4

Junction "D"

7546

7874

10,000 Waves

1874

Hyde Park Road / Route 475

7874

Sierra del Norte

Dale Ball Trails Sierra del Norte Trailhead
begin Section 1-4

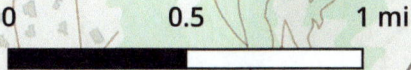

0   0.5   1 mi

S1-5: Little Tesuque Creek / Juan Trail (399) to Winsor Trail (254)

1.9 miles. 308 feet ascent. 633 feet descent.

At the intersection of Little Tesuque Trail and Juan Trail (399), take a sharp left and go up. You'll go up a lot. The trail splits at 0.3 miles from marker "F." The left trail is "Carol Connector." Take the right to stay on Juan (399).

About 0.3 miles from the split at the Carol Connector, after the trail has leveled out somewhat, you'll come to a second marked split. The right is Saddleback Trail (232). Don't take it. Stay on Juan Trail, going left and down into Juan Canyon. You have just crossed into the Santa Fe National Forest.

After you walk down through Juan Canyon with its oak trees and little fields, you'll cross an arroyo/wash a few times over the next 0.7 miles as you go through dry, mostly evergreen forest. There is occasional rock work along this part of the trail, mostly set up to manage heavy water flow.

If there have been storms recently, this wash could potentially have significant amounts of water flowing through it. That's unlikely, but it is wise to be aware of the weather when you go through arroyos. Santa Fe rain can be fickle; it can pour hard at one point while a quarter of a mile away gets no precipitation. Arroyos can have water even if it hasn't rained where you are.

Just a bit beyond Juan Canyon, the trail splits. The left fork is the "Juan Connector." Don't take it. Stay on the right fork. (The Juan Connector would also get you to Winsor Trail and Big Tesuque Creek. It's just less direct.)

After another half mile or so along dry trail, you'll come to Winsor Trail (254). You may be able to hear Big Tesuque Creek. You have completed Section 1-5.

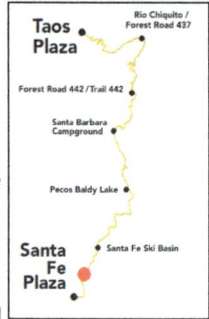

Juan Trail (399) coming down into Juan Canyon.

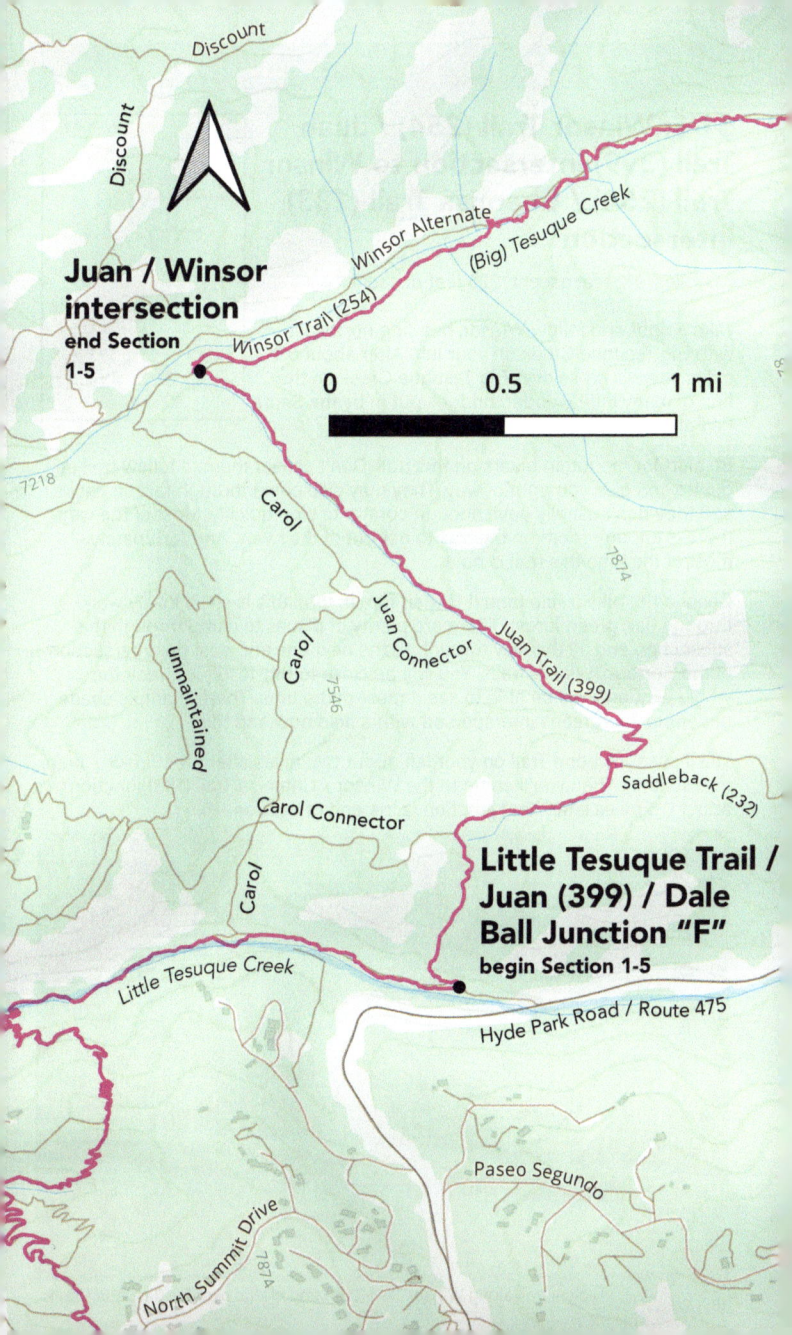

Juan / Winsor intersection
end Section 1-5

Discount

Discount

Winsor Alternate

(Big) Tesuque Creek

Winsor Trail (254)

7218

Carol

Carol

Juan Connector

Juan Trail (399)

7874

7546

unmaintained

Saddleback (232)

Carol Connector

Little Tesuque Trail / Juan (399) / Dale Ball Junction "F"
begin Section 1-5

Carol

Little Tesuque Creek

Hyde Park Road / Route 475

Paseo Segundo

North Summit Drive

7874

0   0.5   1 mi

S1-6: Winsor Trail (254) / Juan Trail (399) intersection to Winsor Trail (254) / Chamisa Trail (183) intersection

3.3 miles, 912 feet ascent. 226 feet descent.

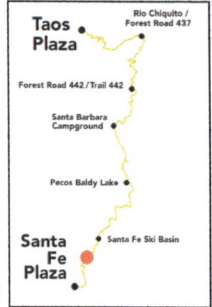

Take a right and follow Winsor, heading northeast with Big Tesuque Creek on your left. After about 0.5 miles you will cross over Big Tesuque Creek on the first of many little wooden bridges put in by the Santa Fe Fat Tire Society.

Be alert for mountain bikers on this trail. Don't expect them to follow trail etiquette and give you right of way. They may also come through fast, in packs, and they don't usually have enough control to stop quickly. Most of the way there is enough room on the trail to get out of their way. And fortunately, most of the time this trail is quiet.

Despite the bike traffic (and it is their forest, too), this is still a lovely walk through flat, green forest. There are plenty of places to camp through this subsection and all the way through to the next one and past the intersection of the Borrego/Winsor trails. You will be close to Big Tesuque Creek the whole way, and will be able to see it most of the time. There is ample shade under big evergreens interspersed with a field now and then.

You'll pass Jawbone Trail on your left about two miles after the Winsor / Juan intersection. Then you'll come to the Winsor / Chamisa Trail (183) junction about 0.6 miles later. That junction is the end of Section 1-6.

Typical trail along Winsor Trail (254) and bridge over Big Tesuque Creek.

**Chamisa (183) /
Winsor (254)
intersection**
end Section 1-6

Chamisa Trail (183)

8530

Jawbone

Jawbone

8530

Chamisa Trail (183)

Chamisa
Trailhead

8202

Saddleback Trail (232)

**Juan (399) /
Winsor (254)
intersection**
begin Section 1-6

7874

Winsor Trail (254)

Discount

Juan Trail (399)

Hyde Park Road

0   0.5   1 mi

7218

Bauer Ro

Lodge

Lodge

Bent Hill

Paseo Primero

S1-7: Winsor Trail (254) / Chamisa Trail (183) intersection to Winsor Trail (254) / Borrego Trail (150) intersection

1.9 miles. 615 feet ascent. 9 feet descent.

From the Chamisa Trail intersection, continue straight ahead, heading northeast on Winsor Trail. This will be very much like the prior section, with big trees and stream crossings. There are plenty of places to camp or rest. The trail starts to get busier, and you may see more mountain bikers. Still, it's fairly quiet, at least on weekdays.

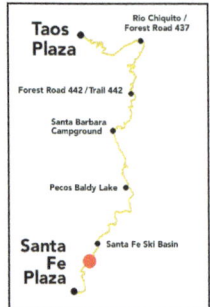

You're relatively close to Santa Fe, but there is wildlife around. This is the only place I have seen a bear in the entire 20+ years I have lived in Santa Fe, including all my travels in the backcountry in northern New Mexico. Please don't panic over wildlife if you are lucky enough to encounter any. The animals would much rather leave you alone. 99% of the time they will disappear as soon as possible.

The trail will get busier after you pass Bear Wallow Trail (182) on your right, which is just before yet another creek crossing over a wooden bridge. The triangle/loop that makes up the Winsor, Borrego and Bear Wallow Trails is popular. You may see people every few minutes in the afternoon on a summer weekend. The trail can also get a little tight in a couple of pinchpoints, and there are a few blindspots. Cillian Murphy (the actor) very nearly crashed into me coming out of a grove of willows on a bike.

You will be near Big Tesuque Creek the entire time you're on this sub-section. When you reach the intersection with Borrego Trail (150) coming in on your right, you're at the end of this subsection. This is the last water access you'll have for an hour or so.

There is a nice field just past the intersection on the right (about 400 feet north of Big Tesuque Creek), but it's not terribly quiet. If you want quieter camping, get water here, then walk up along Winsor (and on to the next subsection) and enjoy the fields there, less than 0.25 miles further along the trail.

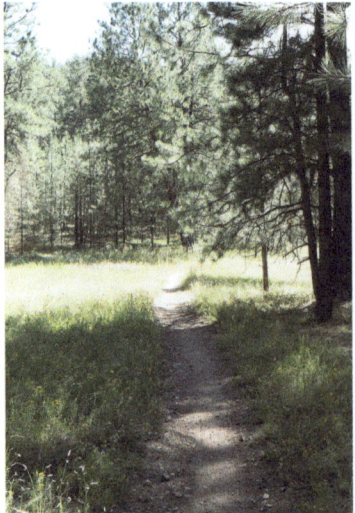

Along Winsor Trail (254).

0   0.5   1 mi

9186

8858

Hyde Park Road / Route 475

9514

9186

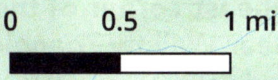

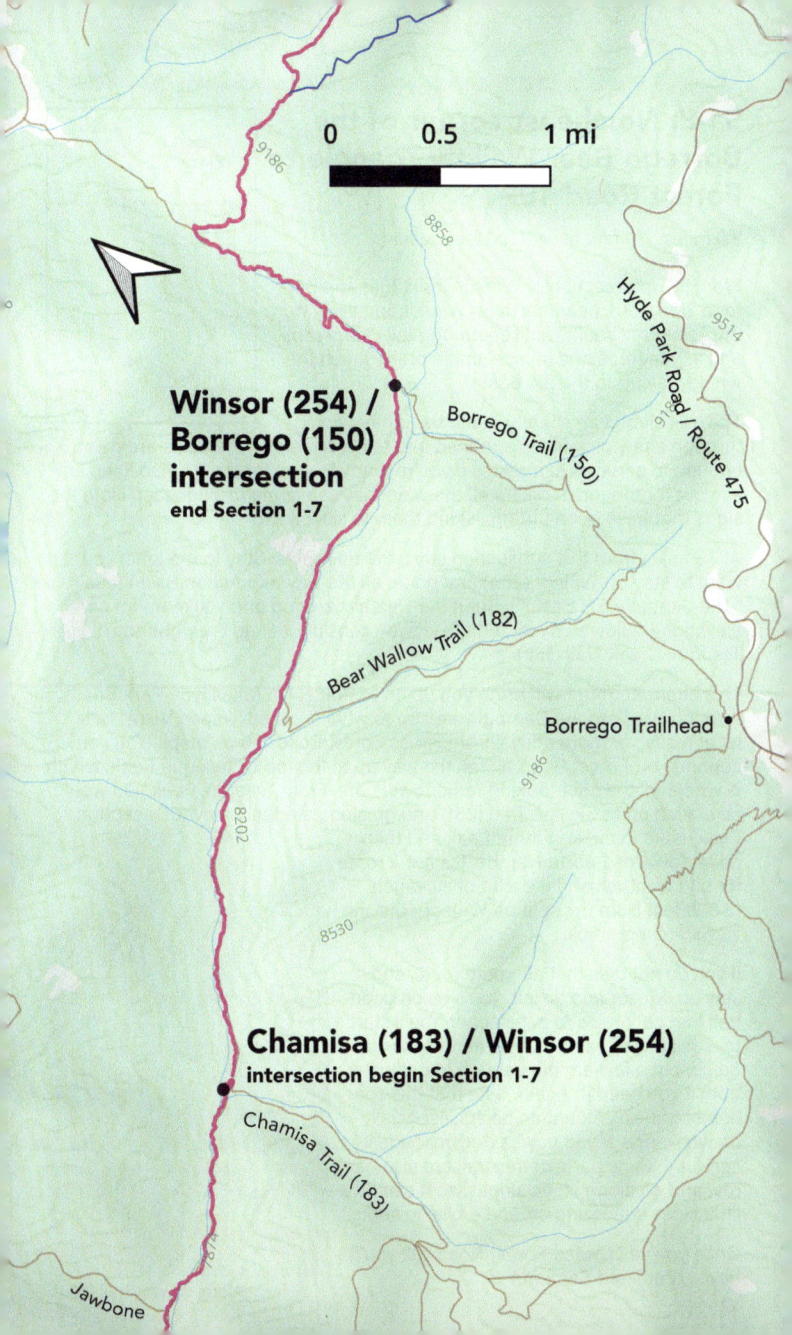

Winsor (254) / Borrego (150) intersection
end Section 1-7

Borrego Trail (150)

Bear Wallow Trail (182)

Borrego Trailhead

8202

8530

Chamisa (183) / Winsor (254)
intersection begin Section 1-7

Chamisa Trail (183)

Jawbone

S1-8: Northeast corner of the Borrego Bear Wallow Triangle to Forest Road 102

2.0 miles. 761 feet ascent. 20 feet descent.

From the intersection of Winsor Trail (254) and Borrego Trail (150), head north on Winsor and away from Big Tesuque Creek. You'll be among tall evergreens and aspen trees and in nice shade pretty much the whole way up to the Ski Basin.

The trail climbs up slightly at the beginning, going through a few nice fields and then into tall evergreens. The fields are quiet enough to serve as campsites if you're ready to stop for the day. Do keep an eye out for mountain bikers all the way; they can come through fast. Note the signs that have been put up asking them to slow down.

At 1.3 miles from this subsection start, the trail splits. Stay to the left if you want to stay on Winsor (254) and go up all the way into Aspen Basin (aka "The Santa Fe Ski Basin"). But if the weather is good and you're up for some elevation—followed by incredible views—consider taking the right onto Tesuque Creek Trail (152).

This alternate route will bring you up on to Route 475 (aka Hyde Park Road), through Big Tesuque Campground, up to what is called "Aspen Vista", but is "actually", or more officially shown as Forest Road 150 on maps. You can continue on Forest Road 150 all the way up to the top of Tesuque Peak, which is where all the cool-looking radio towers are. From Tesuque Peak you would take a left on to Skyline Trail (251) and go along a ridgeline over Deception Peak, Lake Peak, Penitente Peak and then down towards Puerto Nambe. It's not a route for bad weather, and it's a lot of elevation (3,000 feet from the split off Winsor), but the views are incredible.

If you do not take that alternate route, and stay on Winsor and go left, you'll be on good trail that continues to get steeper. You'll start to cross tiny streams (seeps, almost) as you go up, but a few are big enough to get water from if you need it. Again, note that this section of trail has mountain bikers, especially on weekends. If you have a dog, manage it carefully. Many parts of this trail are also narrow and go along steep slopes, so it can be a little close squeezing around a bike in spots.

Once you've crossed Forest Road 102 you'll have completed Section 1-8.

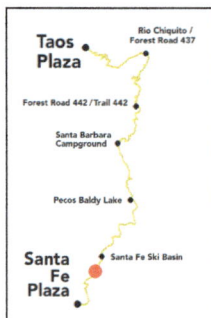

Along Winsor Trail (254).

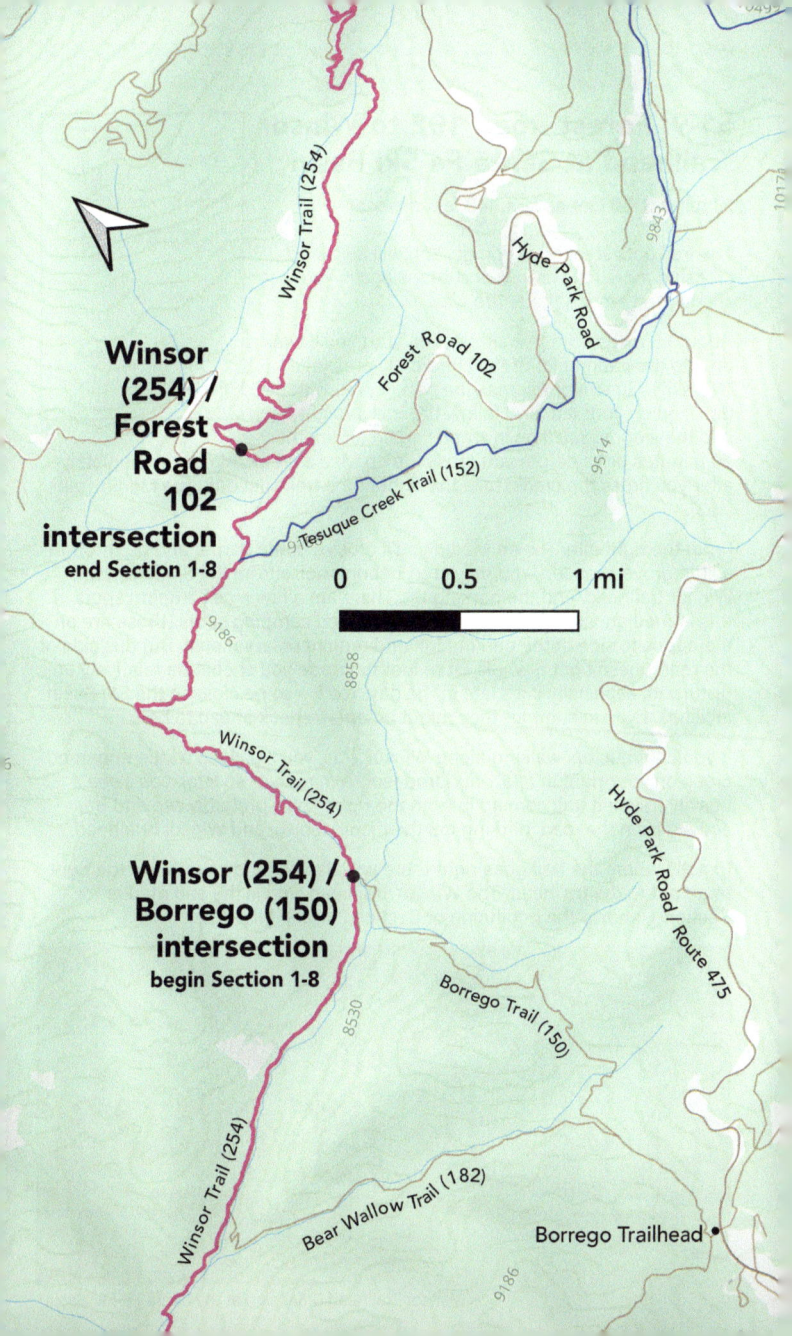

Winsor Trail (254)

Hyde Park Road

Winsor
(254) /
Forest
Road
102
intersection
end Section 1-8

Forest Road 102

Tesuque Creek Trail (152)

9514

9186

0   0.5   1 mi

8858

Winsor Trail (254)

Winsor (254) /
Borrego (150)
intersection
begin Section 1-8

Hyde Park Road / Route 475

8530

Borrego Trail (150)

Winsor Trail (254)

Bear Wallow Trail (182)

Borrego Trailhead

9186

S1-9: Forest Road 102 to Winsor Trailhead at Santa Fe Ski Basin

3.1 miles. 1,136 feet ascent. 143 feet descent.

The trail gets steeper as you go. You will also start crossing more little creeks and seeps again. You're in shade pretty much the entire way.

About 1.6 miles from this subsection start you'll walk up into the parking lot of the Nordic Ski area (aka "Norski"). Go straight across the parking lot, with the trail sign on your left, and follow the trail straight back into the woods. You'll be in woods again for another 20 minutes or so before you cross Rio en Medio creek. Almost immediately after you cross the creek, take the right at the trail split onto Rio Medio Trail (163).

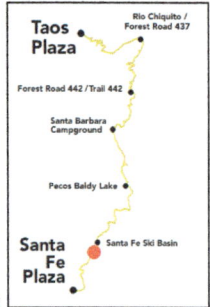

From the right after Rio en Medio you'll cross a cattle barrier and go through a little grove of aspen. You may start hearing noise from the Ski Basin, the Winsor trailhead, and the parking lot. There are a few nice camping spots in this immediate area. These are not designated camping spots (those are on the opposite side of the parking lot, and require reservations). But this side of the road doesn't get a whole lot of foot traffic, so you should be relatively undisturbed, especially if it's late in the day. You'll also be close to the Ski Basin facilities. Even in summer they might be open; check ahead to be sure.

If you continue on, walking along Winsor Trail, you'll pick up a little unnamed creek on your right in a few hundred feet. A minute or so later, you'll see a heavily traveled trail coming in from the right. You'll probably see and hear activity from the road, parking lot, the picnic tables, and Winsor Trailhead.

Exactly where the trail goes right there will also be a trail sign. Take the right to go out to the trailhead. The Winsor Trailhead sign is the end marker for Section 1, and/or the beginning of Section 2 of the thru-hike.

Winsor Trailhead (254) sign at the Santa Fe Ski Basin.

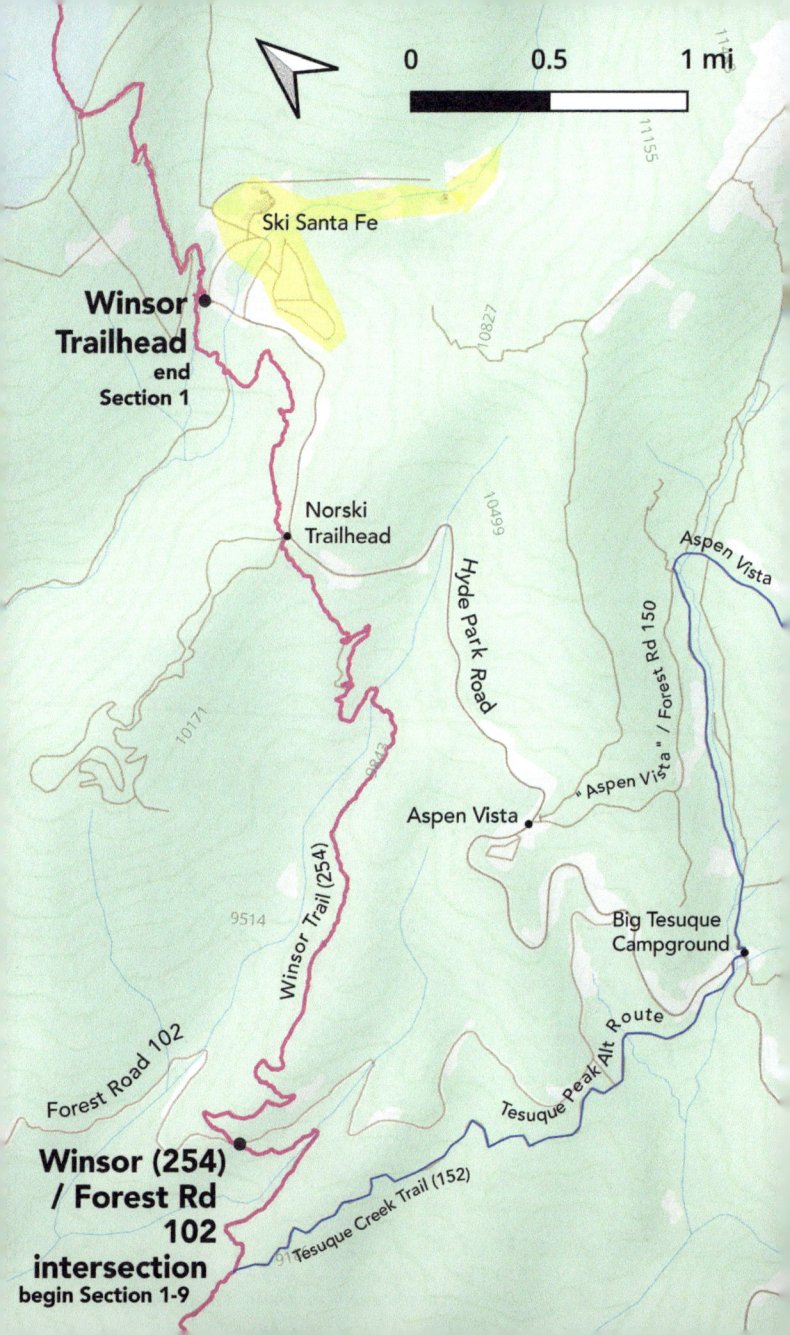

Winsor Trailhead
end
Section 1

Ski Santa Fe

Norski Trailhead

Hyde Park Road

"Aspen Vista" / Forest Rd 150

Aspen Vista

Aspen Vista

Big Tesuque Campground

Winsor Trail (254)

Forest Road 102

Tesuque Peak Alt Route

Winsor (254) / Forest Rd 102 intersection
begin Section 1-9

Tesuque Creek Trail (152)

0   0.5   1 mi

Good field for camping just north of the Winsor Trail (254) / Borrego Trail (150) junction.

The ridgeline that the Tesuque Peak alternate route goes over.
View from near the communications towers. September 2016.

Alternate route: Tesuque Peak

9.45 miles. 4,026 feet ascent. 1,985 feet descent.

Overview: Instead of taking Winsor (254) all the way up to the Ski Basin, you take Tesuque Trail (152) through Big Tesuque Campground, up Aspen Vista, and over Deception, Lake, and Penitente Peaks down into Puerto Nambe. The route goes along Tesuque Trail (152), Aspen Vista/FR 150, and then Skyline Trail (251). There are incredible views along the four peaks, but be mindful of the weather. *This is not a route for bad weather.*

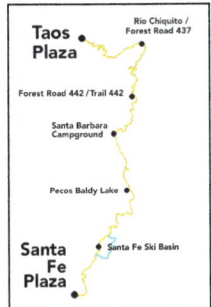

Water access: Water is available for 1.5 miles of this route along Big Tesuque Creek, then there are three spots for water as you go up Aspen Vista (aka FR 150). There might be water at Tesuque Peak from the infrastructure associated with Ski Santa Fe (this is not verified so don't count on it). There is no water from where you start on the ridgeline all the way down into Puerto Nambe. There are several rills (again, a "rill" is a tiny stream about 1-2 feet wide) on the far side of Puerto Nambe and going down from Puerto Nambe.

Camping: Big Tesuque Campground and the northwest side of FR 150 from where you come up to it from Tesuque Trail would work for dispersed camping. You might also find a quiet spot off Aspen Vista/FR 150 about a mile to two miles short of Tesuque Peak.

Details of the Tesuque Peak alternate route

From Section 1-8, at the intersection of Winsor Trail (254) and Tesuque Creek Trail (152), take Tesuque Creek Trail east/southeast for 1.4 miles until you come out at Hyde Park Road. You'll come out at a tight bend in the road with Big Tesuque Campground on the opposite side of the road. Be mindful of cars as you cross; they won't be expecting you to come out at this point.

Walk over into Big Tesuque Campground and look for the trail about 30 feet to the right of Big Tesuque Creek. Follow that trail (which is still Tesuque Creek Trail) up for the next 0.8 miles. You will come out on Aspen Vista, which is technically Forest Road 150. Take a right onto Forest Road 150. You'll go up this all the way to Tesuque Peak.

About 0.1 of a mile after you've gotten on to Aspen Vista you'll walk over Big Tesuque Creek. There are decent places to camp on the east side of Aspen Vista, on either the north or south side of the creek. You'll probably notice the side trails that go up and off to the left just before and after the creek. Finding a flat spot is a little tricky, but they're there, and there's water here, and so this is a good enough area to crash for the night if you need it.

Continuing on Aspen Vista, you'll be walking on a service road up through aspens with nice views mostly to the west, but really all around. There's another little creek/active seep that crosses Aspen Vista about 0.8 miles from where you crossed Big Tesuque when you came on to Aspen Vista/FR150.

You may hear water again when you get to a tight, steepish turn on FR 150 another 0.9 miles from the second seep. From here the water situation is dicey; you might be able to get water at the Tesuque Peak buildings, but otherwise you'll be without water until you either reach the far side of Puerto Nambe or go all the way to Spirit Lake. If you are heading to Lake Katherine (returning to the standard route of the thru-hike), there's no water until Lake Katherine unless you go to one of the little rills on the far side of Puerto Nambe.

FR 150 continues up through into evergreen forest. There's a terrific view about 1.4 miles from the tight turn. There are semi-sketchy but usable places to dry camp off FR 150 after it flattens out on the approach to Tesuque Peak. Do not go too far west from FR 150 to camp or you'll be in the watershed area and liable for a $2,000 ticket. I only recommend crashing here if it's near dark and thus obviously not a good time to be going over a ridgeline. Don't light a campfire here; the fire risk to the upper watershed is too great.

About 1.7 miles from the first big view (and another tight turn in the road), you'll walk into the infrastructure on top of Tesuque Peak. Most of this is part of Ski Santa Fe, but if you went a bit further you'd also walk up to the communications towers. We're not going to the comms towers, though, so look for a left to take Skyline Trail (251) northeast over the ridgeline. It's just a bit south of Tequila Sunrise Glade, as marked on Gaia app maps, or as it's known among skiers. Skyline goes almost all the way to Las Vegas (NM), 67 miles, and is probably the best well-known trail in the Pecos. You will follow it for the next 1.3 miles as you walk over first Deception Peak (12,305 ft), then Lake Peak (12,372) and finally Penitente Peak (12,205) before you make your way down from Penitente 2.1 miles to where Skyline Trail meets Winsor Trail. Wave hello to Santa Fe Lake on your right as you pass it around Deception Peak... just mind the dropoff. The views from the ridgeline are epic. The wind and the weather can be pretty epic, too. Be careful.

By the time you reach Winsor Trail (254) you will be back below the treeline. Take a left onto Winsor to get to Puerto Nambe and pick up the standard route of the thru-hike. Take a right on Winsor to go to Spirit Lake.

If you hit bad weather along the ridgeline

If the weather turns while you are near Tesuque Peak, skip the ridgeline and just follow Ski Basin service roads or ski trails down to Aspen Basin and the Winsor trailhead. Then take Winsor as described in Section 2-1.

If the weather turns while you are on the ridgeline, take Raven's Ridge Trail (near the southwest side of Deception Peak) down. That 1.2 mile trail will bring you to Wilderness Gate and Winsor Trail, where you can pick up the standard route of the thru-hike. Do not take the side trail that heads north-west from Lake Peak (along the ridgeline), as that doesn't go down; it just takes you to another peak and view.

If the weather turns while you are past or near Penitente Peak, continue on Skyline to Winsor. Don't take the unmaintained trail off Skyline that goes down, south/southeast from Penitente. That will only take you to a dead end on the border between the Pecos Wilderness and Santa Fe National Forest.

Pacheco
Canyon
Fire
burn scar
June, 2011

11483

12467

12199

11811

Skyline Trail

Winsor Trail (254)

11155

10827

Puerto Nambe
end Section 2-2,
begin Section 2-3

11483

12199

La Vega

Penitente Peak

Nambe
Lake

Lake Peak

The Y

12409

Winsor Trail

11811

Deception Peak

Raven's Ridge

Santa Fe Lake

Lower Nambe 403

Tesuque Peak

Wilderness
Gate

Alternate Route

Ski Santa Fe

Winsor Trailhead
end Section 1

Norski Trailhead

Aspen Vista

Aspen
Vista

11483

Big Tesuque
Campground

9186

Forest Road 102

0   1   2 mi

Winsor / Forest Rd 102
begin Section 1-9

Tesuque Creek Trail

Hyde Park Road

8588

9186

Section 2: Santa Fe Ski Basin to Pecos Baldy Lake

26.4 miles

S2-1: Ski Basin / Winsor (254) Trailhead to the Y. 2.4 miles.

S2-2: "The Y" to Puerto Nambe. 2.2 miles.

S2-3: Puerto Nambe to Lake Katherine. 2.8 miles.

S2-4: Lake Katherine to Winsor Ridge (271) / Skyline Trail (251) intersection. 3.6 miles.

S2-5 Winsor Ridge (271) / Skyline Trail (251) intersection to Skyline Trail (251) / Cave Creek (288) intersection. 2.9 miles.

S2-6: Cave Creek (288) / Skyline Trail (251) intersection to Cave Creek (288) Dockweiler Trail (259) intersection. 3.3 miles.

S2-7 Dockweiler Trail (259) / Cave Creek Trail (288) intersection to Dockweiler Field and rill. 4.1 miles.

S2-8: Dockweiler Field and rill to intersection of Dockweiler (259) and Jack's Creek Trail (257). 2.5 miles.

S2-9: Intersection of Dockweiler Trail (259) / Jack's Creek Trail (257) to Pecos Baldy Lake. 2.6 miles.

Alternate route: Puerto Nambe to Spirit Lake to Winsor Creek / Winsor Trail.

Get a GPX file of Section 2 at https://SantaFeToTaos.org/gpx-files/

Along Winsor Trail (254), about a third of a mile up from the Winsor Trailhead.

Pecos Baldy Lake
end Section 2

Jack's Creek Trail (257)

11811

11811

12139

11155

Rito Perro
Field

Dockweiler Trail (259)

9843

Jaroso Fire
burn scar
June, 2013

10499

11483

Horsethief
Meadow

Cave Creek Trail (288)

11514

Panchuela
Campground

Skyline Trail (251)

Winsor Ridge Trail (271)

11483

Lake Johnson

10827

Stewart Lake

11811

Lake Katherine

Spirit Lake

Holy Ghost Trail (283)

Pacheco
Canyon
Fire
burn scar
June, 2011

11155

Puerto Nambe

Tesuque Peak Alt. Route

The Y

0   2   4 mi

**Winsor
Trailhead**
**Santa Fe Ski Basin
begin
Section 2**

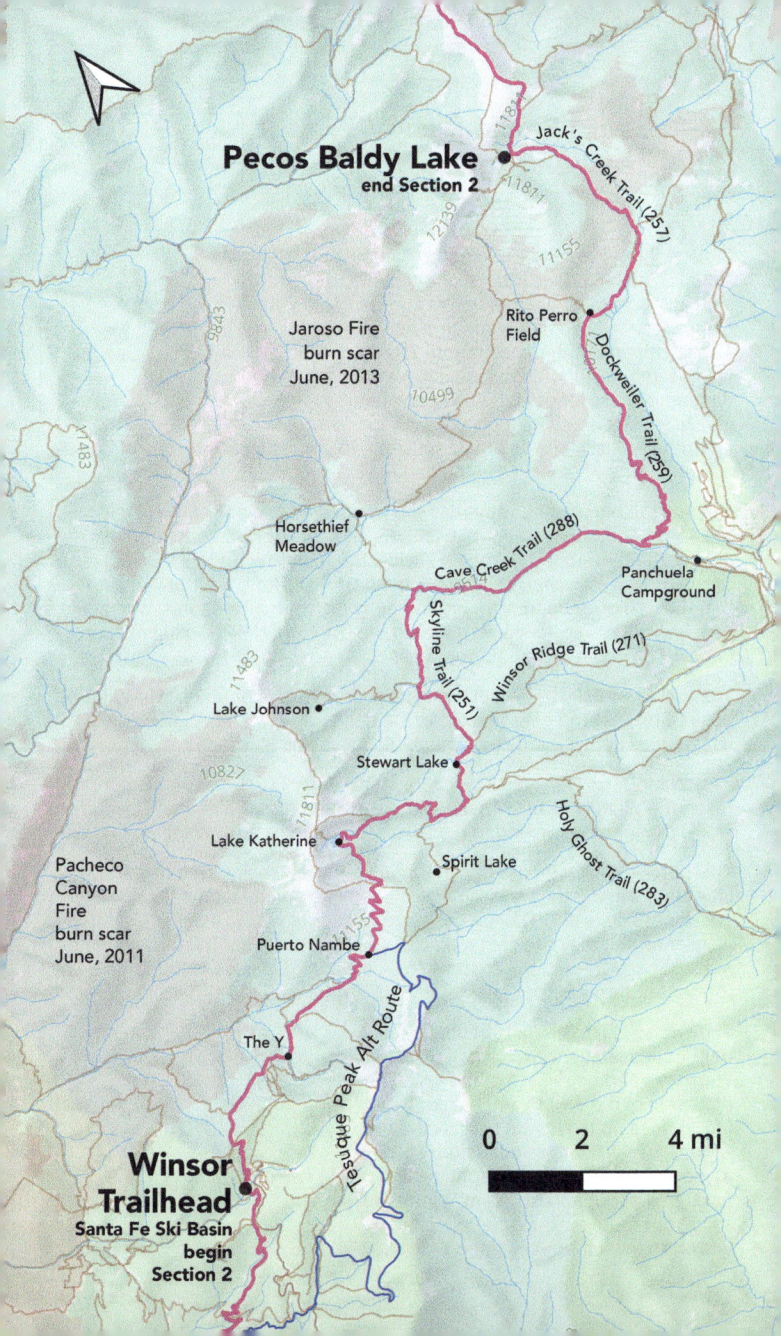

S2-1: Santa Fe Ski Basin / Winsor (254) Trailhead to the Y

2.4 miles. 580 feet ascent. 350 feet descent.

Start at the Winsor Trailhead at the Santa Fe Ski Basin (aka "Aspen Basin"). See a photo of the trailhead sign on page 24. There's water here, parking lot-style campsites, bathrooms, and a large free parking lot. This is your last water access until you reach Rio Nambe just past the Y. You could leave your car in the parking lot here for up to two weeks with no problems. This is a good resupply point if you have come up from the Plaza and you have someone to bring supplies to you, or if you placed a car with supplies in the parking lot.

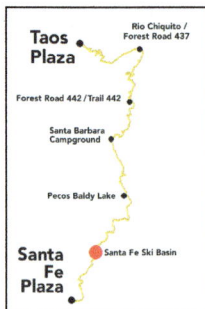

Go past the big trailhead sign into the woods and cross the little creek over the 4-foot-wide bridge about 30 feet beyond, then take a right immediately after at the trail sign. You'll be on a wide, thoroughly worn trail that will cross a large new dirt access/utility road about 0.1 miles from the trailhead. After that the trail goes up (quite a bit) as you go through mixed forest and make your way up the switchbacks, passing the "Be Here Now" sign shown on page 30 on your way up. There's a bench along the way.

The trail eventually levels out. About a quarter mile later you get to Wilderness Gate. Past the gate, you are in the Pecos Wilderness. All wilderness usage rules apply—namely no mountain bikes and no drones.

Past Wilderness Gate you'll be on Winsor Trail for 30-40 minutes before you reach the Y. Do NOT take Trail 403 (Lower Nambe Trail, aka the "Elevator Trail") that goes down and to the left about 0.4 miles from Wilderness Gate.

This part of Winsor Trail is generally flat with a few rocky stretches and little slopes along the way. You'll be among evergreens for the first bit after Wilderness Gate. Pretty soon the evergreens give way to aspens. On busy weekends you may see someone every 15 minutes or so. This is one of the most popular trails in the area. You may also see glimpses of Santa Fe Baldy to your left through the canopy.

The Y is a split in the trail about 200 feet before Rio Nambe, aka "Nambe River." You may hear the river from the split. The right side of the split (Nambe Lake Trail (400)) goes up to Nambe Lake. Nambe Lake is lovely, but it's a dead end. There is a good campsite off to the right of Nambe Lake Trail about a third of a mile from the split. Your route for the thru-hike continues on to the left branch of the Y.

Wilderness Gate.

Rio Nambe

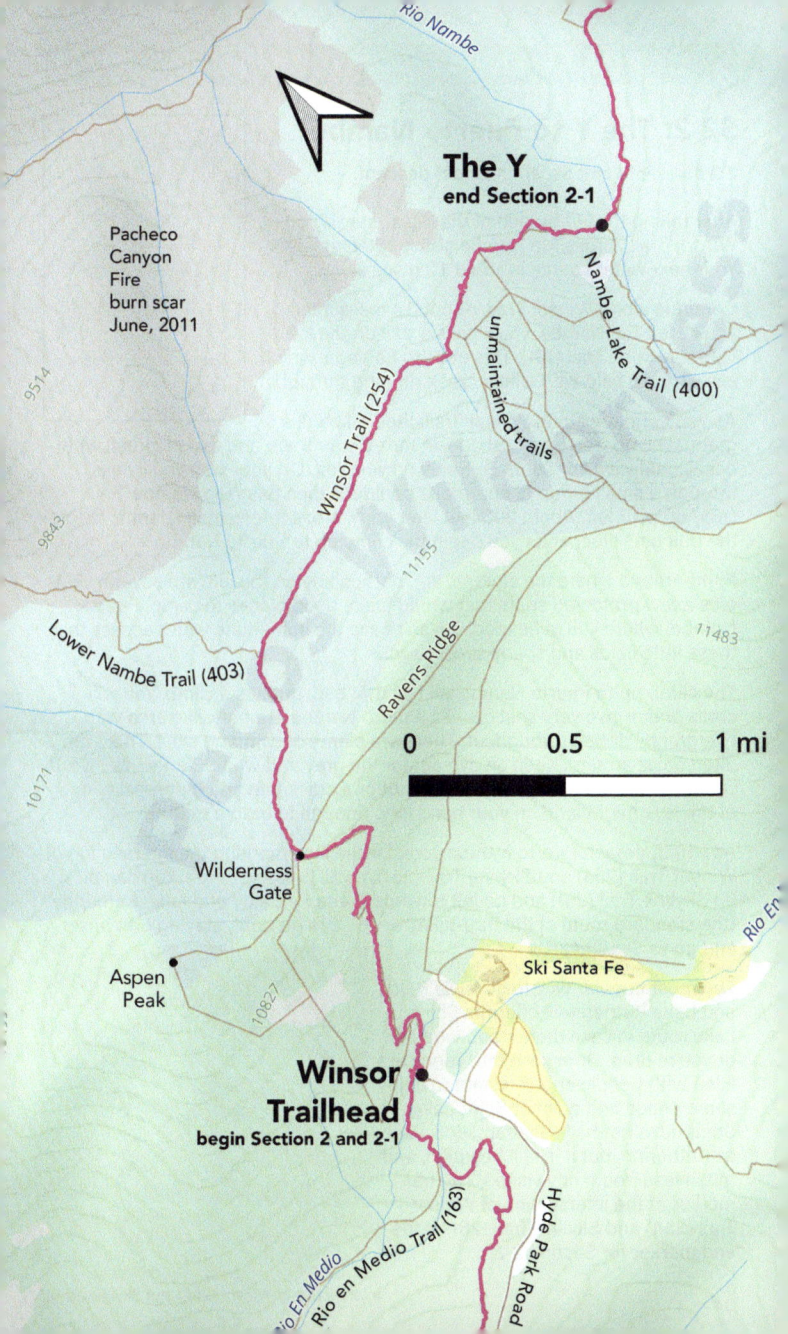

The Y
end Section 2-1

Pacheco
Canyon
Fire
burn scar
June, 2011

9514

Nambe Lake Trail (400)

Winsor Trail (254)

unmaintained trails

9843

11155

Lower Nambe Trail (403)

Ravens Ridge

11483

0   0.5   1 mi

10171

Wilderness
Gate

10827

Aspen
Peak

Ski Santa Fe

Winsor
Trailhead

begin Section 2 and 2-1

Rio En Medio Trail (163)

Rio En Medio

Hyde Park Road

Rio En

S2-2: The Y to Puerto Nambe

2.2 miles. 514 feet ascent. 107 feet descent.

After taking the left branch of the Y (i.e., staying on Winsor Trail), cross Rio Nambe about 200 feet later. Your next water source is about 1.2 miles away.

Continue along Winsor Trail. About 0.4 miles after you've left Rio Nambe, you'll pass a trail on the left, Upper Nambe Trail (101). This goes to La Vega, which is a very big field with a little creek running through it.

As you continue along Winsor Trail, the trail begins a gradual climb. You'll be in shade, in mixed evergreen and aspen forest, with occasional views of Santa Fe Baldy on your left. On your way you'll pass through a small group of enormous boulders, then pass Rio Nambe Trail (160) on your left. About 200 feet later you'll cross three small streams before the trail gets steeper as you begin the climb up to Puerto Nambe.

Right around where the streams are, particularly on the left, are several fields plus a few protected spots that would make good places to camp. Puerto Nambe, where you're headed, doesn't have the immediate water access that these little fields and shady spots have.

The climb up to Puerto Nambe isn't all that bad, but it is a climb. You will cross one or two very shallow rills. Puerto Nambe is a park-like area with evergreens dotted throughout. There are plenty of camping sites. There are often cows around. Keep an eye out for the grey and white Clarkson's Jays. If you are patient, and hold still with a nut or a cracker in your open palm, one of the jays might land on your hand long enough to grab a treat.

As you approach Puerto Nambe, look for the sign marking the intersection of Winsor Trail (254) and Skyline Trail (251). It will be on your left. You can pick up Skyline Trail (251) and go left towards Santa Fe Baldy and Lake Katherine (the standard route of the thru-hike), or you can go right, staying on Winsor, and go to Spirit Lake.

The most popular way to go is via Baldy and Lake Katherine. I offer the Spirit Lake route in case there's bad weather or you're tired. Or in case the woods are filled with people and you want to enjoy some peace and quiet at Spirit Lake. Spirit does not have as dramatic a view as Katherine, but it is still beautiful, and much less frequently visited. The trail marker at the intersection of Winsor Trail (254) and Skyline Trail (251) is the end marker for Section 2-2.

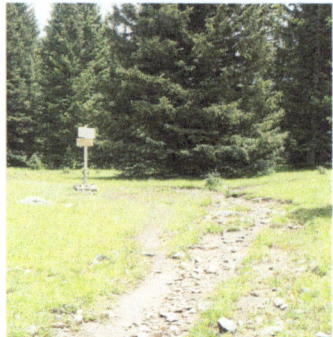

Intersection of Winsor (254) and Skyline (251).

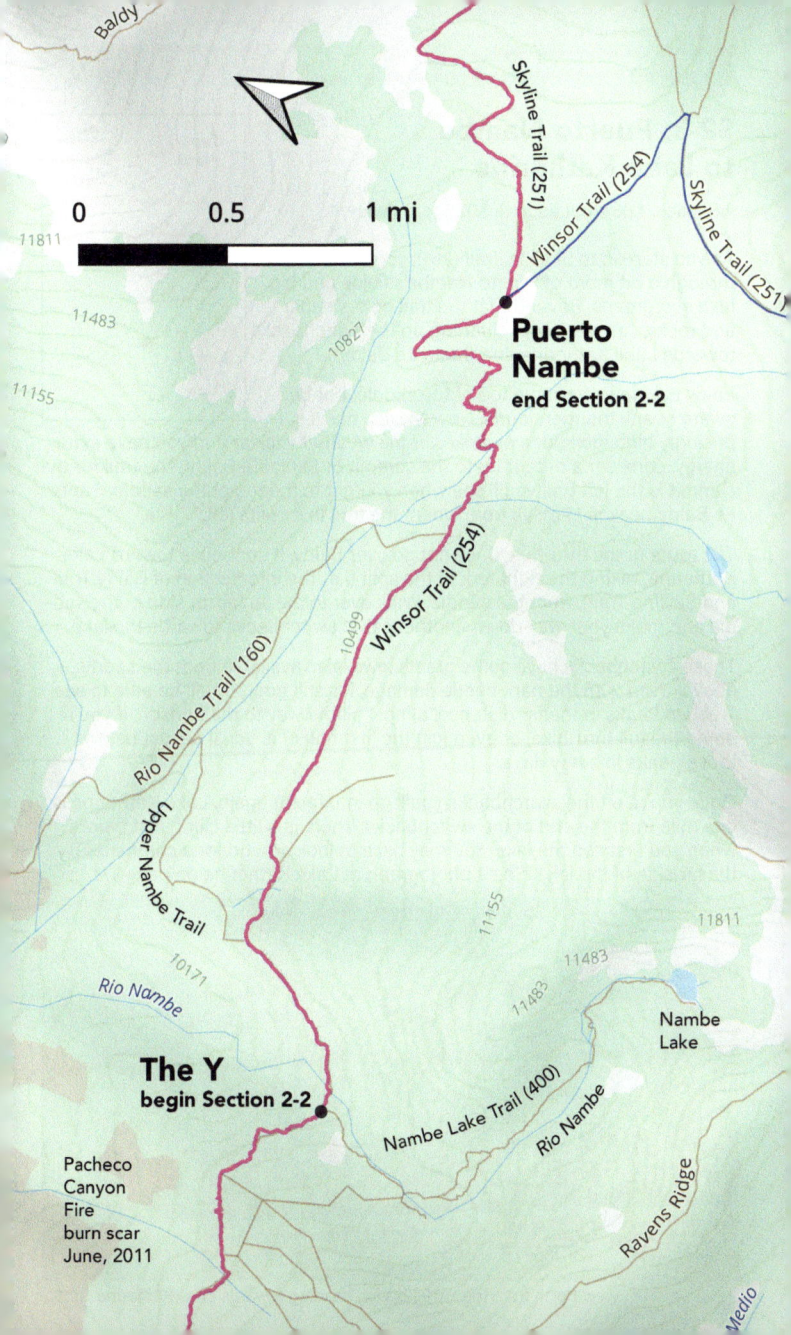

Skyline Trail (251)

Winsor Trail (254)

Skyline Trail (251)

Puerto Nambe
end Section 2-2

Winsor Trail (254)

Rio Nambe Trail (160)

Upper Nambe Trail

Rio Nambe

The Y
begin Section 2-2

Pacheco
Canyon
Fire
burn scar
June, 2011

Nambe Lake Trail (400)

Rio Nambe

Nambe
Lake

Ravens Ridge

Medio

Baldy

0   0.5   1 mi

11811

11483

11155

10827

10499

10171

11155

11483

11483

11811

S2-3: Puerto Nambe to Lake Katherine

2.8 miles. 1,881 feet ascent. 1,028 feet descent.

As you step on to Skyline Trail (251), you'll walk through a bit more of Puerto Nambe's fields and big lush evergreens. Beyond that the trail gets steeper and rockier as you begin climbing up the switchbacks towards Lake Katherine and Santa Fe Baldy.

Enjoy the views from the top of the saddle, but be aware of any thunderclouds. New Mexico has a surprisingly high incidence of strikes. If the weather is clear and you have extra energy, consider a detour up to the summit of Santa Fe Baldy. The trail for the summit is the left trail you'll see when you get to the top of the saddle. Santa Fe Baldy peak is 1.1 miles from where the trail to it splits left.

The route of the thru-hike does not go over Baldy. It continues toward Lake Katherine, taking the right fork of the split (i.e., the intersection of Baldy Trail and Skyline Trail), from the saddle. Walk over to the far/north side of the saddle and make your way down another set of switchbacks towards the lake.

These switchbacks have some great views, also available from the saddle above. Even with the bark beetle damage, it's still good. You'll be able to see Truchas Peaks in the far distance, almost all the way to the horizon. If you're doing the full thru-hike, or even just the first half of it, you'll be just below those peaks in a few days.

Once you're off the switchbacks you'll go into forest again. Lake Katherine is one mile from the end of the switchbacks. There is a little climb just before when you first see the lake. You may have to look around for a campsite. Try the far side of the lake. See a photograph of Lake Katherine on page 171.

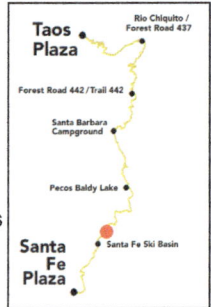

View north from the switchbacks, heading towards Lake Katherine. 2018.

Rito Oscu...

11811

Lake
Katherine
**end
Section
2-3**

Skyline Trail (251)

Winsor Creek

Winsor Trail (254)

Skyline Trail (251)

Spirit
Lake

12467

Santa Fe Baldy
summit

Baldy Trail

unmaintained trail

10827

11155

Winsor Trail (254)

Skyline Trail (251)

**Puerto
Nambe
begin Section 2-3**

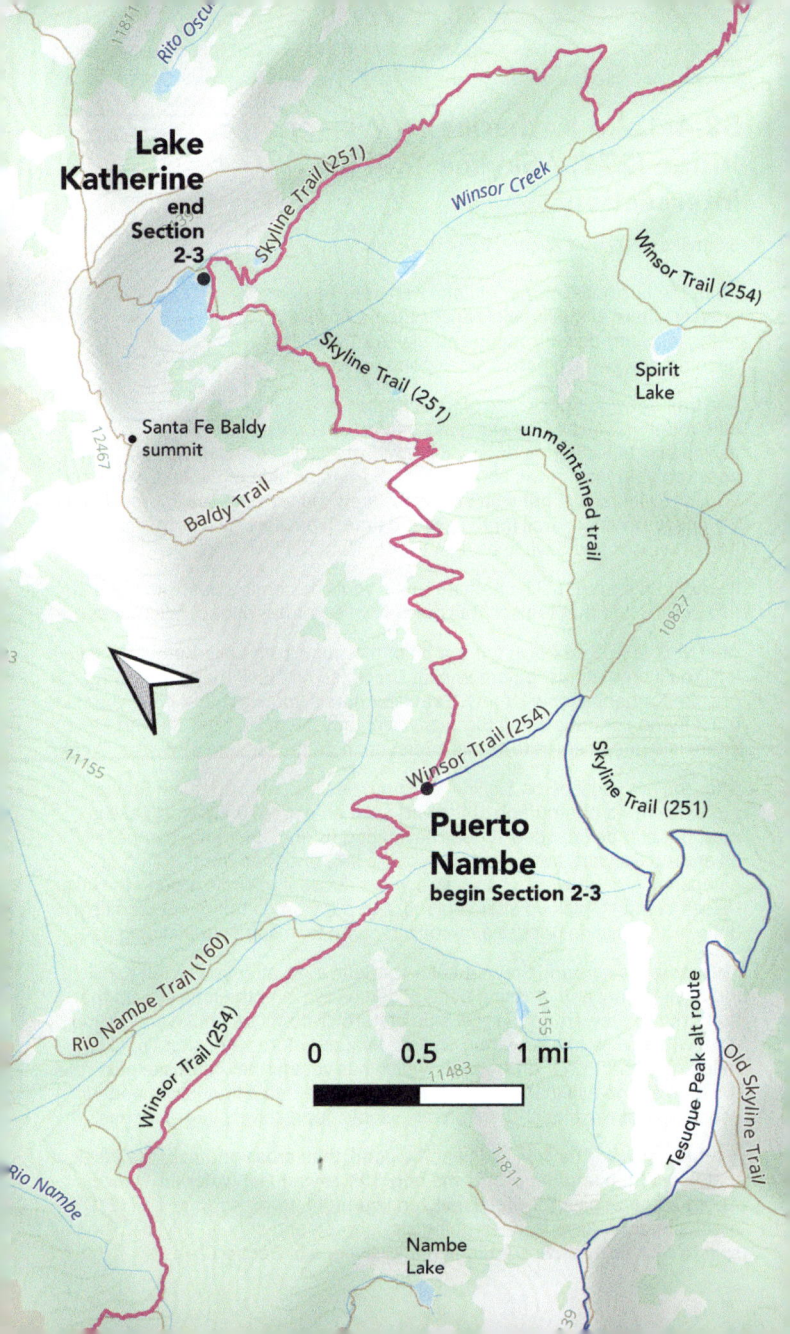

Rio Nambe Trail (160)

Winsor Trail (254)

11155

Tesuque Peak alt route

Old Skyline Trail

0	0.5	1 mi

11483

Rio Nambe

11811

Nambe
Lake

39

S2-4: Lake Katherine to Winsor Ridge (271) / Skyline Trail (251) intersection

3.8 miles. 1,372 feet ascent. 2,914 descent.

From the northeast corner of Lake Katherine, approximately where a little creek (Winsor Creek) flows out of the lake and down, continue on Skyline Trail (251), heading down. You'll pass a small pond on your left.

The trail down the back side of Lake Katherine is a little rough in places. You won't see as many people
as you saw at Katherine or on your way to it. You'll cross over Winsor Creek again on your way down, about 0.4 miles from the side of the lake. You'll see Winsor Creek again, but won't cross it, when you arrive at the intersection of Skyline and Winsor Trail for the second time. (You were also at the intersection of Winsor and Skyline back at Puerto Nambe.)

If you did the Spirit Lake alternate route, you'll be coming out from there at this point. Note that Winsor Trail down from Spirit has a lot of fallen trees.

After you've walked down the last bit of the slope from Lake Katherine, take a left. You'll turn left just before Winsor Creek (same creek that was flowing out of Lake Katherine, now larger). Get water here if you want, but once you take the left and continue along Skyline, you're only 0.6 miles from Stewart Lake. There is a good campsite at this intersection on the far side of Winsor Creek.

After the left you'll be on Skyline Trail for 0.6 miles until you reach Stewart Lake. There's a photograph of Stewart Lake on page 170. Stewart Lake is nice, but can be crowded. It does have good fishing. There are campsites all around Stewart, both with views of the lake and then another ring of campsites around what's basically a wider concentric circle around the lake. Please be quiet, pick up after yourself, and put your campfire out (or skip it entirely). Please do not use a motorized pump to inflate your sleeping pad.

The campsites around Stewart Lake continue even after you've left it, following Skyline Trail and crossing the wooden bridge over the little stream that flows out of Stewart on the east side of it. You'll continue on Skyline as you walk with a view of a large bog on your left (and more campsites) until you reach "Stewart Pond" on your left, which has yet another campsite next to it. There are no fish in this pond, but there are neotenic tiger salamanders, which look like axolotls. There are also some impressively large leeches.

Continue on Skyline Trail just past the pond, then cross another little creek that flows from another part of the bog. This is your last water for 1.1 miles. About 200 feet past the little creek, on your right, Winsor Ridge Trail (271) breaks off from Skyline. Keep going straight/left and stay on Skyline. The trail split of Skyline and Winsor Ridge marks the end of Section 2-4.

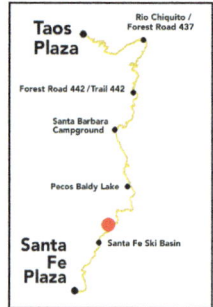

Winsor Ridge (271)

Winsor Ridge (271) / Skyline (251) intersection
end Section 2-4

Johnson Lake Trail (267)

Skyline Trail (251)

Rito Oscuro Creek

Stewart Pond

Stewart Lake

Winsor Creek

Winsor Trail 261

Winsor Trail (254)

Skyline Trail (251)

11155

Winsor Creek

10827

Spirit Lake

12135

Lake Katherine
begin Section 2-4

Santa Fe Baldy summit

2467

unmaintained trail

Winsor Trail (254)

10499

11483

11

11483

0   0.5   1 mi

Winsor Trail (254)

Skyline Trail (251)

11155

911

S2-5 Winsor Ridge (271) / Skyline Trail (251) to Skyline Trail (251) / Cave Creek (288)

2.9 miles. 1,009 feet ascent. 1,389 feet descent.

Continue on Skyline, passing a big bog on your left. You may not see anyone while you're on this subsection. There is some blowdown on the trail. The trees in this subsection, for whatever reason (heat, drought, bark beetles), have taken a beating over the last decade. There are views that weren't there ten years ago.

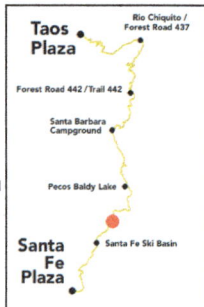

After 1.1 miles along Skyline Trail (251) from the Skyline / Winsor Ridge split, you will cross Rito Oscuro Creek. About 300 feet after Rito Oscuro, you'll see a trail sign and a trail going up and to the left for Lake Johnson. Lake Johnson is a gem, but the trail to it is rough and it's not on the route of the thru-hike.

There is a hidden little campsite right behind your left shoulder, basically, as you're standing on Skyline and looking at the sign for "Johnson Lake". The site is 20 feet or so off Skyline, towards the bog that would be to the left of the trail if you were going up to Lake Johnson.

Continue on Skyline Trail. The trail has blowdown for the next 0.7 miles or so, but it's passable. There's the new view on the right of the trail at a very large boulder that makes for a nice spot to sit and rest at while you take in the view. You'll be able to see East Pecos Baldy, where you're headed, and Truchas Peaks beyond Pecos Baldy.

A bit after you get past most of the blowdown, there's a set of switchbacks as you come down towards another wet area. There is a workable campsite near the bog, just as the trail takes a sharp right. Camp there, or keep walking toward Cave Creek and Cave Creek Trail. The next third of a mile before you reach Cave Creek has quite a few little fields, existing campsites, and good spots to sleep for the night.

When you reach Cave Creek, the trail splits left and right about 20 ft ahead of you on the far side of the creek. This is the intersection/junction of Skyline Trail (251) and Cave Creek Trail (288). Skyline Trail goes to the left ("upcreek," as it were). Cave Creek Trail, and the route of the thru-hike, goes down, following Cave Creek itself down. This junction is the end of subsection 2-5.

A note about the thru-hike route **not** going left, to Horsethief Meadow and then following Skyline Trail to Pecos Baldy Lake: The Jaroso Fire burn scar starts 1.5 miles beyond Horsethief Meadow. It goes all the way to just short of where Rito Perro Trail and Skyline intersect. There is extensive blowdown in this area, even after a lot of trail work by the New Mexico Volunteers for the Outdoors. The 2018 route of the thru-hike went through here, but I changed the route so it uses better trail, has more water access, and is safer.

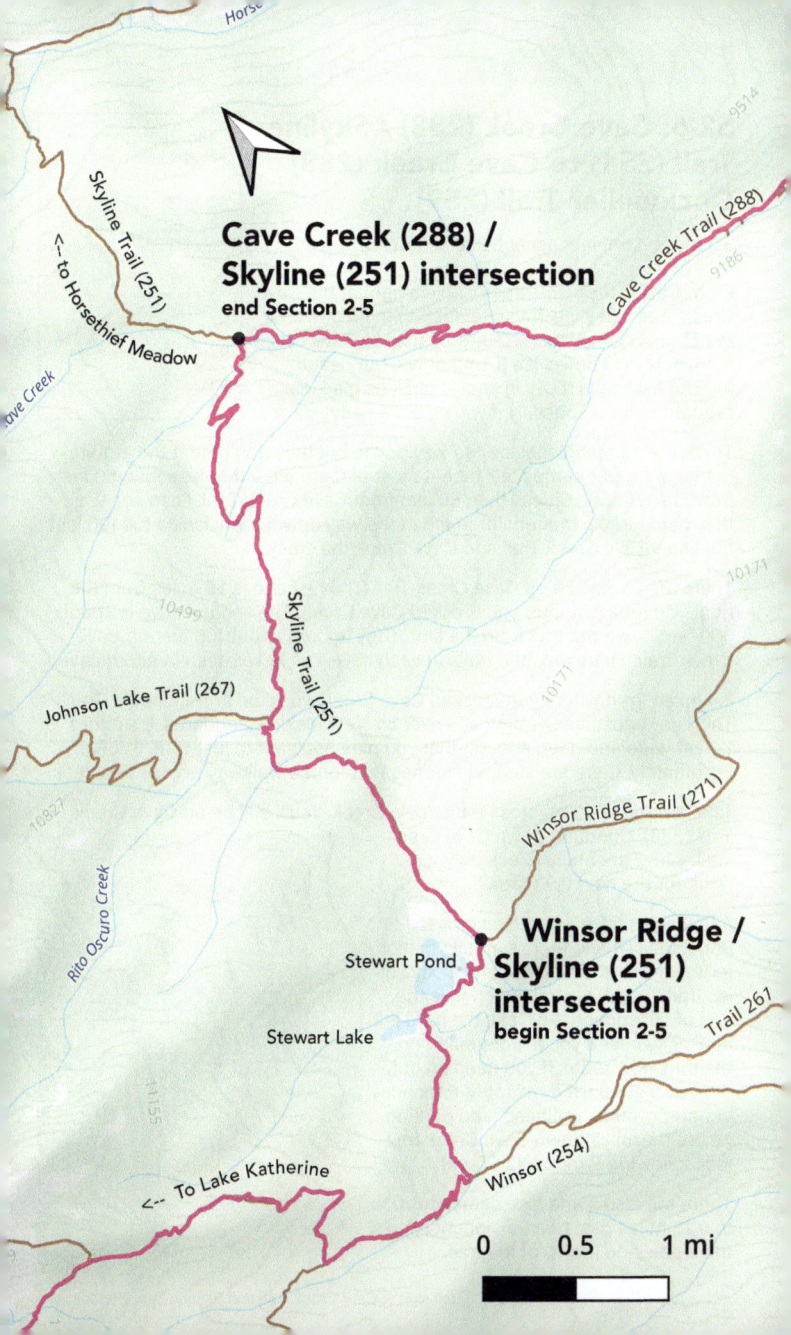

**Cave Creek (288) /
Skyline (251) intersection**
end Section 2-5

Skyline Trail (251)

← to Horsethief Meadow

ve Creek

Horse

Cave Creek Trail (288)

9514

9186

10171

10499

Johnson Lake Trail (267)

16827

Skyline Trail (251)

Winsor Ridge Trail (271)

Rito Oscuro Creek

Stewart Pond

**Winsor Ridge /
Skyline (251)
intersection**
begin Section 2-5

Trail 261

Stewart Lake

91155

<-- To Lake Katherine

Winsor (254)

0   0.5   1 mi

S2-6: Cave Creek (288) / Skyline Trail (251) to Cave Creek (288) Dockweiler Trail (259)

3.3 miles. 1,519 feet ascent. 270 feet descent.

From Cave Creek (the creek), take a right at the Cave Creek Trail / Skyline Trail intersection to go down to Panchuela Campground. You'll be next to Cave Creek the whole way down. It's a long down, but beautiful. The footing is dicey in spots. You'll be glad you brought poles, especially if you've got a heavy pack.

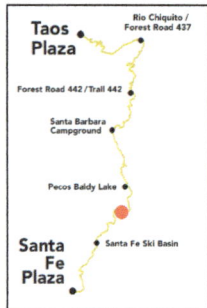

There are camping sites on the way down, but they don't meet the requirements of proper campsites, in that most of them are either less than 50 feet from Cave Creek, or less than 50 feet from Cave Creek Trail. I can see why they came to be, though: for much of the way down, there isn't a full 100 feet between Cave Creek Trail and Cave Creek the creek.

There are caves just off Cave Creek Trail. The first one is 1.8 miles from the right you took just after you crossed Cave Creek. The second cave is about 300 feet down the trail from the first. They're both about 100 feet off Cave Creek Trail. There are little trails to each cave. I've never been in either cave.

2.4 miles from where you crossed Cave Creek, you'll be at Panchuela Creek. This is a robust creek—almost a river by New Mexico standards. It's about 12 feet wide and deep enough that you may not want to just walk through it. Fortunately, there are stepping stones that form a walkway across the creek.

Take a right after you cross Panchuela Creek. You'll still be on Cave Creek Trail (288). Continue down Cave Creek Trail, with Panchuela Creek on your right, for the next 0.9 miles.

At 0.9 miles from where you crossed Panchuela Creek, there's a trail junction for Cave Creek Trail (288) and Dockweiler Trail (259). This trail junction is the end of subsection 2-6. Take the hard left up Dockweiler if you're continuing on the thru-hike route. If you need an out, or even a supported resupply, Panchuela Campground, trailhead, and parking lot are 0.8 miles down Cave Creek trail (still following Panchuela Creek).

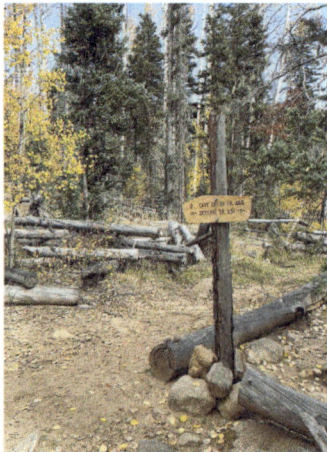

There are also some nice campsites 0.1 to 0.25 miles past this trail junction, on the creek side (right) of the trail.

Trail sign at Cave Creek Trail and Skyline Trail intersection.

NM 63

Jack's Creek

Winsor-Ridge Trail

Panchuela
Campground

8858

Dockweiler Trail (259)

10499

9186

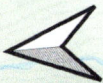

**Cave Creek
(288) /
Dockweiler
Trail (259)
intersection**
end Section 2-6

Panchuela Creek

Cave Creek Trail (288)

9514

9843

Winsor Ridge Trail (271)

10171

Horsethief Creek

**Cave Creek
/ Skyline
intersection**
begin
Section 2-6

Cave Creek

Skyline Trail (251)

Stewart Pond

Stewart Lake

10499

Rito Oscuro Creek

0   0.5   1 mi

10827

S2-7 Dockweiler Trail (259) / Cave Creek Trail (288) intersection to Dockweiler Field and rill

4.1 miles. 1,785 feet ascent. 309 feet descent.

Take Dockweiler up, heading north/northeast and away from Panchuela Campground. This is a long up. From the trail junction with Cave Creek Trail to where Dockweiler finally starts to level off, you'll go 2.1 miles and gain 1,500 feet of elevation.

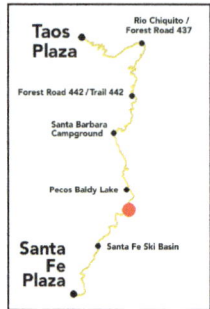

It is pretty, if that helps. For the first mile or so you'll be in dry evergreen forest with very large dispersed trees. There are views as you climb; you'll be able to see to the south and over to the east and some of Jack's Creek Campground and Horse Camp. As you continue to climb you'll cross into some beautiful, if dry, aspen forest. It gets wetter and the trees get healthier as you go. By the time you're where the trail levels off, the undergrowth is thick and the trees are vibrantly healthy.

This is unfrequently traveled trail. You might see someone on the climb up, but after that you are unlikely to see anyone until you get to Jack's Creek (the creek—not the trail or the campground). Trail conditions at the beginning, during the climb, are good. Expect a few fallen trees along the way after that. The biggest "problem" is how lush the undergrowth is. It can obscure the trail, and because this section of Dockweiler gets so little use, it would be understandable if you weren't entirely sure where the trail is at points, especially if we've gotten good moisture and the plants are having a vigorous growth season. So bring a GPS device with downloaded maps that works without cell reception. Please bring a printed map as well (or this guidebook), just in case something happens to your phone.

There is purportedly a side trail to Dockweiler. The maps say so, but I have never been able to find it. Maybe it's there; maybe not. I recommend you stay on the main part of the Dockweiler Trail, even if you find this secret path.

A little bit over a mile from where Dockweiler levels out is Dockweiler Field and rill. The rill is an unnamed little creek about three feet wide running through it. The field spreads out on both sides of the trail. It's not very level, but there are several areas you could place a tent on and enjoy a very nice spot for the night. Or you could just continue on for another 0.9 miles to the intersection of Dockweiler Trail and Rito Perro Trail (256).

Dockweiler Trail (259).

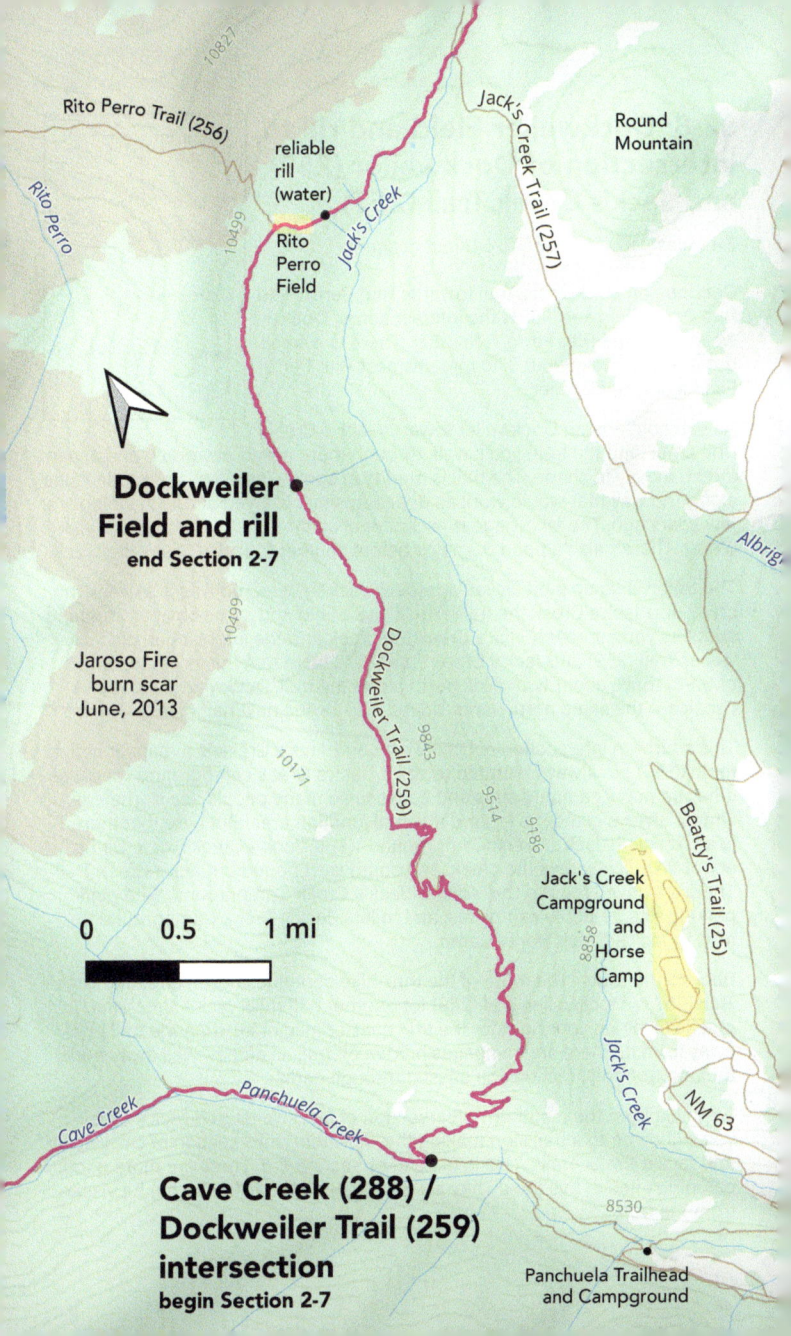

Rito Perro Trail (256)

10827

Rito Perro

reliable rill (water)

10499

Jack's Creek

Rito Perro Field

Jack's Creek Trail (257)

Round Mountain

Dockweiler Field and rill
end Section 2-7

10499

Jaroso Fire burn scar June, 2013

10171

Dockweiler Trail (259)

9843

9514

9186

Albrig

Beatty's Trail (25)

Jack's Creek Campground and Horse Camp

8588

Jack's Creek

NM 63

0   0.5   1 mi

Cave Creek

Panchuela Creek

Cave Creek (288) /
Dockweiler Trail (259)
intersection
begin Section 2-7

8530

Panchuela Trailhead and Campground

S2-8: Dockweiler Field and rill to intersection of Dockweiler (259) and Jack's Creek Trail (257)

2.4 miles. 1,169 feet ascent. 641 feet descent.

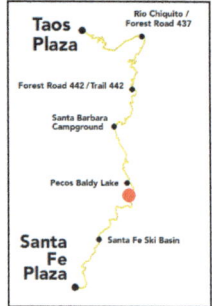

Continue on Dockweiler Trail towards Rito Perro Field. Rito Perro Field surrounds the intersection of Dockweiler Trail and Rito Perro Trail (256). There is a small but reliable creek about 5-10 minutes past Rito Perro Field along Dockweiler.

As you continue on Dockweiler towards Jack's Creek (the creek and the trail) you'll walk through more mixed evergreen and aspen forest, mostly in shade. The trail is muddy in spots. There are a few little fields along the way that would work as dry campsites. I stayed at one in October a few years ago. The fall foliage is exceptional all through this section of Dockweiler. There's also a pond 0.3 miles before you get to Jack's Creek the creek.

The trail will go up a bit as you approach Jack's Creek (both Jack's Creek the creek and Jack's Creek the trail). You'll see a field and some obvious camping spots as you approach Jack's Creek the creek and the intersection of Dockweiler Trail (259) and Jack's Creek Trail (257). Note that this is not the end of S2-8; that's about two miles north along the trail. Dockweiler and Jack's Creek are the same northwards-bound trail for the next half mile.

This southern intersection of Dockweiler and Jack's Creek is a major junction for hikers. I am always tempted to call it "Jack's Creek campground" because it has so many camping sites and because so many people use it. There is almost always someone around this trail junction area. But note that there is an "official" "Jack's Creek Campground" (and "Jack's Creek Horse Camp") about 4.1 miles across the creek, and southward bound on Jack's Creek Trail. There's a paved road to the "official" Jack's Creek Campground, with paid parking lots, rentable campsites, and toilets. Jack's Creek Campground is next to Jack's Creek Horse Camp.

Back to the route: The route of the thru-hike continues north, on Jack's Creek Trail (257) / Dockweiler Trail (259) for another half mile. Jack's Creek the creek will be on your right for the first quarter mile or so, then the trail pulls away from it. There are campsites hidden off trail all along—well away from the primary trail junction you passed through earlier.

0.5 miles from the "southern" intersection of Dockweiler and Jack's Creek you will come to a trail sign making the "northern" intersection of Dockweiler and Jack's Creek Trails. This is the end of Section 2-8. There are more good camping sites in this area. They are just far enough off-trail to not be visible from the trail.

11155

Jack's Creek Trail (257)

Jack's Creek

Dockweiler Trail (259)

**north intersection
of Dockweiler (259) and
Jack's Creek Trail (257)**
end Section 2-8

10827

10499

Jaroso Fire
burn scar
June, 2013

Dockweiler Trail (259)

Round
Mountain

Rito Perro Trail (256)

Rito Perro
Field

Jack's Creek Trail (257)

Jack's Creek

**Dockweiler
Field
and rill**
begin
Section 2-8

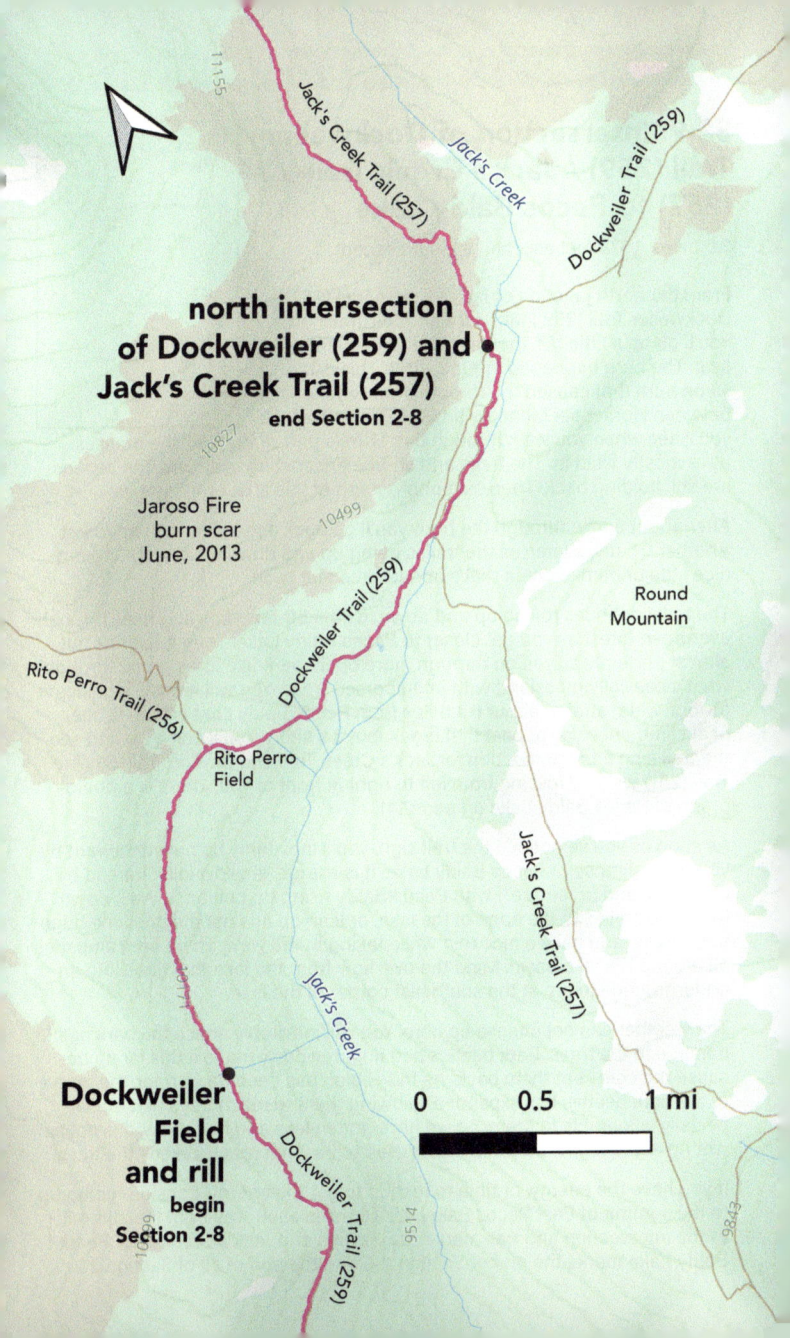

Dockweiler Trail (259)

14156

9843

0   0.5   1 mi

S2-9: Intersection of Dockweiler Trail (259) / Jack's Creek Trail (257) to Pecos Baldy Lake

2.6 miles. 1,678 feet ascent. 799 feet descent.

From the north junction of Jack's Creek Trail (257) and Dockweiler Trail (259), take Jack's Creek Trail north. You'll go up a little hill, then into the Jaroso Fire burn scar. The burn happened in June, 2013. This is the same burn that caused the reroute from Skyline Trail between Horsethief Meadow and Rito Perro Trail. As you'll see when you walk through this 1.1-mile part of the trail, the grasses have mostly filled in. The trees and shrubs are coming in slowly. The aspens are still holding back. There is a photograph of this area on page 140.

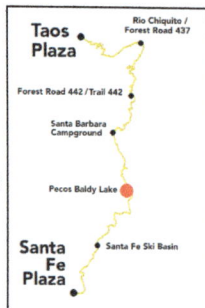

After about a mile through the burn you'll go back into tall evergreen forest. Another 0.5 miles later, as the trail is going up and down a bit, you'll cross a nice little unnamed creek that's about three feet wide.

The trail continues rolling up and down in little 50-foot dips and rises through evergreen forest as you get closer to Pecos Baldy Lake. Then it flattens out almost perfectly as you go through more open, park-like forest, then through what's basically grassland with interspersed trees. You will cross a significant (8-foot-wide) stream about 0.4 miles from Pecos Baldy Lake. There is one final climb once you're past that creek, but it's short. You'll come up and see the trail sign and intersection for Jack's Creek Trail and Skyline Trail. Skyline Trail (251) will be crossing from left to right in front of you. There is a photograph of Pecos Baldy Lake on page 141.

As soon as you've noticed the trail sign, you'll inevitably be pulled forward by your first glimpse of Pecos Baldy Lake. It is a large, shallow lake, framed by a bowl of land (a "cirque") with Pecos Baldy rising up behind it. Walk down the last 0.1 miles to the edge of the lake, or lean up against the one lone huge ponderosa, and have a nice rest while taking in the view. There are campsites all around the lake basin. Mind the overflow from the lake that goes into an underground stream at the southeast corner of the lake.

The weather can get intense up here. You will inevitably notice the bark beetle damage to the trees. Bark beetles had not previously made it this far up because the cold kept them back. As this region has become warmer, the range of the bark beetles has expanded, allowing them to reach trees that are especially vulnerable to them. As we have gotten less and less snow, it is not as wet up in the higher elevations as it used to be. That also weakens the trees.

If you have the energy, or time to rest up to get the energy, consider going up to the summit of East Pecos Baldy. It's 1.3 miles each way from the summit to the intersection and trail marker for Skyline and Jack's Creek Trail. Pecos Baldy Lake marks the end of Section 2-8 and the end of all of Section 2.

Trailriders Wall Trail (164)

11811

11811

12139

Skyline Trail (251)

Jack's Creek Trail

East Pecos
Baldy Peak

Pecos Baldy Lake

end Section 2, 2-9

Skyline Trail (251)

unmaintained

11155

0   0.5   1 mi

Jack's Creek Trail (257)

10827

Jack's Creek

Jaroso Fire burn scar
June, 2013

**north intersection
of Dockweiler (259) and
Jack's Creek Trail (257)**

begin Section 2-9

Dockweiler Trail (259)

Rito Perro Trail (256)

10499

Trail (259)

Section 3: Pecos Baldy Lake to Santa Barbara Campground

19.6 miles

S3-1: Pecos Baldy Lake to Intersection of Skyline (251) and Jose Vigil Trail (351). 2.8 miles.

S3-2: Intersection of Skyline (251) and Jose Vigil Trail (351) to Truchas Lakes. 2.5 miles.

S3-3: Truchas Lakes to Santa Barbara Divide. 2.4 miles.

S3-4: Santa Barbara Divide to West Fork Rio Santa Barbara. 5.4 miles.

S3-5: West Fork Rio Santa Barbara to intersection of Middle Fork Trail (24) and West Fork Trail (25). 3.6 miles.

S3-6: Intersection of Middle Fork Trail (24) and West Fork Trail (25) to Santa Barbara Campground free parking lot. 3.1 miles.

Alternate route: Middle Fork Trail (24).

Alternate route: Jicarita Peak / Divide Trail (36).

Get a GPX file of Section 3 at https://SantaFeToTaos.org/gpx-files/

View north/northeast from the top of the Santa Barbara Divide, where Beatty's Trail (25) becomes West Fork Trail (25).

Santa Barbara Campground
end Section 3

● Ripley Point

Calf Canyon
Fire
burn scar
August,
2022

← To Peñasco

Centennial Trail (100)

● Jicarita Peak

Alt route: Jicarita Peak Divide Trail

East Fork Trail (26)

Alt route: Middle Fork Trail (24)

West Fork Trail (25)

West Fork Rio Santa Barbara

North
Truchas
Peak

● Santa Barbara Divide

Skyline Trail (251)

Middle
Truchas
Peak

Truchas
Lakes

Trailriders Wall

0   1   2 mi

● **Pecos Baldy Lake** - beginning of Section 3

Jaroso Fire
burn scar
June, 2013

Calf Canyon Fire
burn scar
August, 2022

S3-1: Pecos Baldy Lake to intersection of Skyline (251) and Jose Vigil Trail (351)

2.8 miles. 605 feet ascent. 401 feet descent.

Section 3 starts at the trail sign that marks the intersection of Skyline Trail (251) and Jack's Creek Trail (257). From the trail sign, head northeast up what is both Skyline Trail and Jack's Creek Trail. You will be walking into small evergreen forest with lots of grassy areas. There is some shade. The trail climbs gradually.

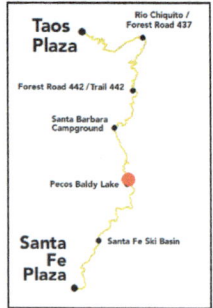

At 0.6 miles from the Jack's Creek / Skyline Trail sign you left from, Jack's Creek Trail will split off to the right. Stay left, on Skyline Trail, as you continue to climb gradually into more open fields.

Within the next 0.3 miles you will be able to see the Trailriders Wall and all the way to Truchas Peaks. It's a fantastic view. Just pay attention as the trail makes a hard left turn. There is an extremely steep slope on the right side of the trail at one point, and the slope drops off within feet of the trail.

Continue on (there are no more spots that tight for a very long way), following the path up to the top of the Trailriders Wall. You may notice another trail coming in from the left and merging with Skyline Trail. This left trail is Trailriders Wall Trail (164). Trailriders Wall Trail ends right here where it connects with Skyline Trail (251). Continue north on Skyline Trail.

For the next 1.4 miles you will have a glorious, almost 360-degree view. Consider taking a rest anywhere along the trail to take in whatever particular view you like best. The Trailriders Wall is probably most accurately described as a long narrow mesa. Elliot S. Barker, in his book *Beatty's Cabin*, called it "a long open hogback, whose east face was marked by remarkably uniform horizontal strata of limestone."

There is a little grove of weathered evergreens about 0.3 miles from the junction with the Trailriders Wall Trail (164). If you wanted shade or quick cover from a thunderstorm, that would be a good spot.

Skyline Trail climbs gradually up then gradually down over the Trailriders Wall, then has one switchback to accomodate a steeper down. You'll see the sign for the intersection of Jose Vigil Trail (351) and Skyline Trail quite a bit before you get to it. It's in the middle of the vast field/open area on the north slope of the Wall. The trails are well-worn over the Trailriders Wall, too, so don't worry about losing the trail. There is also a series of 5-foot-high rock cairns, so you'll be able to see where the trail is headed from quite a way off.

The trail sign marking the junction of Skyline Trail (251) and Jose Vigil Trail (351) is the end of Section 3-1.

Rio Medio

11811

12139

Unmaintained trail

12467

Skyline Trail (251)

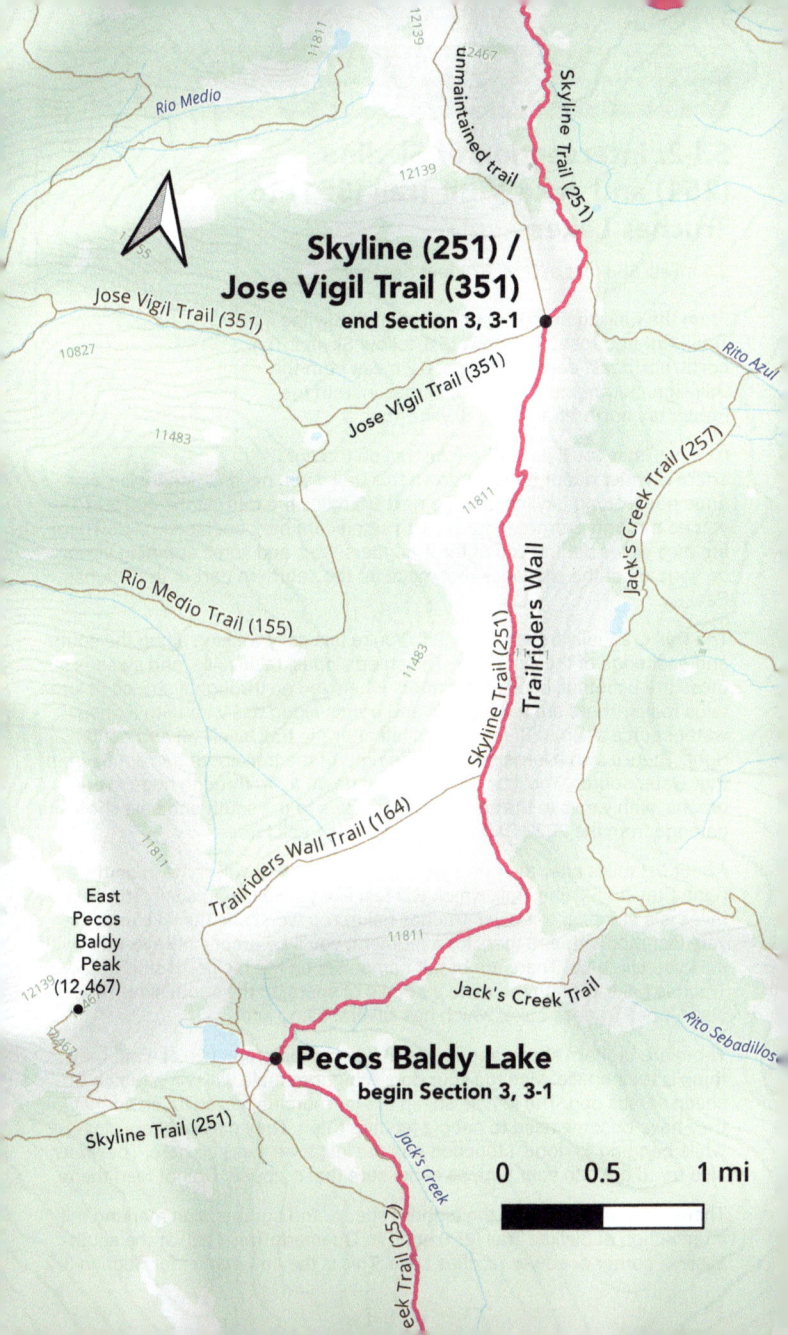

Skyline (251) /
Jose Vigil Trail (351)
end Section 3, 3-1

Jose Vigil Trail (351)

10827

Jose Vigil Trail (351)

Rito Azul

11483

Jack's Creek Trail (257)

11811

Rio Medio Trail (155)

Trailriders Wall

Skyline Trail (251)

11483

Trailriders Wall Trail (164)

11811

East
Pecos
Baldy
Peak
(12,467)

12139

11811

Jack's Creek Trail

Rito Sebadillos

Skyline Trail (251)

Pecos Baldy Lake
begin Section 3, 3-1

Jack's Creek

Creek Trail (257)

0   0.5   1 mi

S3-2: Intersection of Skyline (251) and Jose Vigil Trail (351) to Truchas Lakes

2.5 miles. 588 feet ascent. 376 feet descent.

From the trail sign marking the junction of Skyline Trail (251) and Jose Vigil Trail (351), follow Skyline Trail north/northeast down the slope. 0.2 miles from the trail sign, South Azul Trail (258) comes in from the right. Stay north/straight on Skyline Trail.

0.1 miles later you'll pass Rito Azul trail on the right. There is water about 500 feet down this trail if you need it. Otherwise, continue north along Skyline. For the next 0.8 miles the trail climbs 400 feet as you go through evergreen forest with significant bark beetle damage. There are nice views behind you of the Trailriders Wall, and some stunning views on your left of the cliff faces that make up the southern part of the Truchas Peaks.

The trail gradually bends to the left. You're basically walking along the south and east edge of the cliff faces. The steep slopes, talus piles, and sweeps of grass are beautiful. Look for marmots when you go through a stretch of large talus rocks. There are a few pools and ponds along this way, with a good water source about 500 feet on the left after the trail levels off and bends right. There's also a large pond on the right of the trail about half a mile from that water source. You'll be going up and down a bit, through huge evergreens, with views to the south. The far views to the south and east show the damage from the 2022 Calf Canyon/Hermits Peak Fire.

About 0.3 miles after the pond, North Azul Trail (264) will come in on the right. Stay on Skyline Trail, which will feel like you're taking a left. The next 0.2 miles is a climb up to Lower Truchas Lake. You won't see the lake until the very last moment, and then, for a moment, you'll be practically eye-level with it as you climb up. There are better campsites on the far, north side of Lower Truchas Lake, though there are a couple of spots on the south side. There is also Upper Truchas Lake, which has several camp sites.

There are bighorn sheep about. The males can be protective of what they think is their space. Manage your dog. A bighorn male will win a match of sheep versus dog. The female sheep are far more docile, so much so that they have become used to people feeding them. They may get very close while begging for food. I touched one the last time I was up here. They may also try to get into your tent, so make sure that's zipped. Do not feed them.

There is a trail sign about the bighorn sheep, and another sign marking the intersection of Skyline Trail (251) and Rio Quemado Trail (153) at the southeastern corner of Lower Truchas Lake. This is the end marker for Section 3-2.

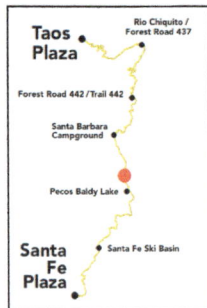

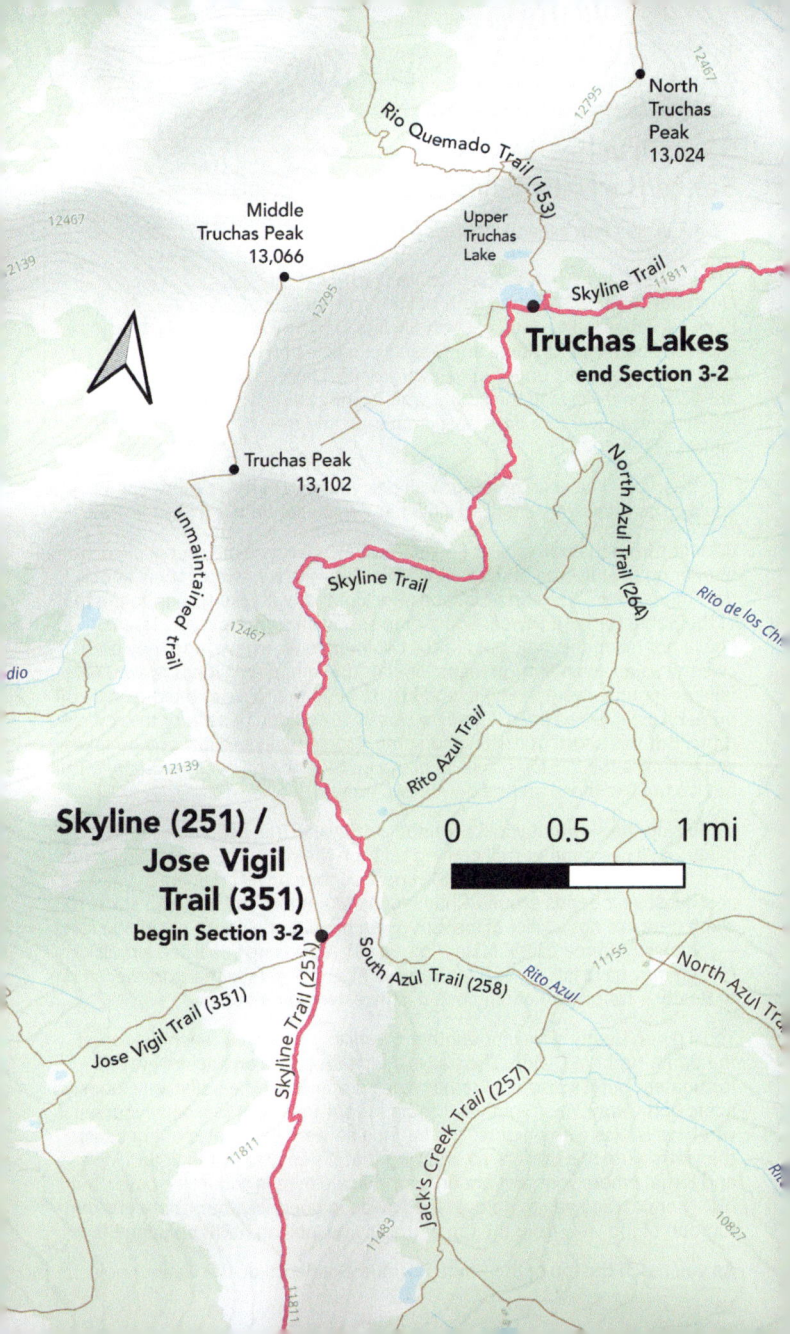

North Truchas Peak
13,024

Rio Quemado Trail (153)

Middle Truchas Peak
13,066

Upper Truchas Lake

Skyline Trail

Truchas Lakes
end Section 3-2

Truchas Peak
13,102

North Azul Trail (264)

Rito de los Ch...

unmaintained trail

Skyline Trail

Rito Azul Trail

Skyline (251) /
Jose Vigil
Trail (351)

begin Section 3-2

0   0.5   1 mi

Skyline Trail (251)

South Azul Trail (258)

Rito Azul

North Azul Tra...

Jose Vigil Trail (351)

Jack's Creek Trail (257)

12467

12795

12139

12467

12795

12467

12139

11811

11811

11155

11483

10827

S3-3: Truchas Lakes to Santa Barbara Divide

2.4 miles. 395 feet ascent. 335 feet descent.

Start at the trail marker for Skyline Trail (251) and Rio Quemado Trail (153) at the south-eastern corner of Lower Truchas Lake. Head east on Skyline Trail. You'll skirt the south side of some impressive cliff faces on your left as you pass under huge evergreens. There are occasional views to the south, which, unfortunately, now show more bark beetle damage and the effects of the 2022 fire.

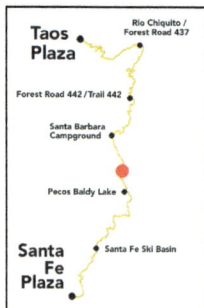

The trees become sparser and smaller as you go. There are more open fields. You'll cross a few very small shallow rills as you continue on Skyline Trail.

0.7 miles from the trail sign at Lower Truchas Lake, you may see a piled stone marker on the left side of the trail. It isn't always there; winter snow knocks the stones over. This marker is for a shortcut that will take you up to the top of the Santa Barbara Divide. Some maps show this shortcut as "Trail 264." I have not taken this trail, but I know two people who have, and they both swear it's fine, even though maps label it "unmaintained." It has looked very faint every time I've gone by it, and I try to keep the route of the thru-hike on primary, established trails wherever possible, so I don't use it for the "official" route. But this shortcut exists, and some people really like it. If you do take it, you will miss the fan-tas-tic views going up Skyline and over on Beatty's Trail, but it's not like those are the only views around.

If you skip the shortcut you'll continue on Skyline Trail heading east. In 0.2 miles you'll see another trail coming up from the right. This is our old friend Jack's Creek Trail (257). Stay on Skyline Trail, which will briefly take you southeast as it bends around Chimayosos Mountain. The trail also starts to climb here. It's not a killer climb, but given the altitude you're at—11,800 feet —you may get tired a little faster than usual. A ways up you'll see a trailsign (which may have fallen over) for Beatty's Trail (257). Take the extreme left on to Beatty's Trail, now heading in a northwesterly direction.

You'll be on Beatty's Trail for another 0.8 miles before you reach the top of the Santa Barbara Divide. The trail is a little dicey. It's on packed gravel, fortunately, but it's also on a rather steep slope. Even the trail itself slopes for some of the way. You might want to have your poles out to steady yourself if you have issues with heights. You might also want your poles out because the views from this trail are so amazing that it's easy to just look and look and forget where your feet are once or twice. There is some tree cover, but I highly encourage you to go over the Divide in good weather. There is a photograph of the view from the top of the Divide looking north on page 50.

As you reach the top of the Santa Barbara Divide, enjoy the views. Look for that shortcut trail coming up from the south side. Have someone take a photo of you standing next to the trail sign. That trail sign is the end marker for Section 3-3.

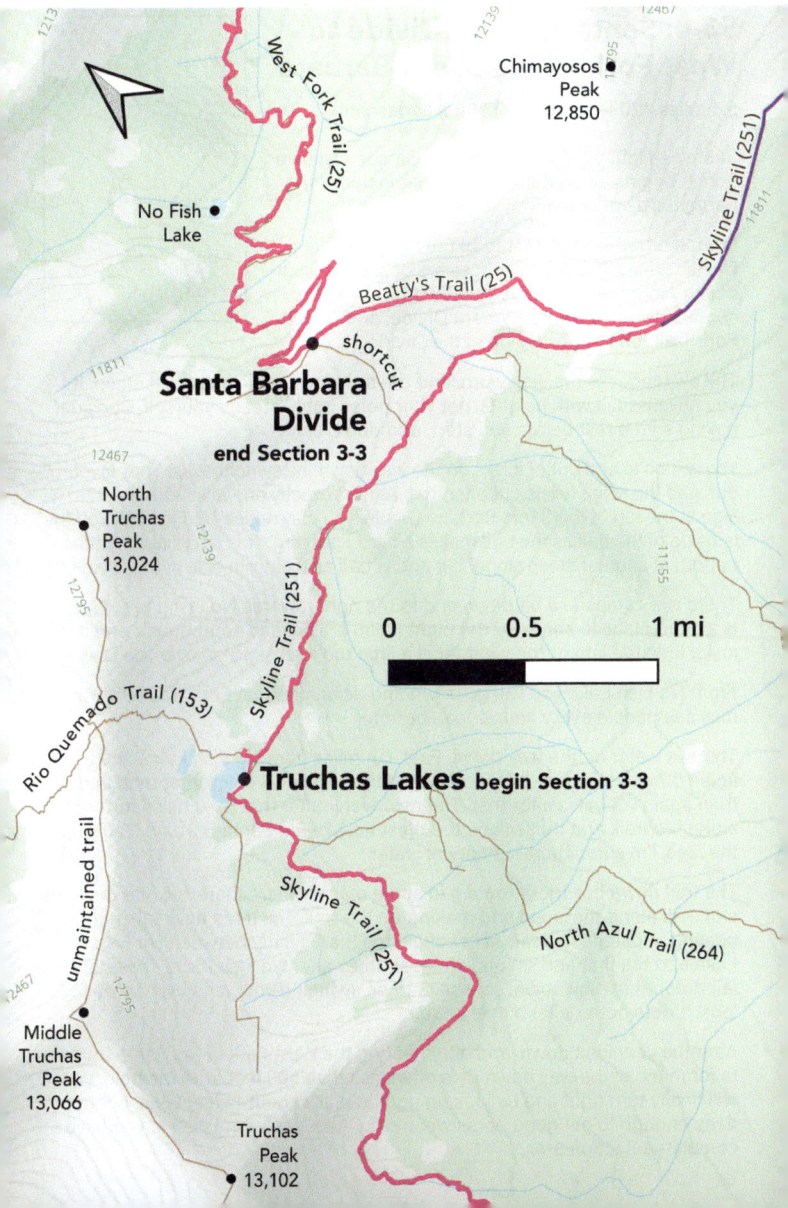

West Fork Trail (25)

Chimayosos
Peak
12,850

Skyline Trail (251)

No Fish
Lake

Beatty's Trail (25)

11811

shortcut

**Santa Barbara
Divide**

end Section 3-3

12467

North
Truchas
Peak
13,024

12139

12795

Skyline Trail (251)

11155

0   0.5   1 mi

Rio Quemado Trail (153)

Truchas Lakes begin Section 3-3

unmaintained trail

Skyline Trail (251)

North Azul Trail (264)

12467

12795

Middle
Truchas
Peak
13,066

Truchas
Peak
13,102

S3-4: Santa Barbara Divide to West Fork of Rio Santa Barbara

5.4 miles. 120 feet ascent. 2,095 feet descent.

Santa Fe National Forest ends and Carson National Forest begins along the ridgeline that includes the Santa Barbara Divide.

From the trail sign at the top of the Santa Barbara Divide, follow Trail 25 down a series of steep switchbacks. Note that Trail 25 is "Beatty's Trail" on the south side of the Santa Barbara Divide, and "West Fork Trail" on the north side of the Divide.

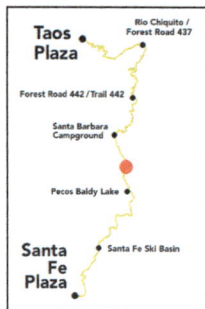

The switchbacks are well worn, and the trail down is clear. It's just steep. If you have issues with heights, get your poles out to steady yourself. Consider having a little rest before you start, and don't rush.

You will go in and out of forest on the way down the switchbacks. They level out, and the slope levels out after that. Almost exactly one mile from the trail sign at the top of the Santa Barbara Divide, you may notice No Fish Lake off the left side of the trail as the trail makes a hard right turn. This small lake is at the bottom of another steep slope, but not as bad as the north side of the Divide.

There is a campsite a bit down and to the right towards No Fish Lake. This is a good place to camp for the night if you are headed southbound and it is just a little too late or the weather is a little too intense to go over the Divide.

From No Fish Lake you will go down and down on West Fork Trail (25). You may see people every hour or so... or not.

There is water on the way down. First, 0.4 miles from No Fish Lake, and then again 0.7 miles from No Fish Lake. And then again 1.7 miles after that, and then again 0.3 miles after that. The next water after that is 1.0 miles further along the trail, and that will be the West Fork of Rio Santa Barbara. You get the idea, I'm sure: There's plenty of water.

The trail down has tricky footing in some places where there is white crushed stone all along the slope and making up the trail. The trees have taken a beating in patches on this subsection, too, particularly between No Fish Lake and the first and second water sources after No Fish Lake. There is a fair amount of blowdown, so expect to be swinging your legs over some high logs. It gets better after a mile or so.

After the very long down, and after hearing the West Fork of Rio Santa Barbara for much of the way down (it is often less than 500 feet from the trail), you will finally turn right and be looking right at it. It's about 14 feet wide, but not deep enough to get good boots wet inside. After you've crossed it, you have completed Section 3-4.

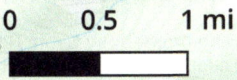

West Fork of Rio Santa Barbara
end Section 3-4

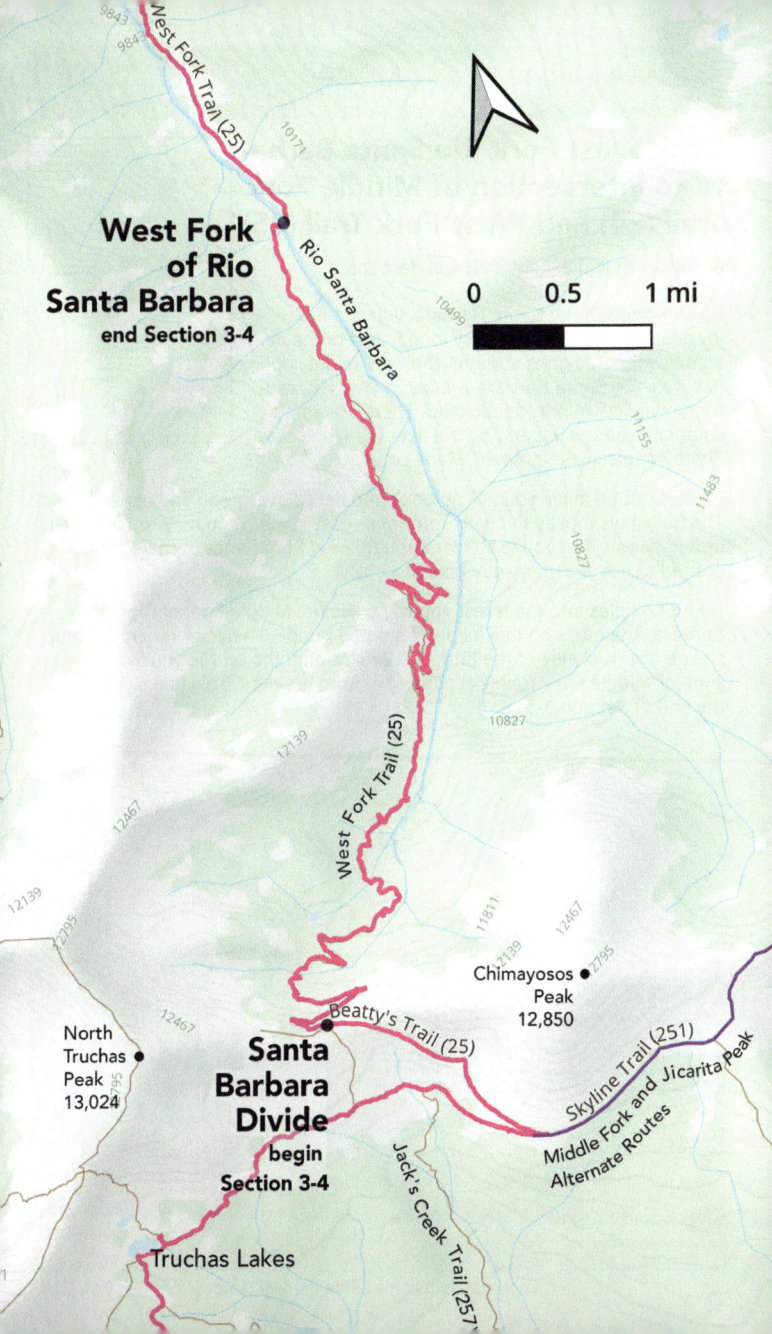

West Fork Trail (25)

Rio Santa Barbara

9843
984
10171
10499
11155
11483
10827
10827
12139
12467
12139
2795
12467
11811
12139
12467
2795

West Fork Trail (25)

Chimayosos Peak
12,850

Beatty's Trail (25)

Santa Barbara Divide
begin
Section 3-4

North Truchas Peak
13,024

2795

Skyline Trail (251)

Middle Fork and Jicarita Peak
Alternate Routes

Jack's Creek Trail (257)

Truchas Lakes

0   0.5   1 mi

S3-5: West Fork Rio Santa Barbara to intersection of Middle Fork Trail (24) and West Fork Trail (25)

3.6 miles. 21 feet ascent. 554 feet descent.

Having crossed Rio Santa Barbara, you can now enjoy a long walk through a very long field. For the next 1.5 miles the trail goes straight, through a huge, open flat area. Rio Santa Barbara will be on your left, usually only a few hundred feet away. There are ample campsites on the left and by the river the whole way. There are also usually cows. Many cows.

After about 1.5 miles you will go back into mixed evergreen and aspen forest. The trail stays mostly flat with some very easy slopes. You may run into one or two people, but you're still far enough away from Santa Barbara Campground to not see many day hikers.

About 1.6 miles into the forest you will cross the Middle Fork of Rio Santa Barbara. The crossing has a cool V-shaped bridge. There's a very nice campsite on the west side of the bridge. 0.2 miles after the bridge you'll see the sign for Middle Fork Trail (24) coming in from the right. This trail sign marks the end of Section 3-5.

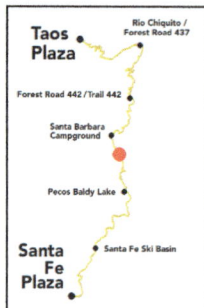

Looking south at the Santa Barbara Divide from West Fork Trail.

Intersection of West Fork Trail (25) and Middle Fork Trail (24)
end Section 3-5

Middle Fork Trail (24)

Middle Fork Rio Santa Barbara

9514

9843

10499

10827

10171

0   0.5   1 mi

Rio Santa Barbara

11155

811

West Fork Trail (25)

9843

Trampas Lakes Trail (31)

Rio de las Trampas

Intersection of West Fork Trail (25) and West Fork of Rio Santa Barbara
begin Section 3-5

S3-6: Intersection of Middle Fork Trail (24) and West Fork Trail (25) to Santa Barbara Campground free parking lot

3.1 miles. 699 feet ascent. 1,239 feet descent.

Your long walk towards Santa Barbara Campground continues along well-maintained trail with Rio Santa Barbara nearby on your left the whole way. You'll go through patches of nice big grassy fields, with campsites sprinkled along the way next to the river.

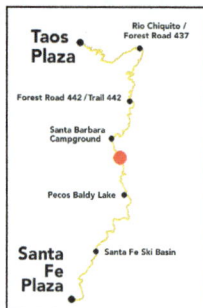

As you approach Santa Barbara campground, the hills on either side of the trail get higher and higher, rockier and rockier. Eventually, you're in a full-on canyon, with rock cliffs on either side, and Rio Santa Barbara crashing down through the middle of it. There is another bridge—wooden, wide, and in good shape—0.7 miles after the first bridge (the one in the last subsection, S3-5).

Once you cross this second bridge you are 1.4 miles from the edge of Santa Barbara Campground. As you get closer to the campground, you'll probably start to see a couple of people. There's good fishing in Rio Santa Barbara, so a lot of fishers walk up the trail to get to the quieter spots. You may also notice the "Chili Waters" fishing sign as you get closer to Santa Barbara Campground. Also note the sign marking the edge of the Pecos Wilderness. These signs are a little before Centennial Trail (100), which goes off to the left.

When you pass Centennial Trail you are 0.8 miles from the far edge of Santa Barbara Campground. You may also notice a little side trail that splits off from the main trail (Middle Fork Trail 24) to the right, about 0.3 miles from Centennial. This runs parallel to Middle Fork Trail, then veers left to rejoin it just before the gate at the edge of Santa Barbara Campground. Stay on Middle Fork Trail.

You may also notice yet another trail that branches off to the left about 26 feet before you go through the gate into the Santa Barbara campground. This is Jicarita Creek Trail (38). Don't take it. Just go through the gate into Santa Barbara Campground.

If you've parked in the free parking lots at Santa Barbara Campground, on the far side of the campground, you'll walk another half mile through the long skinny loop road of campsites. There is a campground host. If you need information or help, look for their big RV right near the cattle guard, just north of the loop of the camping grounds road. There are public toilets and a potable water source within sight of that cattle guard, too.

Congratulations. You have completed Section 3 of the thru-hike. You are halfway to Taos.

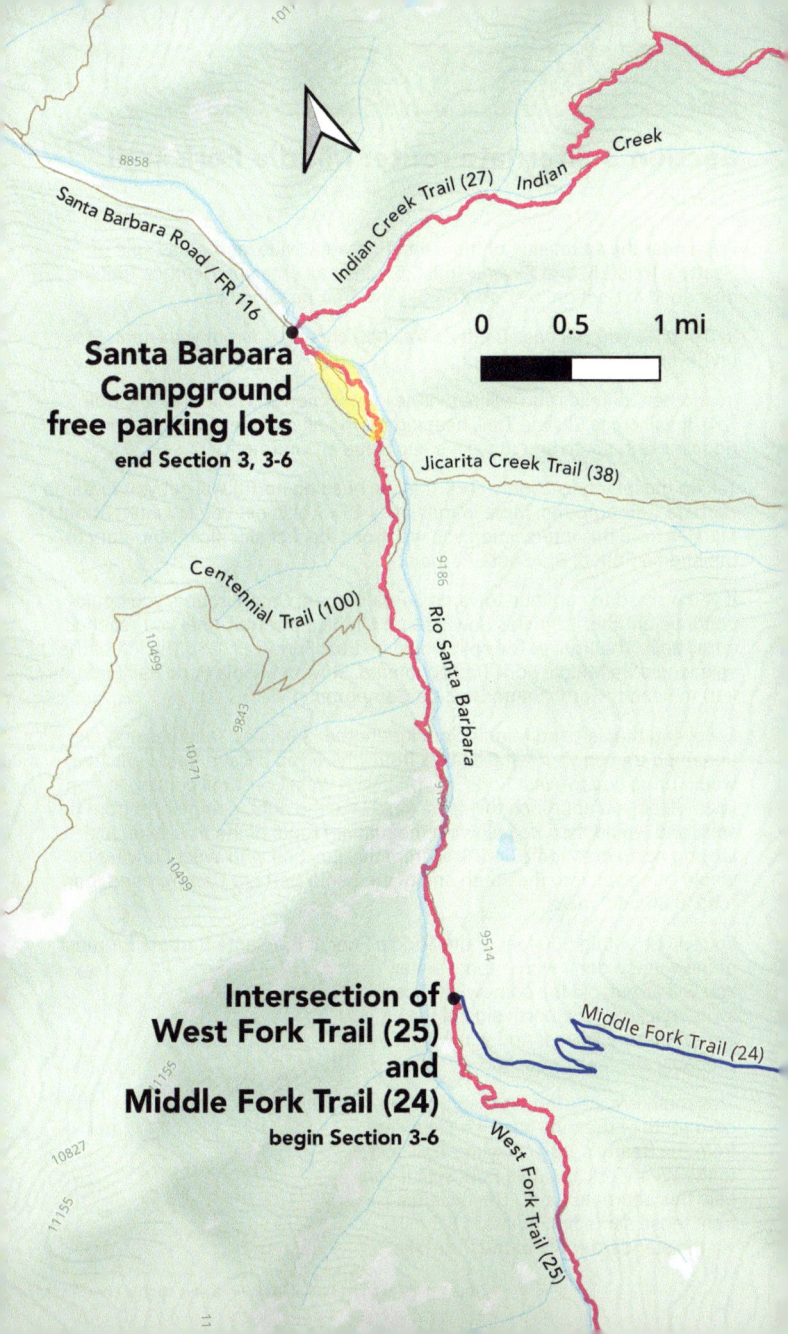

Santa Barbara Campground free parking lots
end Section 3, 3-6

Indian Creek Trail (27)   Indian   Creek

Santa Barbara Road / FR 116

8858

101

0   0.5   1 mi

Jicarita Creek Trail (38)

Centennial Trail (100)

10499

8886

10171

10499

9186

Rio Santa Barbara

9514

Intersection of West Fork Trail (25) and Middle Fork Trail (24)
begin Section 3-6

Middle Fork Trail (24)

West Fork Trail (25)

10827

11155

11

Section 3 alternate route: Middle Fork Trail

12.1 miles.

From near the south side of the Santa Barbara Divide, at the trail split of Beatty's Trail (25) and Skyline Trail (251), instead of taking Beatty's Trail (as described in Section 3-3), stay on Skyline Trail, heading east.

In 0.6 miles you will pass Beatty's Trail (25) coming up from your right. Stay on Skyline Trail and keep going.

In another 2.5 miles you will reach the intersection with Middle Fork Trail (24). It will cross Skyline Trail, heading north and down on your left from the ridgeline and south and down a steep slope on your right.

Taking the left on to Middle Fork Trail (so heading north) will get you to Santa Barbara Campground. More immediately, it will also get you to water; about 1.1 miles from this intersection you will cross the first significant tributary to the Middle Fork of Rio Santa Barbara.

If you wanted to continue towards Santa Barbara Campground, you could continue another 3.9 miles down, all on Middle Fork Trail, until you reached a trail split. The right of the split would be East Fork Trail (26). The left of the split would be Middle Fork Trail continued. Stay on Middle Fork Trail (i.e., go left) to head towards Santa Barbara Campground.

Following that left and Middle Fork for another 3.9 miles, (and passing an unnamed trail on your left 0.8 miles from where you passed East Fork Trail) would bring you to West Fork Trail (25), with West Fork Trail coming in from your left as you approach the split. You'd take the right, going north from this split, and would then be following the primary route of the thru-hike. Just staying north on Middle Fork Trail from this junction with West Fork Trail would bring you into the south end of the Santa Barbara Campground loop road in about 2 miles.

You will be within 500 feet of the Middle Fork of Rio Santa Barbara for most of the way, so don't worry about water. You will also avoid the somewhat dicey switchbacks on the north side of the Santa Barbara Divide. And you will probably see fewer people.

This route is a little longer than the standard route of the thru-hike. It's 12.1 miles from the Beatty's Trail / Skyline Trail split to the West Fork / Middle Fork split if you take this alternate route. The distance from those same two points is 8.8 miles via the standard route of the thru-hike.

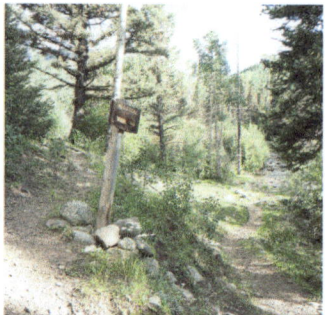

Trail sign at the junction of West Fork and Middle Fork Trails.

Santa Barbara Campground
end S3 / begin S4

Santa Barbara Divide

Ripley Point

Los Esteros

Divide Trail (36)

Jicarita Peak
12467

Serpent Lake

Serpent Lake Trail (19)

small pond just off
Divide Trail

East Fork Trail (26)

Middle Fork Trail (24)

Middle Fork Rio Santa Barbara

West Fork Trail (25)

Middle Fork Trail (24)

Divide Trail (36)

Skyline Trail (251)

Skyline Trail (251)

Calf Canyon
Fire burn scar
August 2022

Calf Canyon Fire burn scar
August 2022

0   1   2 mi

9186

9843

10171

12139

12139

12139

11155

11483

11811

Section 3 alternate route: Jicarita Peak

From near the south side of the Santa Barbara Divide, at the junction of Beatty's Trail (25) and Skyline Trail (251), instead of taking Beatty's Trail (as described in Section 3-3), stay on Skyline Trail and keep heading east. In 0.6 miles you will pass Beatty's Trail (25) as it veers off to your right. Stay on Skyline and keep going east.

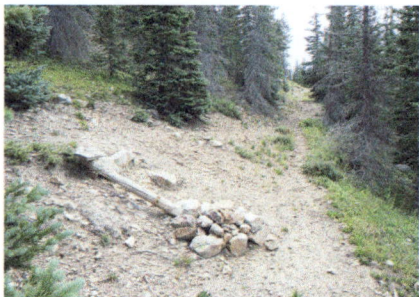

Fallen trail sign at the junction of Skyline Trail (251) and Beatty's Trail (25).

In another 2.6 miles you will reach the intersection with Middle Fork Trail (24). Middle Fork Trail goes left (north) and down from Skyline Trail. Pecos Trail (also 24) goes south and down a steep slope on your right. This is a whiff confusing, because it's going to look like this is just the same trail intersecting with Skyline Trail, but Middle Fork (24) goes north and left. Pecos Trail (also 24) goes south and right. This is very similar to how Beatty's Trail (25) switches over to West Fork Trail (25) right at the Santa Barbara Divide.

Note that there's water 1.2 miles from the ridgeline if you took the left (thus heading north) on to Middle Fork Trail (24). That's also a good out if the weather is shifting on you and it's time to get off the ridgeline. If you don't need water and the weather is still good, just stay on Skyline Trail and keep going, as Skyline Trail now bends northeast.

In another 0.4 miles along Skyline Trail you will come up to another trail on your right. This is where Skyline Trail veers off. It eventually bends down to the south and continues all the way down to near Barillas Peak, which is about the same latitude as Las Vegas, NM. We are not going to Las Vegas, so say goodbye to Skyline Trail (251) and keep going straight, thus picking up the beginning of Divide Trail (36).

Note that Divide Trail is not the Continental Divide Trail; that trail is more than 30 miles east of this point. Divide Trail probably refers to the Santa Barbara Divide. Fun fact, though: The Continental Divide Trail does also go through Carson National Forest.

Continue on Divide Trail, still heading northeast, from where it splits away from Skyline Trail. 1.0 miles later you will come up to East Fork Trail (26) on your left.

If you wanted to, you could take East Fork Trail down and get to Santa Barbara Campground by a very similar route to the Alternate Route via Middle Fork Trail (see page 64). Note, also, if you needed water, you could just zip down East Fork Trail for 0.8 miles and get some water at the tributary to the

East Fork branch of Rio Santa Barbara that crosses the trail. You could also follow that little tributary a mere 100 feet up and off trail to a little pond that is about 80 feet wide and in a fairly flat area. That might be a sweet spot to stay for the night or a good place to rest until a storm passes. There's another little pond, even closer to the trail just a few feet further down and along East Fork Trail from the first pond. These ponds are so close to the trail you will probably see them from the trail.

Assuming you do not need water, a place to sleep, or cover from weather, continue on Divide Trail (36) heading east/northeast.

As you continue over the ridgeline, the trail bends north. Right about where this gradual left/north bend is, you may see Middle Fork Lake off the right side of the trail. In another 0.8 miles from this turn, you'll pass Trouble Mountain on your right. North Fork Lake will also pass by on your right in another half mile or so (you probably won't be able to see it), followed by Horseshoe Lake on your right, about another 0.7 miles along the Divide Trail.

1.5 miles from where Horseshoe Lake was directly on your right, you will reach the intersection of Divide Trail and Serpent Lake Trail (19). The Divide Trail continues straight ahead. Serpent Lake Trail crosses it, so Serpent Lake Trail goes both left (west) and right (east).

If you need to get off the ridgeline or you need water, take the right down Serpent Lake Trail. There's a little pond 0.1 miles from the intersection with the Divide Trail. This is your last water access for 6.0 miles, when you reach Los Esteros. Note that if you wanted to get to Santa Barbara Campground, you'd take the left from this intersection, heading west down Serpent Lake Trail.

0.3 miles from the Divide / Serpent Lake intersection, the trail splits. The right branch will take you to the summit of a mountain that is not Jicarita Mountain in 0.5 miles. The left branch is Divide Trail (36).

From that split, it is another 0.9 miles to the split for Jicarita Peak (12,808 feet). There is an unmaintained trail that goes down from the peak and rejoins the Divide Trail on the other side. If you don't take the peak route, it's 1.3 miles from the split to get around Jicarita Peak to the point where the peak route rejoins the Divide Trail. If you do take the peak route, it's 0.8 miles point to point.

Note that there is a little split in the Divide Trail in this same area where the peak route rejoins the Divide. It's only 300 feet from the Divide Trail, and the unmaintained little "diversion" rejoins the Divide Trail in about 700 feet. Either trail will do; just be aware that you may see several trail variants while you're up on Jicarita Peak.

From where the little diversion rejoins the trail, you'll start down, still heading north. It's a gradual down that is basically flat for a while. About one mile on you will go back below the tree line. Another mile after that you will walk up to where Indian Creek Trail (21) comes in on the left. This is also where you rejoin the standard route of the thru-hike.

Note that this Jicarita alternate route does not take you into Santa Barbara Campground. If you need to get to Santa Barbara Campground but want to do as much of this alternate route as possible, go down via Serpent Lake Trail, taking the left (west) from where it intersects with Divide Trail.

Section 4: Santa Barbara Campground to Forest Road 442

18.6 miles

S4-1 Santa Barbara Campground free parking lot to intersection of Indian Creek Trail (27) and Bear Mountain Trail (28). 2.1 miles.

S4-2: Intersection of Indian Creek Trail (27) and Bear Mountain Trail (28) to intersection Indian Creek Trail (27) and Divide Trail (36). 2.6 miles.

S4-3: Intersection Indian Creek Trail (27) and Divide Trail (36) to Los Esteros. 1.5 miles.

S4-4: Los Esteros to intersection of Agua Piedra Creek, Trail 19A and Trail 22. 3.8 miles.

S4-5: Trail 19a/22/Agua Piedra Creek to Agua Piedra Campground entrance. 1.9 miles.

S4-6: Agua Piedra Campground bridge to La Cueva Canyon/Trail 492. 0.9 miles.

S4-7: La Cueva Canyon / La Cueva Trail (492) to intersection of La Cueva Trail (492) and Ojitos Maes Trail (182). 1.7 miles.

S4-8: Intersection of La Cueva Trail (492) and Ojitos Maes Trail (182) to intersection of Ojitos Maes Trail (182) and La Cueva 8. 1.4 miles.

S4-9: Intersection of La Cueva 8 and Ojitos Maes Trail to FR 442. 2.7 miles.

Get a GPX file of Section 4 at https://SantaFeToTaos.org/gpx-files/

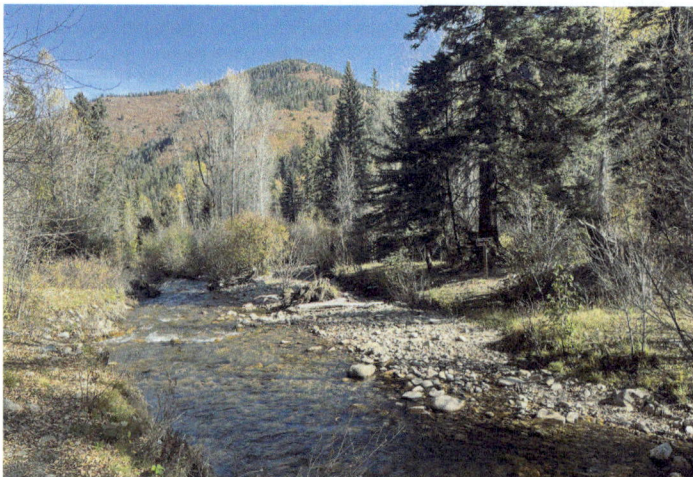

Rio Santa Barbara, from near the day parking lot at Santa Barbara Campground.

Forest Road 442
end Section 4

FR 442

10499

Ojitos Maes Trail (182)

La Cueva Lake

La Cueva Field

Santa Fe to Taos Thru-Hike Members' Resupply

8858

TRES RITOS

9514

Indian Lake

New Mexico Highway 518

Rio del Pueblo

Sipapu Ski & Summer Resort

Agua Piedra Campground entrance bridge

8530

8202

9514

FR 183

9843

Trail 7

10171

0   1   2 mi

10171

9843

10499

Trail (22)

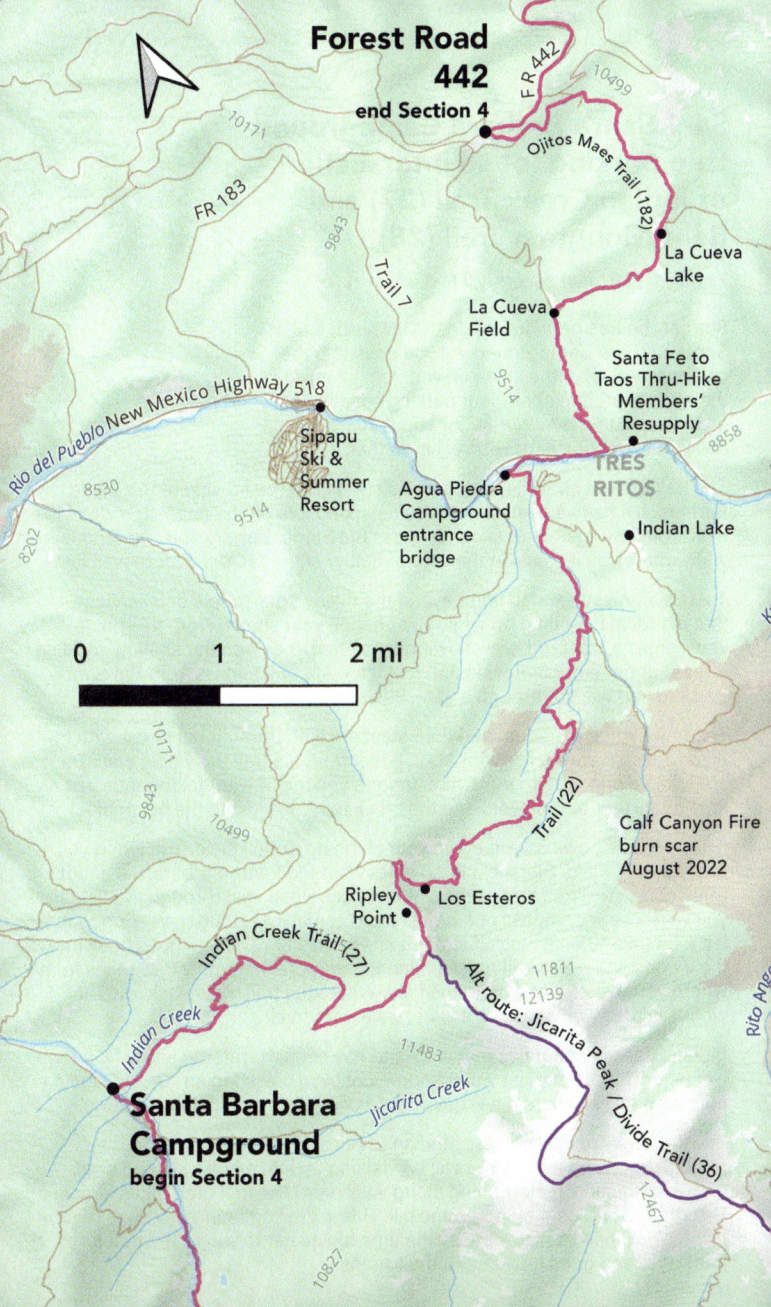

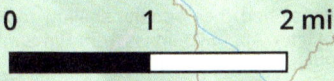

Calf Canyon Fire burn scar August 2022

Ripley Point

Los Esteros

11811

12139

Indian Creek Trail (27)

Indian Creek

Alt route: Jicarita Peak / Divide Trail (36)

Rito Ange

Ke

11483

Santa Barbara Campground
begin Section 4

Jicarita Creek

10827

12467

S4-1 Santa Barbara Campground free parking lot to intersection of Indian Creek Trail (27) and Bear Mountain Trail (28)

2.1 miles. 1,692 feet ascent. 25 feet descent.

Start at the free parking lots on the far north end of Santa Barbara Campground. As you drive into the campground area, they'll be on your left, alongside the river. There are about four parking spaces right off the road, then another lot for about 20+ cars about 100 feet north (downriver) from that.

The trail marker for Indian Canyon Trail (27) is on the far side of Rio Santa Barbara. It's halfway between the two parking lots on the opposite side of the river. You may want river shoes to cross Rio Santa Barbara. It is about 15 feet wide where you'll cross. In the spring melt or after rain, the river moves fast.

There's a grassy area 30 feet beyond the river with a couple of fallen logs that are ideal for sitting on while you change your shoes. From this point, you'll cross a wet but barely flowing creek bed, then another shallow trickling "creek" about eight feet wide 500 feet later. About 0.2 miles from Rio Santa Barbara you will go through a gate. Please close it behind you.

The trail begins a gradual and then steeper climb through tall forest with Indian Creek on your left, about 50-250 feet from the trail the whole way. There are spots along here to put a tent, though you might want to continue just a little bit further to Bull Field and the creek that runs just to the north of it.

Expect to see cows as you begin your climb up to Bull Field, and when you arrive at Bull Field. Bull Field is 0.8 miles from Rio Santa Barbara. It's about three acres. The trail is faint through the field. Head east through the field if you've got your compass out, or just head somewhat straight, veering to the left a bit (like 10 on a clock if straight ahead was 12). The trail goes back into the woods again and will cross Indian Canyon Creek roughly 0.25 miles from where you first stepped on to the field. Where the trail goes back into the woods is pretty obvious. It's a wide, well-worn track.

Indian Creek is about five feet wide and has enough water to easily fill a Nalgene. This is your last water source until you cross Indian "Creek" again in about 2.5 miles, where it will have about one fourth as much water flow.

Indian Creek Trail (27) crosses Indian Creek and then begins a climb up through full-sized aspen. You will be walking up into a bowl-shaped area, now with Indian Creek running along your right. The trail then takes almost a U-turn here left, continuing up the hill. This is the beginning of a considerable climb. You'll have a nice view by the time to you get to where the trail turns hard right and goes further into the aspens.

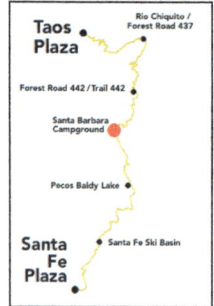

The trail flattens out briefly, then climbs through aspens and evergreens.

Expect fallen trees. You'll be able to see the far side of Indian Canyon through the trees in spots. After the climb—832 feet of elevation in the 0.8 miles from where you crossed Indian Creek—you will walk up to a trail split. Bear Mountain Trail (28) goes off to the left. Indian Creek Trail (27) continues on to the right. This is the end marker for Section 4-1.

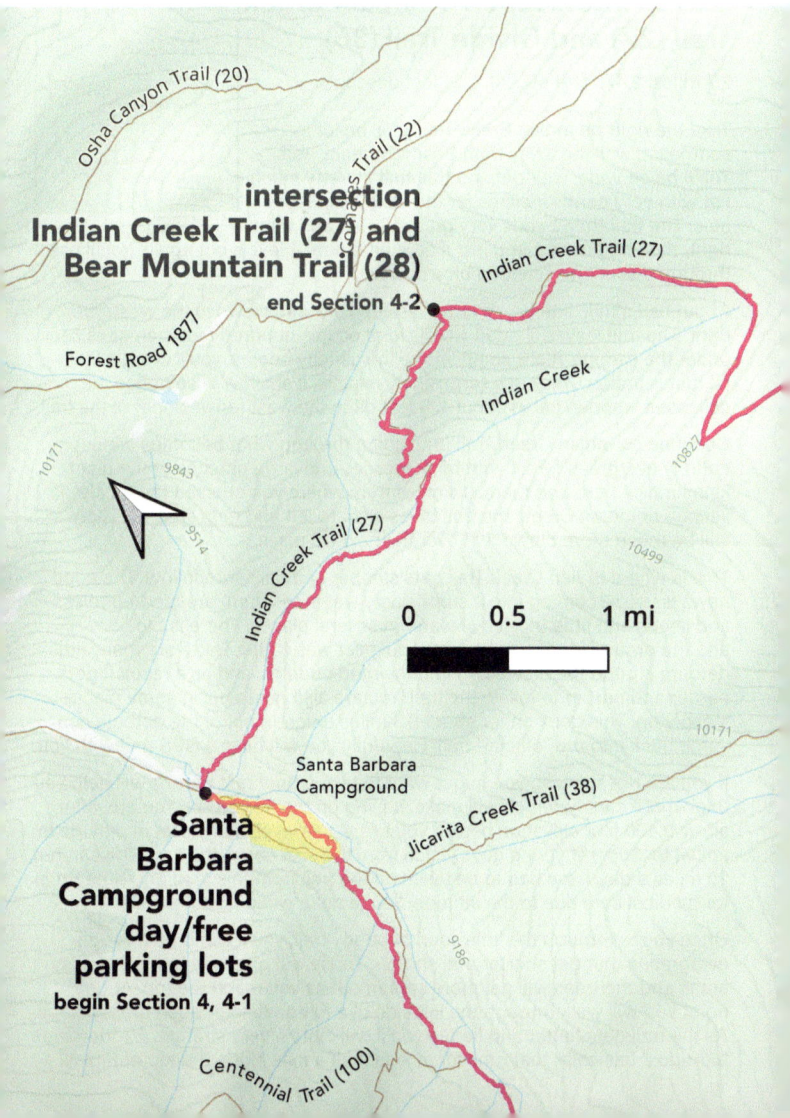

Osha Canyon Trail (20)

Trail (22)

intersection Indian Creek Trail (27) and Bear Mountain Trail (28)
end Section 4-2

Indian Creek Trail (27)

Forest Road 1877

Indian Creek

Indian Creek Trail (27)

10171

9843

9514

10827

10499

0   0.5   1 mi

Santa Barbara Campground

Jicarita Creek Trail (38)

10171

Santa Barbara Campground day/free parking lots
begin Section 4, 4-1

9186

Centennial Trail (100)

S4-2: Intersection of Indian Creek Trail (27) & Bear Mountain Trail (28) to intersection of Indian Creek Trail (27) and Divide Trail (36)

2.7 miles. 2,470 feet ascent. 1,191 feet descent.

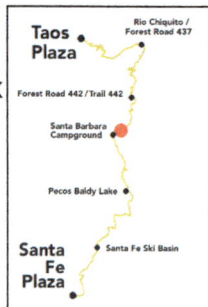

Take the right on Indian Creek Trail (27), heading southeast, walking away from Bear Mountain Trail. You'll be on wide, well-defined trail that's pretty much flat with very gentle inclines for the next 0.3 miles plus. The trail then bends very gradually left and then right, then begins to climb just a little bit before it levels out again. You'll pass through a section of cleared blowdown.

About half a mile later you'll cross a steep field with views to the west/your right. The trail leaves shaded woods for a couple hundred feet then goes back under the canopy. Right about where the canopy begins, you'll cross a little rill that is Indian Creek. It's surprisingly reliable, if shallow. Also notice the collapsed wooden cabin about 150 feet off to the west (downslope) of the trail.

Continue on Indian Creek Trail (27), going through what becomes almost entirely evergreen forest with thick mosses and large patches of the plant kinnikinnick here and there. 0.4 miles from where you crossed the trickly version of Indian Creek, the trail takes a sharp left and gets steeper. There will be much more blowdown over the next 0.6 miles.

This is where Indian Creek Trail gets steeper and harder to follow. The good news is you're coming into a surprisingly wet area. There are mud puddles and seeps and little trickles of water in several places. There is blowdown, and the ground is torn up by what I suspect was cattle. There are many little detours around the blowdown and the mud puddles, and as a result it gets harder and harder to follow the trail. You are also going up, in some places steeply up. This goes on for about 0.3 miles before most of the detours converge back into the "official" trail. Hopefully you will have a GPS unit with you.

If you are not superfit, you might want to take a brief rest here. It will help you think more clearly, which will make staying on the trail easier. You are, after all, at 11,400 feet elevation here. If you live at sea level, that's a lot of altitude to adjust to. Superfit young guys just in from the east coast, the sort who can run 20 miles a day, have had to be taken off the trail from this area and brought in for medical care due to the altitude. You're not a wimp if you're tired.

Once you're through the little snarl of boggy trail, you'll climb up through evergreens that get shorter and shorter. These will give way to more grassy areas and the trees will get more spread out as you reach the top. At one point you will walk through the left side of a full-on field or open grassy slope. As the trail gets flatter and flatter, you'll walk into a very strange, 40-foot-wide "corridor," basically, that runs for at least half a mile along the top of Ripley

Point. The corridor has been created because all the trees in it have been torn up. I cannot discern how this happened, and it happened in the last couple of years. I didn't see any clean cuts, like from a chainsaw... it's like all the trees were just churned up. I didn't see any tracks from machinery.

In the middle of this mess, as you walk into it, is the trail marker for the intersection of Indian Creek Trail (27) and the Divide Trail (36) (It's not the Continental Divide Trail). If you took the alternate route over Jicarita Peak in Section 3, this is where you'll rejoin the standard route of the thru-hike.

This trail marker marks the end of Section 4-2.

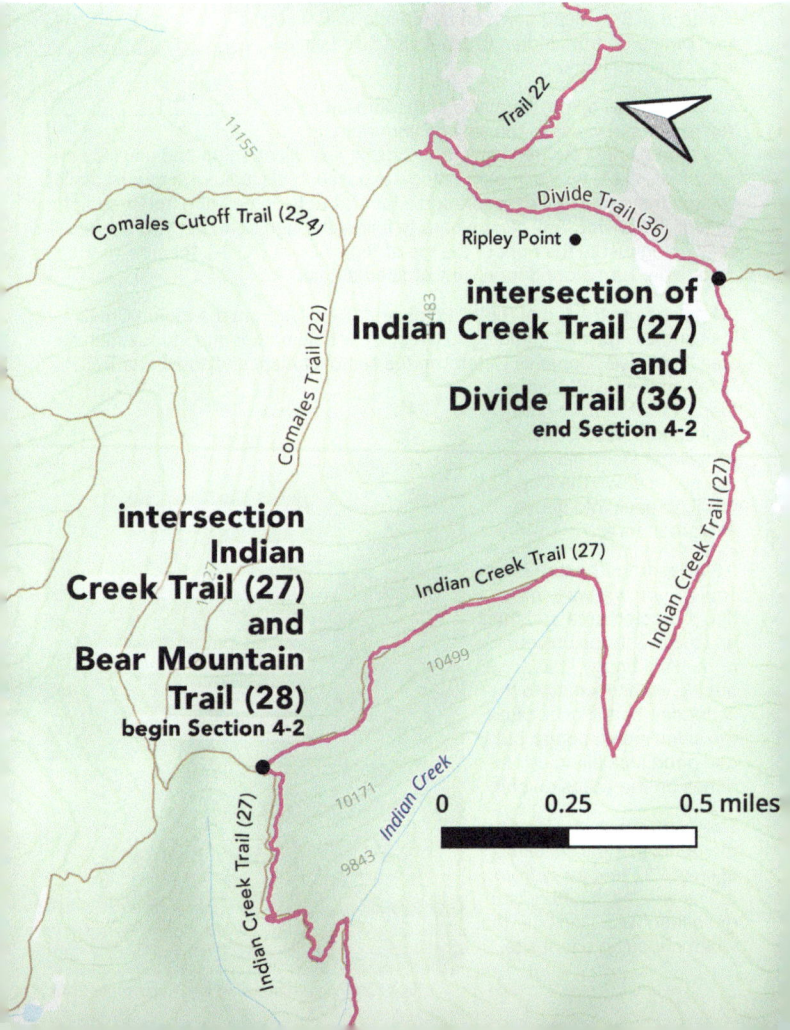

Trail 22

Divide Trail (36)

11155

Comales Cutoff Trail (224)

Ripley Point •

intersection of Indian Creek Trail (27) and Divide Trail (36) end Section 4-2

Comales Trail (22)

Indian Creek Trail (27)

intersection Indian Creek Trail (27) and Bear Mountain Trail (28) begin Section 4-2

Indian Creek Trail (27)

10499

10171

9843 Indian Creek

Indian Creek Trail (27)

0   0.25   0.5 miles

S4-3: intersection of Indian Creek Trail (27) and Divide Trail (36) to Los Esteros

1.6 miles. 551 feet ascent. 966 feet descent.

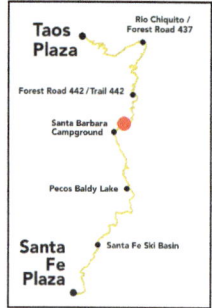

From the intersection of Indian Creek Trail (27) and Divide Trail (36), head north on the Divide Trail. If you are coming up from Indian Creek Trail, you'll take a left at the trail marker.

Follow the trail on the right side of the torn-up trees. You'll have big views to the east on your right. In less than 0.1 mile the trees on either side of you will open up and you'll be on what feels like a typical mountaintop—exposed, rocky soil, with much smaller twisted trees. You will pass through a fence, but keep heading north/straight ahead. The Divide Trail can be hard to follow through here, but you are basically going just to the right of the top of Ripley Point (11,791), then down the other side. Turn around for a view of Jicarita Peak.

0.4 miles from the top of Ripley Point, and 0.9 miles from the Indian Creek Trail and Divide Trail marker, you'll reach the trail marker and intersection for Trail 22 (called "Comales Cutoff" on the National Map, and shown as Trail "22a" on the USFS Visitor map). Take the right onto Trail 22 and head down a somewhat steep slope. As you come down the slope you'll go back into dense evergreen forest.

0.5 miles from the turn onto Trail 22 you will walk into a flat, protected area and then up to Los Esteros on your right. It's a boggy little pond, but it's water. Getting to the water can be tricky because the sides are so boggy, but I had good luck filling up Nalgenes on the east side of it.

There are campsites around the pond, just please camp at least 200 feet away from it. The weather up here can get a little wild. Consider that when choosing a tent site.

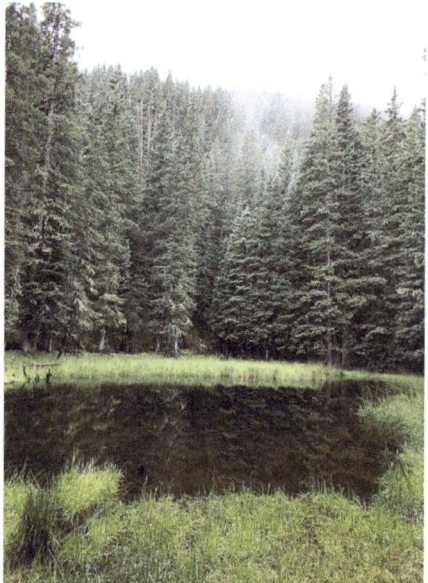

Los Esteros with morning fog, September 2018.

Comales Trail (22)

11483

Trail 22

Los Esteros
end Section 4-3

Los Esteros

Ripley Point •

11155

Divide Trail (36)

| 0 | 0.25 | 0.5 mi |

intersection of
Indian Creek Trail
(27) and
Divide Trail (36)
begin Section 4-3

Indian Creek Trail (27)

11811

S4-4: Los Esteros to intersection of Agua Piedra Creek, Trail 19A and Trail 22

3.8 miles. 58 feet ascent. 2,120 feet descent.

From Los Esteros you'll make your way down towards Agua Piedra (the creek and the campground) through some lovely country. It's the usual mix of aspen and evergreens with lots of shade plus many large fields.

The trail is fairly good, if faint in spots. There is some blowdown. You'll also go through a burn scar from the Calf Canyon Fire for about half a mile.

2.6 miles from Los Esteros you'll cross a nice unnamed creek that's a good reliable water source and a good place to camp. Another 0.9 miles from there you'll cross a tributary to Agua Piedra creek.

100 feet after crossing that tributary, you'll come to the trail marker of Trail 22 and Agua Piedra Trail (19A). This is the end point for Section 4-5.

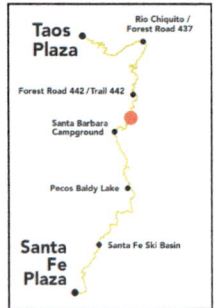

Coming down Trail 22 from Los Esteros.

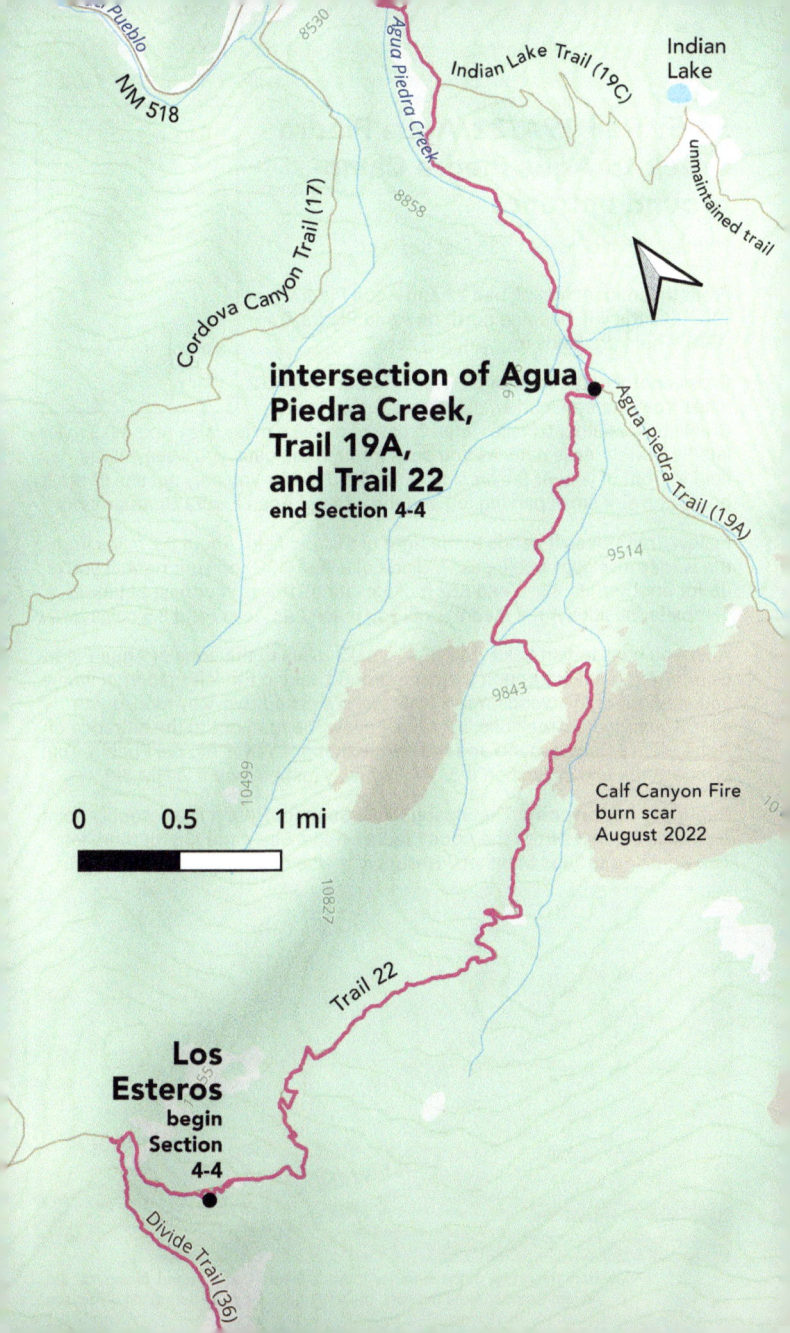

Pueblo

NM 518

8530

Agua Piedra Creek

Indian Lake Trail (19C)

Indian Lake

unmaintained trail

Cordova Canyon Trail (17)

8858

intersection of Agua Piedra Creek, Trail 19A, and Trail 22
end Section 4-4

Agua Piedra Trail (19A)

9514

9843

10499

Calf Canyon Fire burn scar August 2022

0   0.5   1 mi

10827

Trail 22

Los Esteros
begin Section 4-4

Divide Trail (36)

S4-5: Trail 19A/22/Agua Piedra Creek to Agua Piedra Campground entrance

1.9 miles. 55 feet ascent. 735 feet descent.

From the intersection of Trail 22 and Agua Piedra Trail 19A, take the left, heading north on Agua Piedra Trail (19A). There are fields for camping here.

Cross another little tributary to Agua Piedra Creek 0.2 miles from the trail marker, then cross Agua Piedra Creek itself another 0.1 miles later. Cross it again 0.4 miles later. About 0.3 miles later is a wilderness gate. As you pass through the gate, you'll see a large field in front of you. At the far side of this field (so far you may not see it) are a horse corral, a small parking lot, and the edge of Agua Piedra Campground.

Follow Trail 19A as it bends to the right of this big field. About 0.2 miles from the wilderness gate, you'll pass Indian Lake Trail (19C) on your right. If you're up for another 1.5 miles (and 852 ft of elevation), this is your best bet for a campsite (besides Agua Piedra) until you reach La Cueva Field 3.5 miles away.

After you pass Indian Lake Trail (19C) it's 0.3 miles to the edge of Agua Piedra Campground. Walk through the campground, taking the left road from where you step out of the woods. You'll walk along a paved two-way road, going over Agua Piedra Creek one last time. Follow the road out to the entrance of Agua Piedra Campground and the bridge that goes over Rio del Pueblo. That bridge is the end of Section 4-5. The highway just beyond it is NM 518.

Resupply opportunity: The Sipapu Ski & Summer Resort is a resupply point. Sipapu is 2.2 miles from the Agua Piedra bridge. See page 138 for more info. The Santa Fe to Taos Members' Resupply is also near here, in Section 4-6.

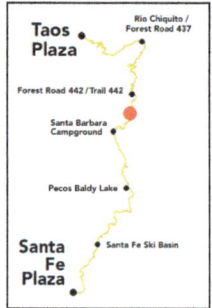

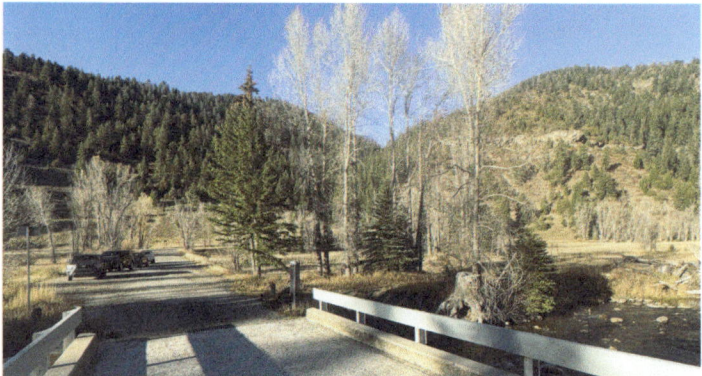

View from the bridge at the entrance to Agua Piedra Campground, facing NM 518, in late October. Note the cars; the entry gate is closed during the off season.

9514

La Cueva Canyon Trail (492)

Santa Fe to Taos Thru-Hike Members' Resupply

8530

Tres Ritos

NM 518

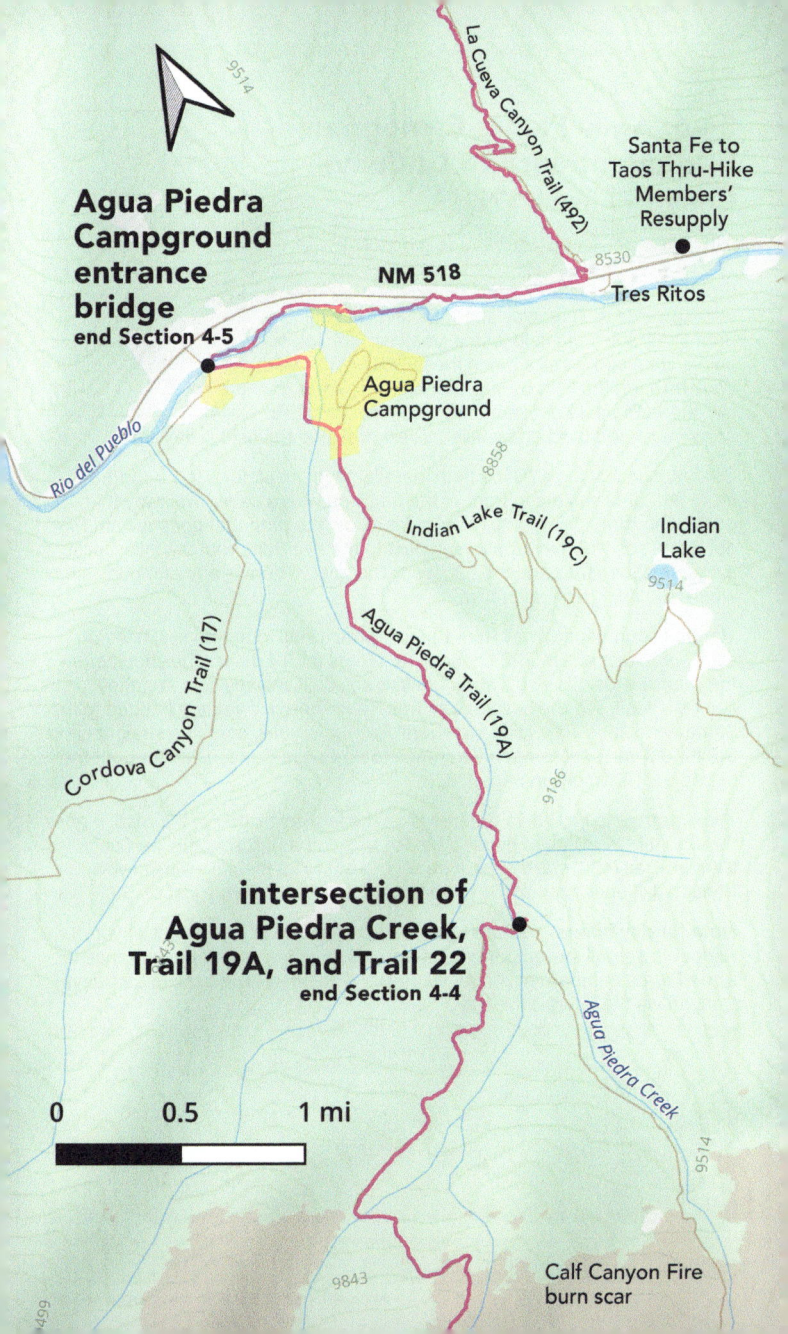

Agua Piedra Campground entrance bridge
end Section 4-5

Agua Piedra Campground

Rio del Pueblo

8858

Indian Lake Trail (19C)

Indian Lake

9514

Cordova Canyon Trail (17)

Agua Piedra Trail (19A)

9186

intersection of Agua Piedra Creek, Trail 19A, and Trail 22
end Section 4-4

Agua Piedra Creek

0   0.5   1 mi

9514

9843

9499

Calf Canyon Fire burn scar

S4-6: Agua Piedra Campground bridge/entrance to La Cueva Canyon / Trail 492

0.95 miles. 377 feet ascent. 273 feet descent.

From the Agua Piedra bridge, facing the highway, walk towards the highway about 50 feet. To your right you'll see a big field with a small parking lot, a picnic area, and a trail sign on the far side of the field. Walk through the field over to that area. (There is a trail along Rio del Pueblo, but after 100 feet or so it's grown over and blocked by fallen trees. Crossing the field is easier.)

Continue east along a paved path, parallel to the river, for a few hundred more feet until you are in front of the trail sign with a paved walkway that goes off in three directions. From there follow the path that goes toward Rio del Pueblo and upriver. You'll walk next to the river for about 0.2 miles, past a couple of benches and the "Gnaw or Die" sign. There is a brief muddy spot where Rio del Pueblo overflowed.

The trail soon bends away from the river. You'll walk out onto 518, heading east/southeast on NM 518 towards Tres Ritos for 0.4 miles. The shoulder on the road is wide. It's also a straightaway, so you'll see any cars and they'll see you. You'll see the buildings of Tres Ritos shortly. If you are headed to the Santa Fe to Taos Thru-Hike Members' Resupply, you'll continue straight on Rt 518 for 0.2 miles, passing the entrance to La Cueva Canyon. More about the Members' Resupply on page 138.

The entrance to La Cueva Canyon is on the left/north side of the road. It goes through a little clutch of houses. Please be quiet and respectful. La Cueva Canyon Trail (492) starts near a trail sign about 700 feet into the canyon. Section 4-6 ends right at the entrance of La Cueva Canyon, just off 518.

Note for day hikers: You can't park at the entrance to La Cueva Canyon. Park at the small, paved parking lot about 0.25 miles east of the entrance to Agua Piedra campground (directly off NM 518), then walk back to La Cueva Canyon via the interpretive trail.

Approaching NM 518 from the interpretive trail.

Santa Fe to Taos Thru Hike Members' Resupply •

Tres Ritos Lodge •

TRES RITOS

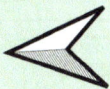

La Cueva Canyon Trail (492)

• **entrance
to La Cueva
Canyon /
Trail 492**
end Section 4-6

0   0.25   0.5 mi

8858

9186

• "Gnaw or Die" sign
along interpretive path

parking for
entrance to
La Cueva Canyon,
picnic tables,
kiosk, bathrooms

Rio del Pueblo

8530

NM 518

Forest Service Road 708

Agua Piedra Creek

**Agua Piedra
Campground bridge**
begin Section 4-6

entrance road
to Agua Piedra
Campground

Cordova Canyon Trail (17)

S4-7: La Cueva Canyon / La Cueva Trail (492) to intersection of La Cueva Trail (492) and Ojitos Maes Trail (182)

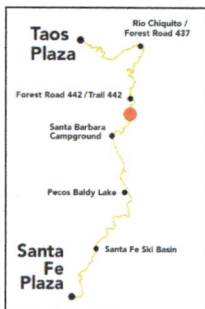

1.7 miles. 562 feet ascent. 90 feet descent.

Walk away from Route 518 into the entrance to La Cueva Canyon, passing a few cabins and houses.

The beginning of the trail is clearly marked, and the trail itself well-worn. There is a small creek that runs along on the left for the first 10 minutes or so. This is your last access to water until you get to La Cueva Field in about 1.5 miles.

It's a bit of a climb for the next half mile, but not too bad. You'll be under mixed aspen and evergreen canopy with an assortment of wildflowers. The trail flattens out after half a mile. It stays flat for the next half mile as you go through some lovely wildflower-strewn fields on your way to La Cueva Field.

By the time you see the old collapsed cabin just off the trail on your left, you'll probably be getting your first views of La Cueva Field. It's big; probably about 15 acres, and long and narrow, like a football field. There is a robust little creek on the left/west side of it; you'll probably hear it as you walk past it.

Continue on the trail, looking for the metal boxspring (like for a bed) that will be on your left. About 150/200 feet beyond the boxspring is the intersection of La Cueva Trail (492) and Ojitos Maes Trail (182), which is the end of S4-7.

Somewhere along the edge of La Cueva Field, particularly toward the back of it, would make a great place to camp for the night.

La Cueva Field.

La Cueva Canyon Trail (492)

large
wooden
bench

Ojitos Maes Trail (182)

**intersection
of La Cueva
Canyon Trail (492)
and Ojitos Maes
Trail (182)**
end Section 4-7

9843

La Cueva Canyon Trail (492)

9514

8858

parking for
entrance to
La Cueva Canyon,
picnic tables,
kiosk, bathrooms

Tres
Ritos
Lodge

Rio del Pueblo

NM 518

8530

**entrance
to La Cueva
Canyon /
Trail 492**
begin Section 4-7

Agua Piedra
Campground

Agua Piedra Creek

0   0.5   1 mi

S4-8: Intersection of La Cueva Trail (492) & Ojitos Maes Trail (182) to intersection of Ojitos Maes Trail (182) and La Cueva 8

1.4 miles. 982 feet ascent. 48 feet descent.

Finding where La Cueva Trail and Ojito Maes Trail (182) intersect can be tricky. This section of Ojito Maes (aka "La Cueva Cutoff") Trail does not exist on many maps, but it does exist on the National Map.

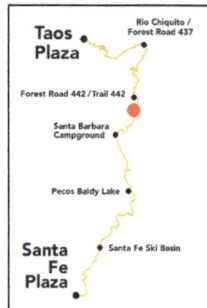

Hopefully you have a GPS device with you, so you'll be able to follow the route with that. If you don't, know that if you've crossed the little creek (that had been on your left when you were about one-third of the way into La Cueva Field), you've gone too far.

To find where the trails meet, look for an old metal boxspring of a bed on the left side of the trail. About 150/200 feet past that boxspring is where you should turn right/east and head up the slope. After walking about 250 feet up the slope, you'll see a large wooden bench. The bench is under a couple of big ponderosas. It is about 12 feet long, sitting on three short tree logs. It is right next to the trail known as La Cueva Cutoff.

The trail from the bench and up to La Cueva Lake is well-defined, but a bit rough and steep. It's become one of those trails that's kind of an earthen chute, with the edges of the trail dropping down steeply toward the center, and the center of the trail being somewhat unwalkable in places.

La Cueva Cutoff levels out in about half a mile. It comes up into a massive field with excellent views and lots of wildflowers. When you get to the field, you have just finished the last significant climb you'll have to do until the very short one just before Forest Road 442. From this field you are also about 0.4 miles from La Cueva Lake. You'll walk through a flat, open grassy area inter-spersed with groves of trees on your way to and from the lake.

La Cueva Lake itself may be a disappointment, but it is open water. It's just boggy. It's in the middle of a very large field, with one lone cottonwood about 300 feet from it, plus a large cottonwood log that makes a great place to con-template how you might get close enough to the "lake" to get water without sinking into the mud/bog. See a photograph of La Cueva Lake on page 150.

I was able to get water with the two-Nalgene method (tip Nalgene #1 sideways enough to capture water, pour what you can get into Nalgene #2, repeat process.). I did have to move around a bit to keep from sinking in, but it worked. The east side of the "lake" might have a better edge for getting water.

Continue on La Cueva Cutoff. About 0.1 miles from La Cueva Lake you will come to a dirt road/forest track on your right. This is "La Cueva" or "La Cueva 8" depending on which map you're looking at. It marks the end of S4-8.

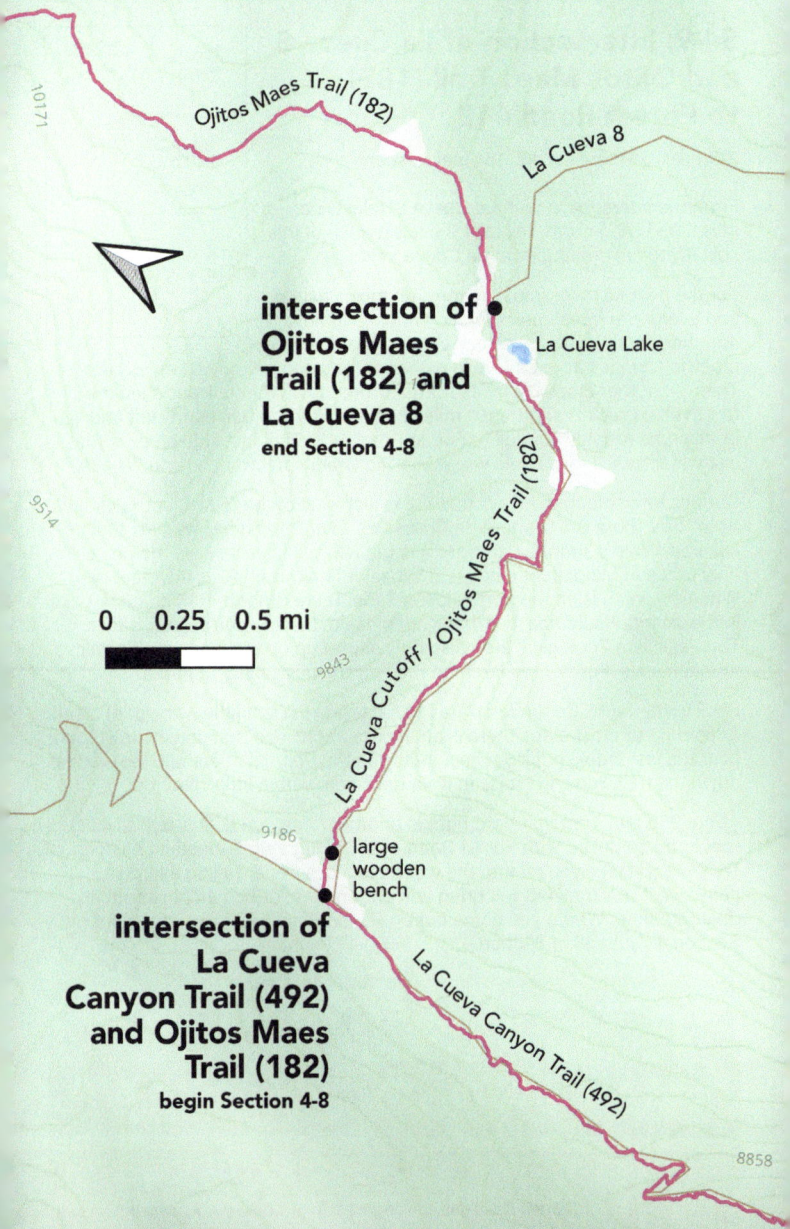

Ojitos Maes Trail (182)

10171

La Cueva 8

intersection of Ojitos Maes Trail (182) and La Cueva 8

end Section 4-8

La Cueva Lake

9514

La Cueva Cutoff / Ojitos Maes Trail (182)

0   0.25   0.5 mi

9843

9186

large wooden bench

intersection of La Cueva Canyon Trail (492) and Ojitos Maes Trail (182)

begin Section 4-8

La Cueva Canyon Trail (492)

8858

S4-9: Intersection of La Cueva 8 and Ojitos Maes Trail (182) to Forest Road 442

2.7 miles. 367 feet ascent. 184 feet descent.

From the intersection with La Cueva 8, take Ojito Maes Trail (182) north. I.e., take the left branch of this split if you are coming from La Cueva Lake.

For the next 1.6 miles you'll go through mixed aspen and evergreen forest interspersed with a field now and then. You'll cross four small creeks. The first little creek is 1.3 miles from La Cueva 8, then there's another one 0.1 miles later. There's another creek 0.2 miles north/further down the trail, and then the fourth little creek is another 0.1 miles further (after the trail bends left and briefly runs roughly parallel to Forest Road 442). That last little creek is the last water for 8.4 miles until you reach Rio Grande del Rancho and FR 439.

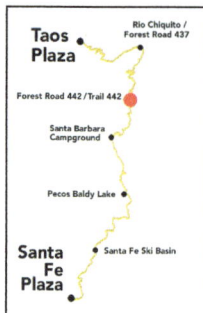

Curious thing along the way: Trail 182 is just west of the "Pea Clam Zoological Area." So... there is a "Sangre de Cristo Pea Clam," *and* it has its own zoological area. What's strange (stranger?) is the NM Wildlife site says the pea clam only exists in Middlefork Lake near Wheeler Peak. Trail 182 is nowhere near Wheeler, which is on the north side of Taos. There is another Middlefork Lake in the Jicarita Peak area, but that's not close to the zoological area, either. The Pea Clam Zoological area also only shows up on the maps my Garmin InReach uses. Further research on the Pea Clam is clearly required.

Back to the route. Continue up Trail 182, passing the last little (very little) creek. According to most maps there is an access track/road that comes down right near the last creek, but if you're actually on the trail, it's about 800 feet further down the trail. You can't miss it; it's a hard right with a little climb up.

About 250 feet from that hard right is another forest track. This is *Trail* 442 (not to be confused with Forest Road 442). Taking a right, heading east, on Trail 442 will take you off into the woods to a dead end. Taking a left (i.e., going west) on Trail 442 will bring you out on Forest Road 442 in about another 500 feet. Where you come out on Forest Road 442 is the end point for Section 4-7 and all of Section 4.

Forest Road 442, looking west from where you'll come out on to it.

Forest Road 442
end Section 4, 4-9

Forest Road 442

10499

Trail 442

99

unnamed

shortcut

Trail 442

1062

10171

Ojitos Maes Trail (182)

9843

9514

intersection of
Ojitos Maes
Trail (182) and
La Cueva 8

begin Section 4-9

9186

La Cueva Cutoff

La Cueva 8

0   0.25   0.5 mi

Section 5: Forest Road 442 to Rio Chiquito / Forest Road 437

26 miles

S5-1: Forest Road 442 to the beginning of the Sardinas Canyon Fire burn scar. 4.73 miles.

S5-2: Beginning of the burn on Forest Road 442 to Forest Road 439 / Rio Grande del Rancho. 4.2 miles.

S5-3: Forest Road 439 / Rio Grande del Rancho to the beginning of the Connector. 4.0 miles.

S5-4: The beginning of the Connector to Forest Road 438. 4.0 miles.

S5-5: Forest Road 438 / end of the Connector to Bernardin Lake. 2.4 miles.

S5-6: Bernardin Lake to Puertocito (intersection of Forest Road 438 and Forest Road 478). 2.3 miles.

S5-7: Puertocito to Rio Chiquito / Forest Road 437. 4.5 miles.

Get a GPX file of Section 5 at https://SantaFeToTaos.org/gpx-files/

Bernardin Lake, Section 5-6.

South Boundary Trail

9843

Rio Chiquito / FR 437
end Section 5

FR 478

Forest Road 437 / Rio Chiquito

10171

10499

10499

Bernardin Lake

Forest Road 438

Rito de la Olla

Luna Fire scar
October 2020

The Connector

8202

8530

10171

11811

Forest Road 440

Forest Road 439

Rio Grande del Rancho

11483

11155

10171

9843

Forest Road 442

9514

Sardinas Canyon Fire scar
July 2018

10827

Forest Road 442
begin Section 5

0   1   2 mi

La Cueva Field

La Cueva Lake

e Hwy 518

9843

9843

9843

S5-1: FR 442 to the beginning of the Sardinas Canyon Fire burn scar

4.7 miles. 376 feet ascent. 250 feet descent.

Start at the intersection of Trail 442 and Forest Road 442. Then take a right, heading north/northeast on Forest Road 442. You'll be on Forest Road 442 for 8.4 miles. The burn starts around 4.4 miles.

The water access through here is poor. There are a few seeps, but nothing good. This is the second-longest distance without water on the thru-hike. You will have good water at the end of the 8.4 miles when you reach Rio Grande del Rancho, and at least you'll be in shade for almost all of this section. There are a couple of good fields for camping along the way.

You are now in the maze-like road system of Carson National Forest. There are forest tracks carved throughout the woods of Carson. They are old logging roads for the sawmills that used to operate in this area. You will see many of these tracks going into the woods as you walk along FR 442.

I have yet to find a reliable map of all of the forest tracks. Some maps are mostly accurate, but not completely. You may notice that the GPS route line of the thru-hike appears to veer off where the map baselayers say the roads are. That's not from me offroading; it's from me driving on the dirt road that is Forest Road 442. The baselayer maps are not entirely accurate.

Also note that you should not drive out here in anything but a high-carriage four-wheel-drive vehicle, preferably with upgraded tires. Bring a saw, because fallen trees across the road are not uncommon. Also note that if you do go out on FR 442, don't try to do it after snowfall or a heavy rain, or before the snowpack has had significant time to melt (like by mid-May). You may be fine so long as you're on the south side of any given hill, but if you're on the north side, the snow and ice won't melt for much longer than you'd think.

Also consider only driving west to east on FR 442 (i.e., in the same direction as the thru-hike directions). For example, if you went up FR 442 from FR 439 / Rio Grande del Rancho, you'd be driving through the "rio", which is about 12 feet wide and six inches deep. Then you'd immediately be going up and over what is basically a large boulder embedded in the road. It's steep enough that on the way down 442, I can't see the road in front of my car for a few moments.

This may be an unnecessary warning if you're used to forest roads. I am mostly banging on for those of you in, say, Subarus, who think "Oh, it can't be that bad, it's May and it's warm and all the snow has melted around Taos, let's just go." So this is your warning. There is also almost no cell service in this area. In some spots you might be able to get a text message out.

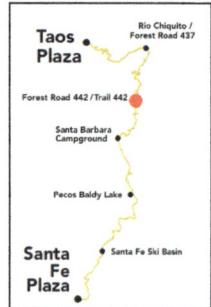

FR 442
where the
burn begins
end Section 5-1

Sardinas Canyon Fire burn scar

F R 439

FR 442

Trail 442

Forest Road 442
begin Section 5, 5-1

Ojitos Maes Trail (182)

FR 442

Flechado Canyon

Trail 7

0   0.5   1 mi

S5-2: Beginning of the burn on FR 442 to FR 439 / Rio Grande del Rancho

4.2 miles. 134 feet ascent. 1,081 feet descent.

Have you been through the burn on the Colorado Trail? Then breathe easy. This burn is going to be *much* easier than that.

This section begins, like the section title says, where the burn starts on Forest Road 442. That probably makes it sound like a grim, unfun section. There is nothing fun about a burn. But fortunately, the burn is fairly short; short enough that you can drive through it in about 2-3 minutes. That does translate to about 0.75 miles of burn.

I think showing the burn through here is important. Fire is a critical element of this landscape. Fire will be a critical element of its future. Maybe seeing a mile of burn might help a few people reconsider having a campfire, or at least motivate them to actually put it out properly (which is dousing it with at least two Nalgenes even after it has burnt down to coals).

There is a "burned area" sign just before the burn begins. You'll see another similar sign from the back (with bullet marks in it) when you're leaving the burn.

Note that maps show Forest Road 442 ending, with a roadless gap, for about 50 feet. In reality the road goes right through. It's just one example of why you should take what the maps say about this area with a grain of salt.

After the burn you'll follow FR 442 downhill. The road curves a lot, and there are some nice views. It should be quiet in terms of traffic. Even on weekends in summer, you're not likely to see more than one or two vehicles going through. You may see a few interesting vehicles, too. Some people bring their tricked-out off-road vehicles, like trikes, out for joy rides on these roads. You'll hear them coming, and there's ample shoulder to get out of the way. Or you may also not see anyone.

When you reach the end of Forest Road 442, you'll cross Rio Grande del Rancho and then come up to Forest Road 439. This is the end of Section 5-2.

There are a few campsite opportunities just short of Rio Grande del Rancho. They're about 500 to 2,000 feet before you get to the rio (which is a decent-sized creek about 12 feet wide). The land flattens out a bit in this area, and if you were to walk a bit away from the road, just far enough into the woods to get out of view, you'd have a reasonably private, flat spot near water to sleep for the night. It's probably not the most beautiful location, but it works well enough.

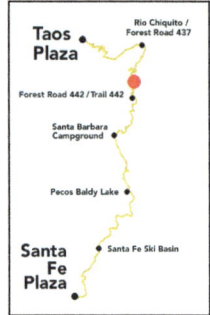

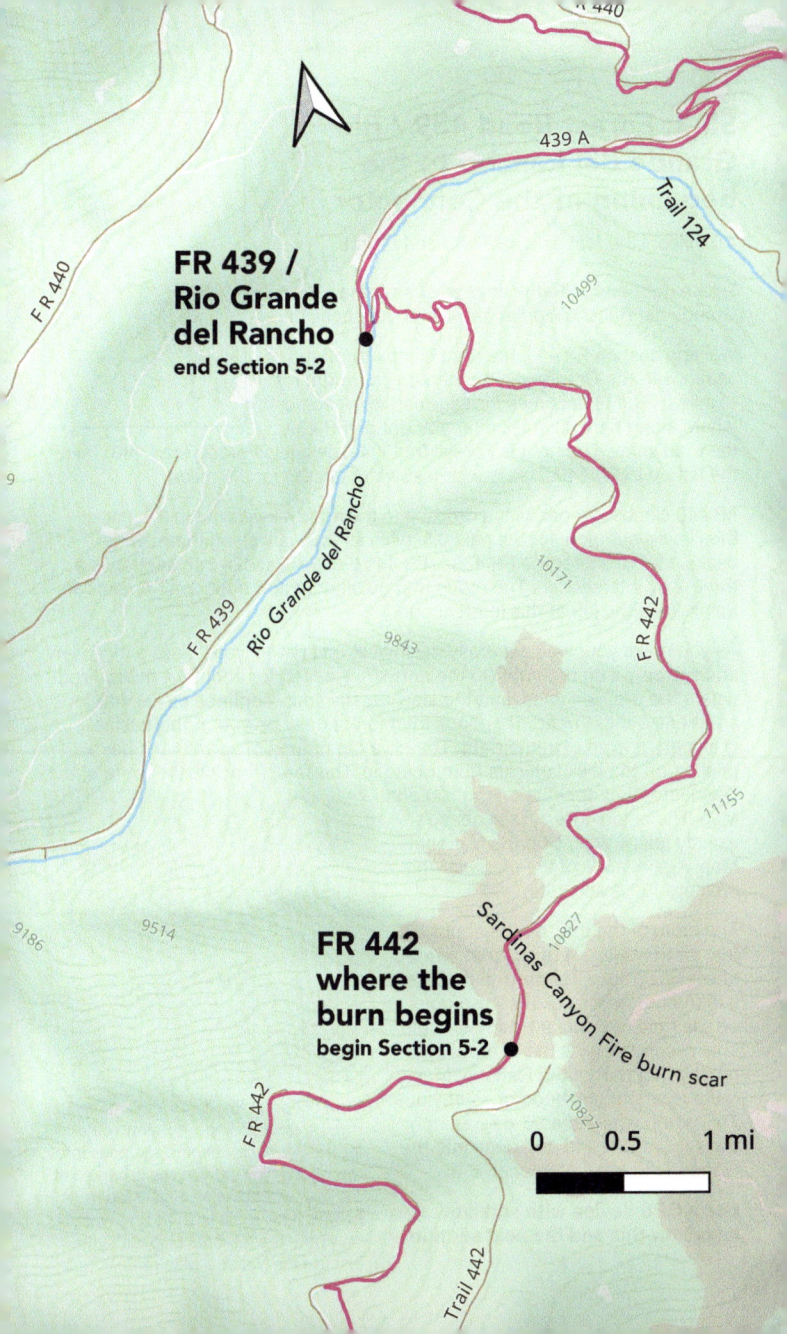

FR 440

R 440

439 A

Trail 124

10499

**FR 439 /
Rio Grande
del Rancho**
end Section 5-2

9

Rio Grande del Rancho

F R 439

10171

9843

F R 442

11155

9186

9514

Sardinas Canyon Fire burn scar

10827

**FR 442
where the
burn begins**
begin Section 5-2

FR 442

10827

0   0.5   1 mi

Trail 442

S5-3: Forest Road 439 / Rio Grande del Rancho to the beginning of the Connector

4.0 miles. 1,010 feet ascent. 379 feet descent.

Take a right on to FR 439 after you've crossed Rio Grande del Rancho. You might want river shoes here.

Walking east on FR 439, the road climbs through aspen with Rio Grande del Rancho on your right for 1.1 miles. FR 439 becomes Forest Road 439A somewhere along here. 1.1 miles after you got on FR 439, the road splits. The right is Forest Trail 124. The left is Forest Road 440. Take the left on to FR 440. This is your last water access for 3.5 miles.

FR 440 climbs steeper with a drop-off to the right. It levels out in 0.6 miles, then levels out more for the next 0.3 miles as you walk along three switchbacks. 1.5 miles after the FR 439A/FR 440/Forest Trail 124 intersection is a three-way intersection. The roads that go straight and right don't appear on maps. Take the left at this intersection.

As you make your way generally northwest on FR 440, you'll pass a nice view and a drop-off on the right (to the north/northeast) for about 0.4 miles. From where the drop-off ends, and the view mostly ends, continue on FR 440 for another 0.5 miles or so. Then look for a forest track on your right (basically a spur). It is an extreme right. There's a big mound of earth that's been pushed up to block vehicles from going in. This forest track is the route of the Connector that appears on the National Map. The actual forest track doesn't exactly follow what's on the National Map. Again, none of the maps for this area are 100% accurate.

The route of the thru-hike is about 250 feet on FR 440 past this extreme right forest track/spur. The thru-hike route is a different forest track that also goes off on the right, but at a 90-degree angle. This second track is the better way to go; the first part of the National Map route is overgrown and not as obvious. This point, where the 90-degree right track leaves FR 440 and goes into the woods, is the end of Section 5-3.

Use a GPS device with satellite layers for this and the next section.

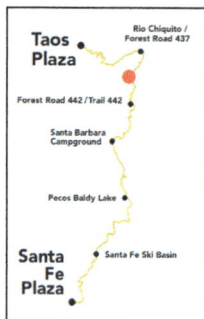

View of Forest Road 440 looking east, if you were standing where my route for the Connector begins and goes into the woods. The car you see is parked at the spur where the National Map route begins. If my route is confusing or if you only have the National Map with you, just use the National Map route.

9186

FR 438

8858

0   0.5   1 mi

The Connector

three-way-split
that's not on
other maps

F R 440

10171

Trail 124

9843

Rio Grande del Rancho

10

**Beginning of the
connector**
end Section 5-3

439-A

Forest Road 442

**FR 439 /
Rio Grande
del Rancho**
begin Section 5-3

F R 440

F R 439

S5-4: The beginning of the Connector to Forest Road 438

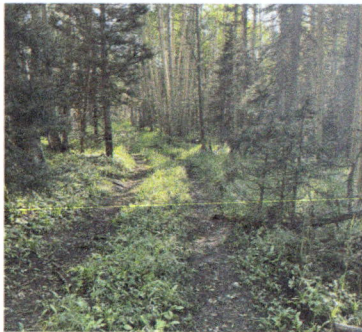

4.0 miles. 143 feet ascent. 1,156 feet descent.

Bring a GPS device with you for this section. You can get a GPX file of this subsection and the full Section at https://SantaFeToTaos.org/gpx-files/.

Step off Forest Road 440 on to the forest track for the Connector. The forest track looks like a road with two tracks for tires. The land is flat and shaded.

Walk northeast for the first 300 feet or so, then 0.1 mile east, always following the track. The track takes a 90-degree right and

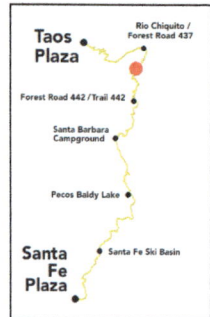

then goes 0.1 of a mile, bending left just a bit. This will take you all the way around, making almost a U, from where you took the 90-degree right.

Go about 0.7 miles north/northeast, then turn right just a bit, heading pretty much due east for 0.3 miles before taking another right and heading south/southeast for 0.3 miles.

The track hugs the contours of the canyonside all along this part. You'll get occasional views of the canyon and far hills to your left. You'll be at

The beginning of my route of the Connector. View a few steps in from Forest Road 440.

9,800 feet elevation. Follow the track, bending left, still on that elevation line, still following the contours of the canyon, still with the views of the canyon on your left for another 0.4 miles.

At this point you will join the track that's on the National Map, and you can follow the National Map route until you reach Forest Road 438.

Continue following the contour of the canyon. In about 0.1 miles that contour will cause the track to take a hard right, then go 0.1

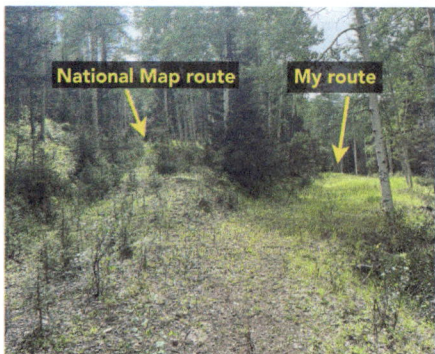

National Map route   My route

Where my route and the National Map route merge. This is looking back if you are Taos-bound, i.e., west/uphill.

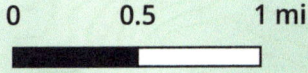

End of the
Connector
end Section 5-4

Palociento Creek

little waterfall
and campsite

Rito de La Olla

F R 438

approximately
where National
Map track is

F R 440

0   0.5   1 mi

Beginning of the
Connector
begin Section 5-4

Rio Grande del Rancho

439-A

F R 442

mile. Then it bends left and goes basically straight for about half a mile. Then there's another 90-degree right, another tenth of a mile, then two 90-degree lefts close together. You'll then be walking almost directly north for 0.2 miles. From there it's a 90-degree left, then 0.1 miles heading west, then an arc around to the right that has you all but going in the opposite direction, but

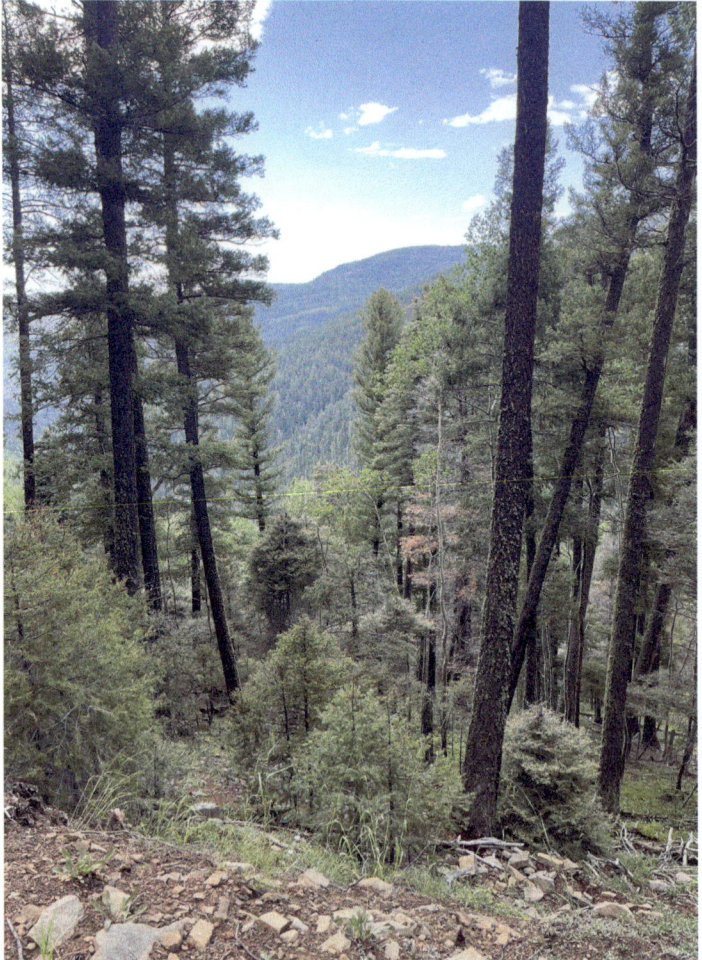

One of the views from the Connector as you walk down into the canyon towards Rito de la Olla and Forest "Road" 438.

heading further and further down into the canyon. You'll now be at about 9,200 feet of elevation.

The trail will take yet another hard left (almost a U-turn). It will go 0.2 miles basically north, and then take a 45 degree right and head almost straight for the next 0.3 miles.

You'll pass a little waterfall on your right, which is a fish gate for Palociento Creek. Walk through a little campsite, take a left, and walk over the old wooden bridge that crosses Rito de la Olla. You will come to Forest Road 438 maybe 150 feet later.

The Palociento Creek fish gate.

If you get lost: Make your way to the bottom of the canyon, as directly as you safely can (you'll be heading north if you are going down into the canyon). In no more than a mile/mile and a half, you'll come to a creek. This is Rito de la Olla. It will be about 6-9 feet wide. It's the only creek in this area anywhere near that big.

Rito de la Olla runs east to west. 30-50 feet beyond Rito de la Olla will be Forest "Road" 438. It's a forest track for most of its distance.

Take the right on Forest Road 438, heading east (upcreek), sometimes southeast, to rejoin the route of the thru-hike. If you take the left on Forest Road 438, you will come out to a crude trailhead in roughly two miles. The "trailhead" is really just where Forest Road 438 ends as a road and begins as a forest track. The road has been blocked with a metal gate and a berm to prevent cars from going through. From the "trailhead," Forest Road 438 becomes an active road with many campsites. Follow it west for approximately 5.5 miles and you'll come out at the Pot Creek Trailhead and Route 518.

Another tip if you get lost, or if you end up on the wrong forest track: Many of the forest tracks are only a few hundred feet apart, so you could bushwack for a few hundred feet to rejoin the route if you get on the wrong track.

S5-5: Forest Road 438 / end of the Connector to Bernardin Lake

2.4 miles. 1,322 feet ascent. 669 feet descent.

Take the right, heading east, on to FR 438. For the next 1.6 miles you will be on a forest "road" technically, but it's more of a forest track. Rita de la Olla will be on your right the whole way. Sometimes it will be as far as 0.2 miles from you, but that will make space for some lovely fields and groves of trees. This is beautiful trail, with lots of spots to camp. Take note of the beaver dams along the way, and look on the side of the trail/"road" for little stumps of slender trees the beavers have decided to take down for their work. You may also see or hear elk.

After 1.6 miles, the trail narrows to about 2 feet wide and climbs to the left on a sandy, somewhat steep slope. It bends left and goes into aspens.

The route gets a whiff tricky here, but only briefly. Veer right once you're just under the aspens, and you should see a rough, overgrown trail that continues somewhat straight. This will bring you out on to the continuation of FR 438 in a couple hundred feet or less. There's a road and a beaver pond a bit further down the road on the left. You should be able to see a couple of campsites or little areas big enough to pull a truck into.

You are headed basically to your left and up the slope from here. There is no optimal trail; you kind of pick your way through the aspen grove left for the new couple of hundred feet. A trail does become obvious. Again, hopefully you'll have a GPS device. The trail becomes a forest track for a few hundred feet, and you may find yourself at a spot with kind of a small quarry almost, to your left, and a track continuing on to your right. Go right.

The track narrows again, and bends left, becoming a narrow little path along a steep sandy slope. Keep going, heading north/northeast. The narrow path then expands to become forest track sized. You'll come up on a large field that slopes up to the right. There's a little stream at the foot of it.

Cross the stream and follow the track that goes up the right side of the field. It is a bit of a climb. You'll continue the climb, veering right, following the track and being briefly back under the trees, until you walk up over the last bit and have Bernardin Lake in front of you. The lake is about 0.2 miles from the north edge of the field. There is a photograph of Bernardin Lake on page 88.

Bernardin Lake is nice, but it has no fish, just salamanders. There are campsites all around it, especially on the south and east sides. There is a very rickety hunting blind on the far side of it, near the boggy cove.

Note that there is a forest road on the north side of the lake. You may see a vehicle going by once or twice. Bernardin Lake is the end of Section 5-5.

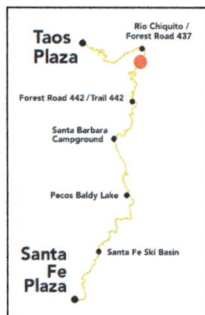

104

FR 153

FR 438

Forest Trail 124

rickety
hunting
blind

beaver
pond

**Bernardin
Lake**

end Section 5-5

Bear Wallow

FR 441

FR 471

10499

9514

Rito de la Olla

FR 438

9186

9843

10171

**End of the
Connector**

begin Section 5-5

FR 438

The Connector

0   0.25   0.5 mi

S5-6: Bernardin Lake to Puertocito (intersection of FR 438 and FR 478)

2.3 miles. 499 feet ascent. 304 feet descent.

From Bernardin Lake, go back down the way you came, alongside that big sloping field, to get back on Forest Road 438 by the beaver pond. Stay on Forest Road 438 past the beaver pond, heading northeast.

There is no reliable water for the six miles between the beaver pond and Rio Chiquito.

This lightly traveled forest road will go through or run next to a few big fields for the next few miles. If you're not going through a field, you'll be shaded by aspen canopy with some evergreens sprinkled in. It is a slight climb, but not bad: 499 feet of elevation gain over 2.3 miles.

As you'll be on forest road, you may see a few vehicles, but probably not more than one every hour or two or so unless it's a holiday weekend. The road has plenty of room to let a vehicle go through.

You'll come to the intersection of Forest Road 438 and Forest Road 478 in 1.92 miles from the beaver pond. This intersection is named "Puertocito" on most maps, including the National Map. Puertocito is the end of Section 5-6.

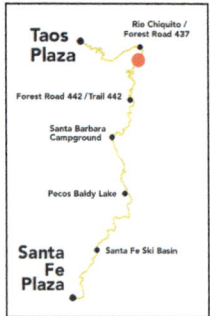

One of the fields off Forest Road 438 between Puertocito and Bernardin Lake.

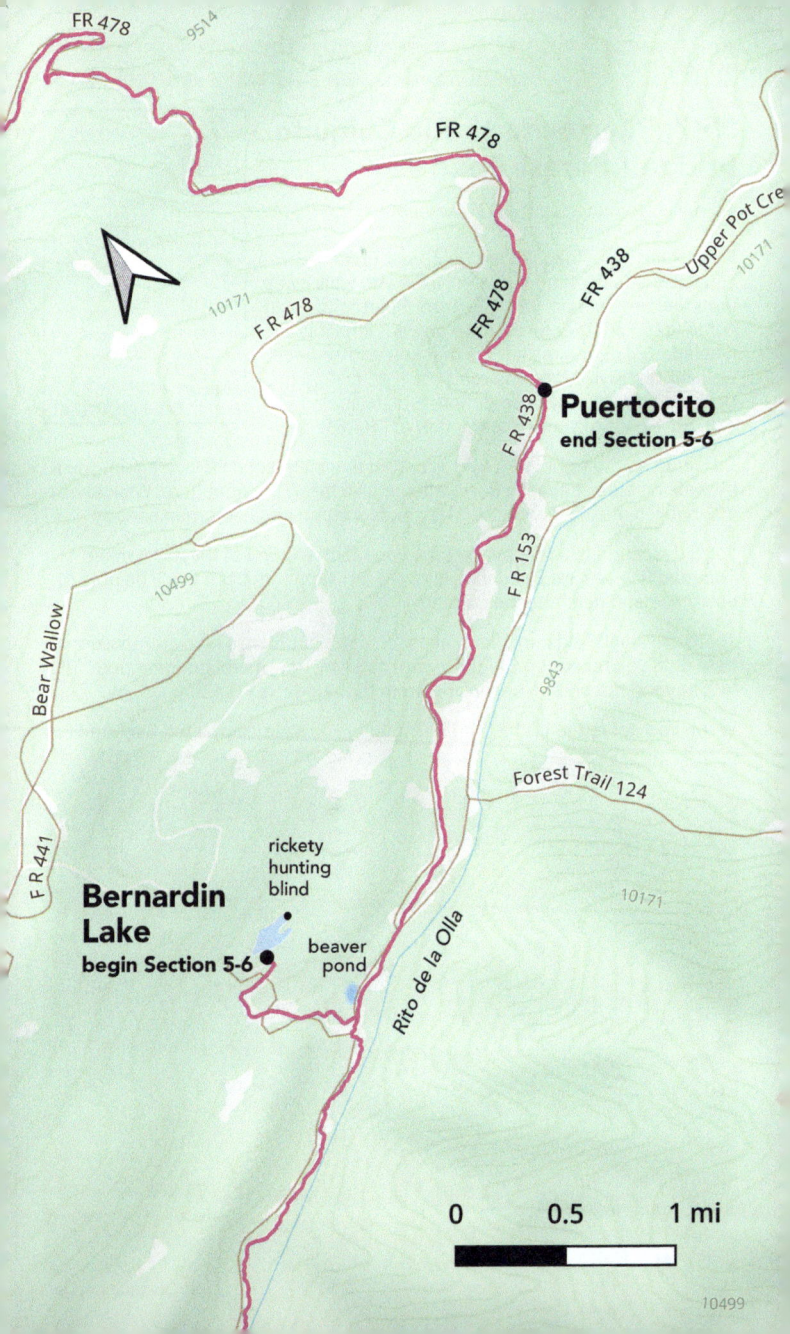

FR 478

9514

FR 478

FR 478

Upper Pot Cre

FR 438

FR 478

10171

FR 478

10171

FR 478

FR 438

Puertocito
end Section 5-6

FR 153

10499

9843

Bear Wallow

Forest Trail 124

10171

F R 441

rickety
hunting
blind

**Bernardin
Lake**

begin Section 5-6

beaver
pond

Rito de la Olla

FR 478

0   0.5   1 mi

10499

S5-7: Puertocito to Rio Chiquito bridge / Forest Road 437

4.5 miles. 46 feet ascent. 1,097 descent.

From Puertocito, take the left on Forest Road 478. You will be going almost due north as you walk away from the intersection. 0.7 miles from Puertocito you'll come up on another forest road on your left. This is labeled FR 478 on maps. Note that you've also been walking on FR 478, and the road you'll be taking, the right side of this new intersection, is also labeled FR 478. So it's a three-way intersection of FR 478.

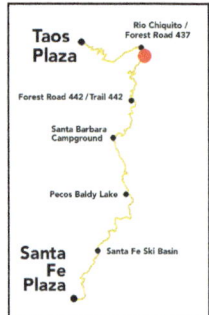

Continue on the right fork of FR 478 from this intersection. Once again, you'll be walking almost exactly north after you've taken the right here. Walk another 3.5 miles mostly downhill under shaded aspen and evergreen canopy.

You'll descend 1,239 feet by the time you reach the end of these 3.5 miles. The road has several switchbacks and a few tight turns, but you'll be able to easily see and hear anyone coming.

There are small fields and flat places to camp, but there's no water through here until you reach Rio Chiquito, with its shiny new metal bridge. About 300 feet beyond the bridge, and visible from the bridge, is FR 437.

When you get to the bridge at Rio Chiquito, you have completed Section 5.

Rio Chiquito bridge.

FR 437

8858

FR 437

Rio Chiquito Bridge

end

Section 5, 5-7

Lagunita Canyon

FR 121 / Rio Chiquito Trail

FR 478

9843

9186

Bear Wallow

FR 441

10171

10499

FR 478

0   0.5   1 mi

FR 478

FR 438

Puertocito

begin Section 5-7

FR 438

438

10171

Trail 124 (west end)

FR 153

10171

Section 6: Rio Chiquito bridge / Forest Road 437 to Taos Plaza

20 miles

S6-1: Rio Chiquito bridge/FR 437 to Buena Suerte Canyon/FR 437. 2.3 miles.

S6-2: Buena Suerte Canyon on Forest Road 437 to Manzanita Canyon on Forest Road 437. 3.0 miles.

S6-3: Manzanita Canyon on FR 437 to Drake Canyon Loop Trail (165) on FR 437. 2.2 miles.

S6-4: Intersection of FR 437 and Drake Canyon Loop Trail (165) to intersection of Drake Canyon Loop Trail (165) and unnamed trail. 3.4 miles.

S6-5 Intersection of Drake Canyon Loop (165) and unnamed trail to intersection of Ojitos Trail (166) and Talpa Ridge Trail. 1.5 miles.

S6-6: Intersection of Ojitos Trail (166) and Talpa Ridge Trail to Ojitos Trail (166) and Ojitos shortcut. 4.1 miles.

S6-7: Intersection of Ojitos Trail (166) and Ojitos shortcut to El Nogal. 1.1 miles.

S6-8 El Nogal to Taos Cow. 1.7 miles.

S6-9: Taos Cow to Taos Plaza. 1.4 miles.

Alternate route: Intersection of 164 and 164B to Witt Road (avoiding Route 64 and El Nogal)

Get a GPX file of Section 6 at https://SantaFeToTaos.org/gpx-files/

Forest Road 437, heading west, just before Drake Canyon.

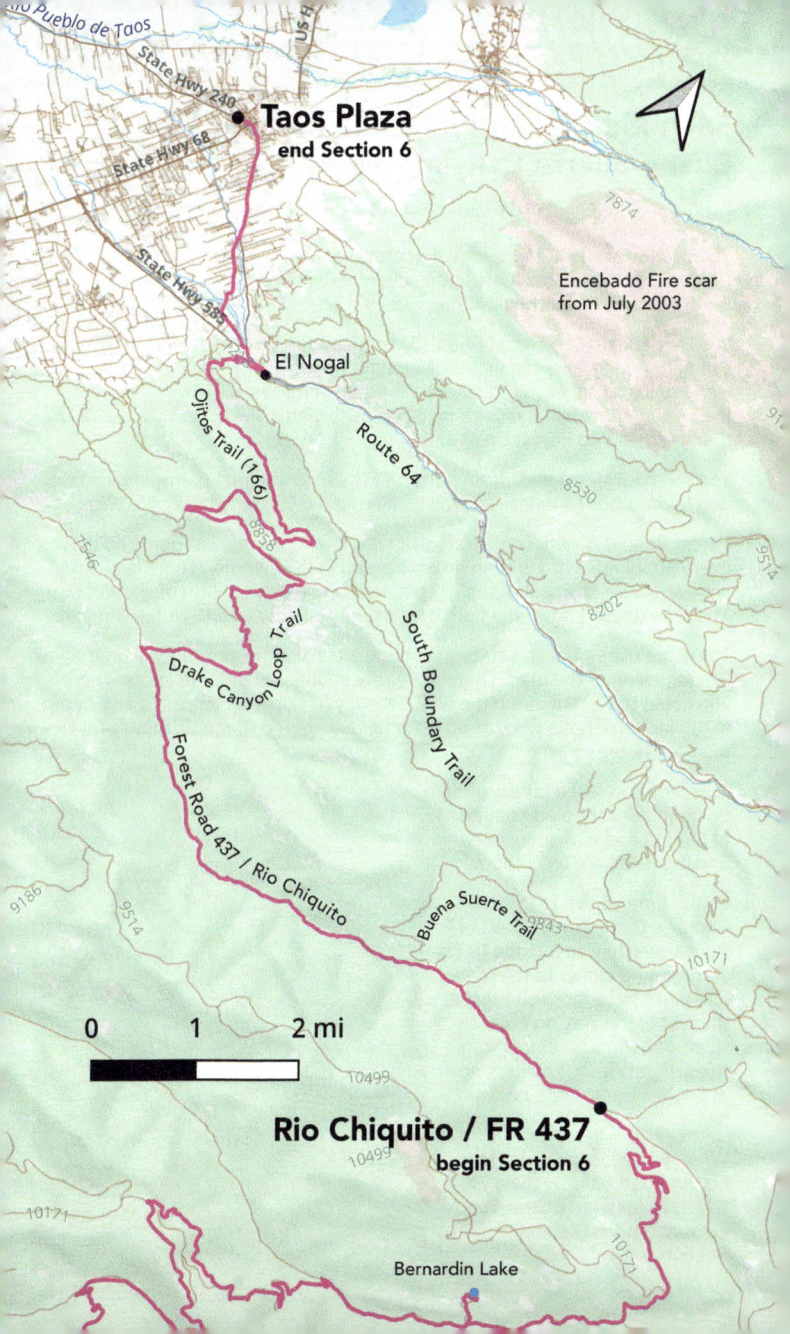

Taos Plaza
end Section 6

State Hwy 240

State Hwy 68

State Hwy 585

Rio Pueblo de Taos

Rio Pueblo de Taos

US-H

7874

Encebado Fire scar
from July 2003

El Nogal

Ojitos Trail (166)

Route 64

8838

8530

9514

91

1546

Drake Canyon Loop Trail

South Boundary Trail

8202

Forest Road 437 / Rio Chiquito

9186

9514

Buena Suerte Trail

9843

10171

0   1   2 mi

10499

10499

Rio Chiquito / FR 437
begin Section 6

10171

10171

Bernardin Lake

S6-1: Rio Chiquito / FR 437 to Bueno Suerte Canyon / FR 437

2.3 miles. 0 feet ascent. 261 feet descent.

The section starts at the bridge that crosses Rio Chiquito, at the approximate intersection of Forest Road 478 and Forest Road 437.

You'll be able to see Forest Road 437 from the Rio Chiquito bridge. You can just walk straight up the slope to it, but it's easier to take the road that crosses the bridge, turns left, passes a nice campsite, and then merges into Forest Road 437.

You will be walking west from here, on FR 437 for the rest of this subsection, and for another 7.3 miles. You will be next to Rio Chiquito the entire way.

Forest Road 437 gets some traffic, but it's "traffic" as in a car going by maybe every 30 minutes or so, even on a weekend in the summer. There is a very wide shoulder for most of the distance—a whole field's worth of shoulder. The road doesn't have any tight bends until you get close to Drake Canyon.

There are over a dozen established campsites along your route, all on the Rio Chiquito side of the road. There are easily another 20 or more spots where you could put a tent along the way. Even if you skip the campsites and camp in the far corner of a field, or on the other side of Rio Chiquito, there's no lack of space here.

This area can feel a bit dry after being in the canopied coolness of FR 438 and earlier sections. The big fields are nice, though.

By the time you've reached Paradise Canyon, just short of Buena Suerte Canyon, the trees start getting closer to the road and you'll have more shade. For the rest of the way on Forest Road 437 you'll be among big trees. It gets lush. I credit some of the lushness to the beaver dams.

When you have walked down Forest Road 437 2.1 miles, you will have reached Buena Suerte Canyon. This is the end of Section 6-1.

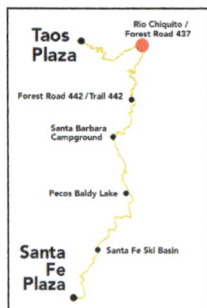

Forest Road 437.

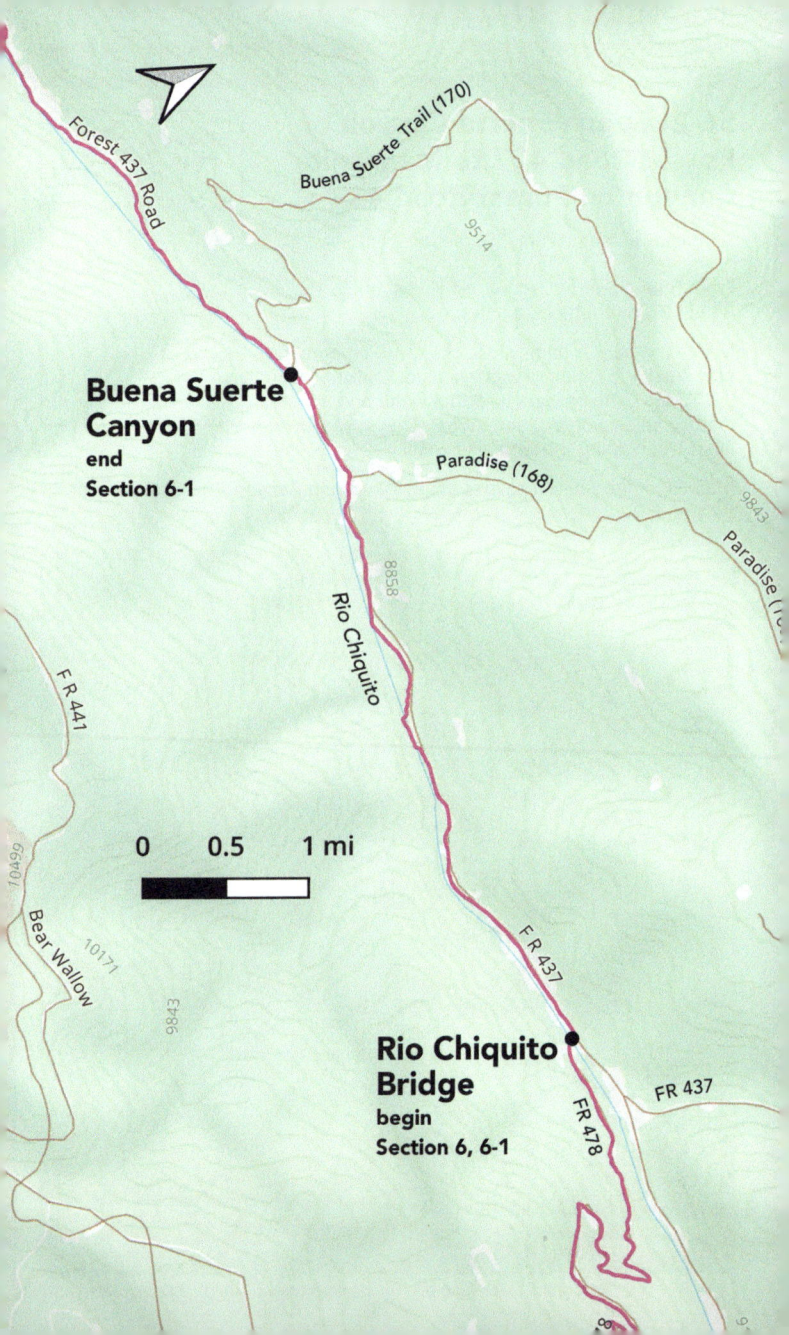

Forest 437 Road

Buena Suerte Trail (170)

9514

**Buena Suerte
Canyon**

**end
Section 6-1**

Paradise (168)

8858

Rio Chiquito

9843

Paradise (16

F R 441

0   0.5   1 mi

10490

Bear Wallow

10171

9843

9896

F R 437

**Rio Chiquito
Bridge**

**begin
Section 6, 6-1**

FR 437

FR 478

8

9

S6-2: Buena Suerte Canyon on Forest Road 437 to Manzanita Canyon on Forest Road 437

3.0 miles. 30 feet ascent. 533 feet descent.

From Buena Suerte Canyon, walk west on Forest Road 437 for another 3.0 miles.

Notice the beaver dams along the way. Remember how small Rio Chiquito was when you walked over the bridge? The beavers took that water and made football fields worth of bog from it. They do an amazing job at helping the land hold water.

After 3.0 miles you will have reached Manzanita Canyon. This is the end of Section 6-2.

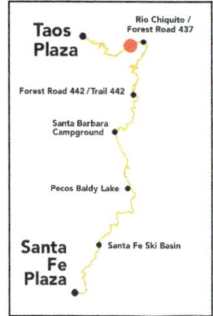

Part of the miles-long bog the beavers have created off Forest Road 437.

Rio Chiquito

**Manzanita Canyon
/ FR 437**

end Section 6-2

8202

8858

9186

8814

0   0.5   1 mi

8530

9843

Forest 437 Road

Buena Suerte Trail (170)

10171

F R 441

10171

9843

10499

**Buena Suerte
Canyon
/ FR 437**

begin Section 6-2

10499

FR 437

Paradise (168)

S6-3 Manzanita Canyon to Drake Canyon Loop Trail (165) on Forest Road 437

2.2 miles. 22 feet ascent. 331 feet descent.

Keep walking west on Forest Road 437 for 2.2 miles. After 2.2 miles, there will be a track on your right going off into the hills at a 90-degree angle. This is Drake Canyon Loop Trail (165). The intersection of Forest Road 437 and Drake Canyon Loop Trail is the end of Section 6-3.

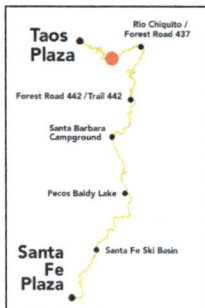

Before you jump into the next section, get water from Rio Chiquito. It's only a couple hundred feet away. This is the last reliable water source you'll have until you get to El Nogal Trailhead, 10 miles away, and it's a good idea to carry enough water to get yourself all the way to Taos Cow, which is 11.6 miles away. So go fill up on water.

You might want to camp near this water spot. I've camped on the far side of Rio Chiquito approximately across from the entrance to Drake Canyon. There are several little fields that are ideal to sleep on. The "rio" is small enough there to cross in good hiking boots and not get your socks wet. This far west along Forest Road 437 you will hear and see more RVs, ATVs, and people, but if you're on the far side of the creek you can get away from them.

Early morning in October at entrance to Drake Canyon and Forest Road 437.

0   0.5   1 mi

Trail 166

7546

8530

**Drake Canyon
entrance
/ FR 437**

end Section 6-3

Drake Canyon Loop Trail (165)

8858

7874

9186

8858

Forest 437 Road

8530

Rio Chiquito

**Manzanita Canyon
/ FR 437**

begin Section 6-3

8202

9514

S6-4: Intersection of Forest Road 437 and Drake Canyon Loop Trail (165) to intersection of Drake Canyon Loop Trail and unnamed trail

3.4 miles. 1,499 feet ascent. 0 feet descent.

The entrance to Drake Canyon is wide and well-worn. You'll walk in on a forest track and go into the woods. You'll be under tall trees interspersed with shorter shrubby oaks and deciduous trees, with a few small fields here and there.

After about 1.2 miles the trail starts to climb and bend left gradually (so heading north then northwest). It will continue to climb up a rocky forest track, heading northwest. As you get higher, the trees thin out a bit and shift into scrub and ponderosa pines.

About 1.2 miles after that gradual bend left the trail will take a 90-degree right turn and continue to climb. 0.9 miles after that right, you'll come upon a split in the trail. The left is still Drake Canyon Loop Trail (165), and this is where you'll be headed. The right is an unnamed trail.

If you are absolutely parched, there is probably some water about a mile away on South Boundary Trail. The water is at American Spring (aka "Bear Spring"). It's sketchy. American Spring is a large metal tube that serves as a holding tank next to a seep. If you really need water, it's there. Also, if you wanted to camp somewhere before you headed into Taos, there are plenty of fields around American Spring. Note that most maps show American Spring in the wrong place. It's actually on South Boundary Trail.

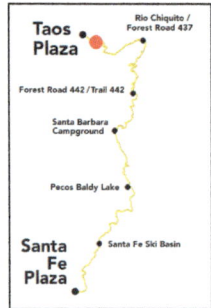

Drake Canyon Loop Trail.

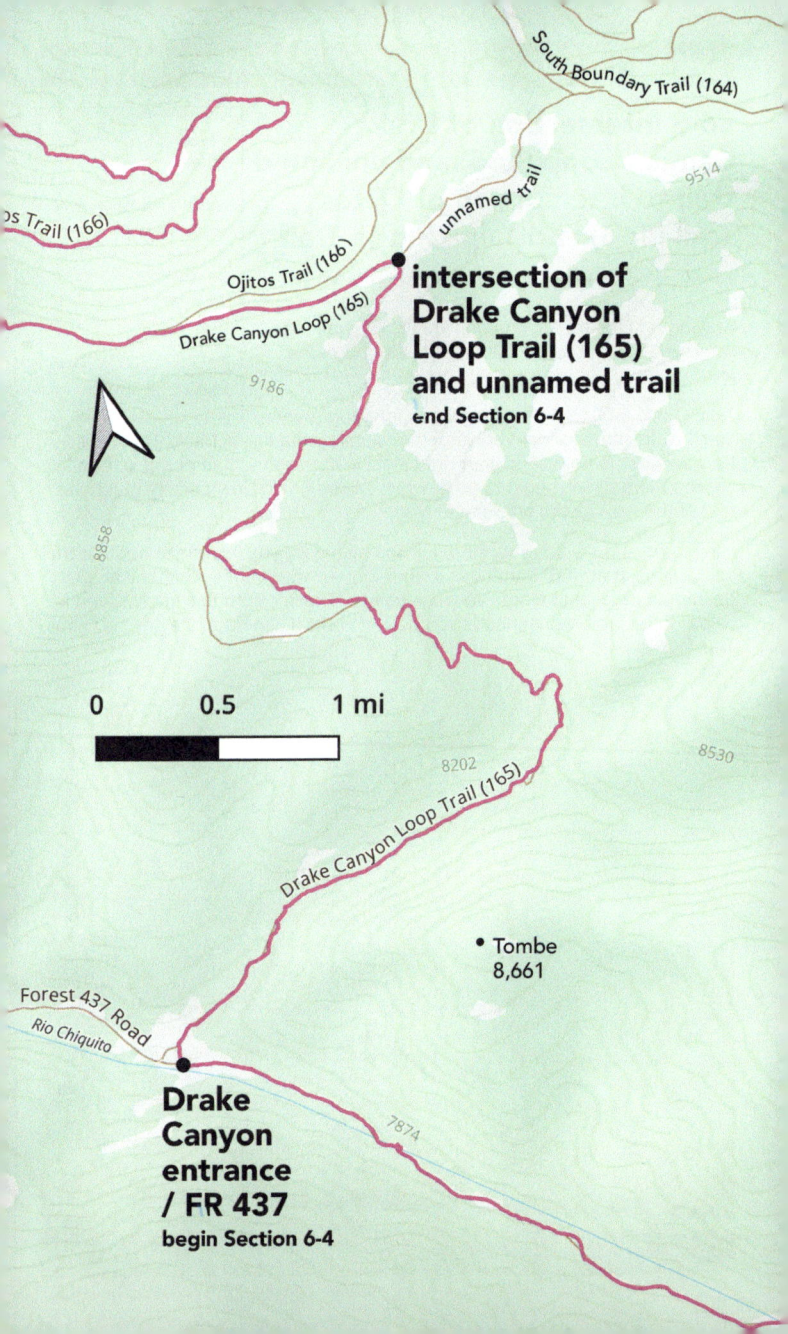

South Boundary Trail (164)

9514

unnamed trail

Ojitos Trail (166)

os Trail (166)

Drake Canyon Loop (165)

**intersection of
Drake Canyon
Loop Trail (165)
and unnamed trail**

end Section 6-4

9186

8858

0   0.5   1 mi

8202

Drake Canyon Loop Trail (165)

8530

• Tombe
  8,661

Forest 437 Road

Rio Chiquito

**Drake
Canyon
entrance
/ FR 437**

begin Section 6-4

7874

S6-5 Intersection of Drake Canyon Loop (165) and unnamed trail to intersection of Ojitos Trail (166) and Talpa Ridge Trail

1.5 miles. 46 feet ascent. 507 feet descent.

Staying on Drake Canyon Loop Trail (165), walking west, you'll come up on Ojitos Trail (166) 0.5 miles later.

Take Ojitos Trail (166), heading west, for another mile. You'll be in shade under very large trees, on a wide forest track. There will be views to the north and your right side. In the second half of this one-mile stretch the trail will begin to go down. It will be going down pretty much the rest of the way, all the way into El Nogal.

Having been on Ojitos Trail (166) for one mile now, you'll come to another trail split. Ojitos Trail (166) continues to the right—a sharp right—that will briefly be almost parallel to where you just walked. The left from this intersection is Talpa Ridge Trail, which heads south. Don't take it. Go right, staying on Ojitos Trail (166).

View coming down on Ojitos Trail (166).

intersection of
Ojitos Trail (166)
and
unnamed trail

end Section
6-5

8530

unnamed trail

unnamed trail

8858

Ojitos Trail (166)

0   0.5   1 mi

9186

Ojitos Trail (166)

Drake Canyon Loop Trail (165)

intersection of Drake Canyon
Loop Trail (165)
and unnamed trail

begin Section 6-5

unnamed trail

S6-6: Intersection of Ojitos Trail (166) and Talpa Ridge Trail to Ojitos Trail (166) and the Ojitos shortcut

4.1 miles. 8 feet ascent. 1,302 feet descent.

Continuing on Ojitos Trail (166), going around the tight bend right, you'll now be going down and down on this same wide forest track, with the same big trees. Now the view is on your left.

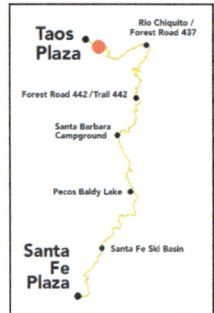

About 1.8 miles from the last trail split, the trail will bend tightly left, then continue down for another 2.2 miles. There will be more small bends here and there as you go, but there's only one primary trail through here, and you're on it. As you go down, it gets drier. By the time you're halfway down, the trees are much smaller and the grasses have given way to bare rocky ground.

After 2.2 miles, you'll have been on a wide, dry, sun-exposed track for a while. You'll have a good view of much of the south part of Taos. Keep an eye out for a trail going off on your right, going up the slope from the track you're on. This "unmaintained trail," which I am calling "the Ojitos Shortcut," will take you over to the intersection of South Boundary Trail (164) and Trail 164B. Avoid the trail just before the right on to this shortcut; if you are heading southeast after taking this trail, you're on the wrong trail. Go out back to Ojitos and go just a wee bit further on it, like 200 feet.

The right turn on to this little unnamed trail is the end of Section 6-6. If you miss that trail, don't worry. Ojitos Trail bends around, basically becoming parallel to the little shortcut you could have taken. Just stay on it and you will walk into "Ojitos Trail Connector", Trail 164B. Take the right.

View of the mountains north of Taos from the Ojitos shortcut, just before the South Boundary (164)/164B trail intersection.

Verde Road

del Ca...

water tower

Ojitos Trail (166)

7218

164B

7546

**intersection
of Ojitos Trail (166)
and another
unnamed trail**
begin Section 6-6

unmaintained trail

South Boundary Trail (164)

unnamed trail

7874

**intersection of
Ojitos Trail (166)
and unnamed trail**
begin Section 6-6

8530

unnamed trail

Ojitos Trail (166)

8858

Drake Canyon Loop Trail (165)

9186

0   0.5   1 mi

S6-7: Intersection of Ojitos Trail (166) and the Ojitos shortcut to El Nogal

1.1 miles. 0 feet ascent. 321 feet descent.

For those of you who did see the little shortcut trail, follow that, going mostly north, with nice views of the Taos mountains, for 0.3 miles. You will walk right into a little intersection of four trails. You will also, suddenly, be on a fairly active trail; you may see someone coming or going on the primary trail to your right even while you're standing at the intersection.

If you are standing facing east at the intersection of Trail 164, 164B, and the little unnamed trail you just came in on, you'll see a trail marker. It is sometimes worn; you may not be able to read the trail numbers. Walk up to it and on to the clearly much more traveled trail, South Boundary Trail (164). Take the left, heading down.

Note that South Boundary Trail (164) is one of the more heavily trafficked mountain bike trails around. Usually the people on bikes have slowed down by this point of the trail, but not always. If you've got a dog on a lead, be careful. Also note that this trail has a few tight spots, so if you've got a mountain biker coming down fast you will need to get out of their way quickly.

The good news is that South Boundary Trail (164) is lovely. It's dry but shaded. It can be busy, but it's pretty, and it's down the whole 0.8 miles to the El Nogal trailhead and parking lot. The trail on the way down has a couple of offshoots; stay on the main trail.

You'll walk down to a little creek on your left, by which time you'll be on flat ground under large willows and cottonwoods. You'll probably be able to see the parking lot in short order. You'll also see the big wooden L-shaped bridge that crosses the creek, Rio Fernando de Taos. Beyond that is the parking lot of El Nogal.

I do not recommend that you drink even treated water at El Nogal (i.e., out of Rio Fernando de Taos) unless you walk upriver about a quarter of a mile past where most people take their dogs. Water near El Nogal parking lot has exceptionally high counts of *E. coli* due to dog owners not picking up after their dogs.

Also note that if it is really dry, Rio Fernando de Taos may not be much more than a mud puddle. I've only seen it like that once, in 2018. The bridge at El Nogal marks the end of Section 6-7.

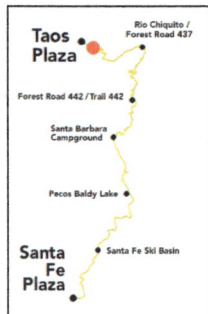

The L-shaped bridge at El Nogal. View from the parking lot.

El Nogal
parking lot
end
Section
6-7

Devisadero Loop Trail (108)

Route 64

El Nogal Nature Trail (181)

Rio Fernando de Taos

Route 64

South Boundary Trail (164)

7218

Road

NM 585
uel Canon East

El Nogal alternate route

unmaintained trail

trail marker for
164 and 164B

7546

intersection of
Ojitos Trail (166)
and
unnamed trail
begin Section 6-7

Ojitos Trail (166)

Talpa Traverse

0   0.5   1 mi

S6-8 El Nogal to Taos Cow

1.7 miles. 0 feet ascent. 155 feet descent.

From El Nogal parking lot, head out toward the road, which is Route 64. Take a left on to Route 64, staying on the left side of the road.

You'll be on Route 64 for 0.3 miles. I hate taking you through here, and there is an alternate way to go if you want to avoid the traffic.

Route 64 has some shoulder most of the way, but it's not ideal for walking. The traffic comes through fast, and there are large trucks and RVs sometimes.

0.3 miles down Route 64, take a left on to Route 585. Do **not** go straight on Kit Carson Road. Take the left instead. You'll be on Route 585 for about 200 feet, then you'll take a right onto the much quieter Witt Road.

Follow Witt Road for 0.4 miles, then follow it further when it bends right at the intersection of Vista del Canon. If you have a dog with you, keep it leashed for the first quarter mile or so. There is an unfriendly dog on the right side of the road just as you get on to Witt Road.

For the next 0.9 miles you'll be on Witt Road, walking through neighborhoods and past fenced fields and the occasional bed and breakfast or church. It's mostly shaded, and while traffic does go through here, it goes slowly. People who live here walk this road a lot.

0.9 miles on you will see Taos Cow on your left. Taos Cow is the end point for Section 6-6. They have water, a bathroom, and excellent food, including tasty ice cream. They are open 7:30 am to 5 pm seven days a week.

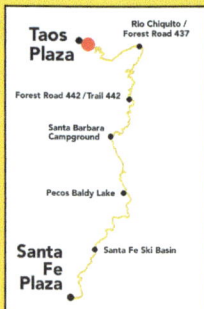

Taos Plaza
Rio Chiquito / Forest Road 437
Forest Road 442 / Trail 442
Santa Barbara Campground
Pecos Baldy Lake
Santa Fe Plaza
Santa Fe Ski Basin

View of the mountains north of Taos from Witt Road.

Kit Carson Road

The Taos Cow
end Section 6-8

Witt Road

Kit Carson Road

Acequia Del Sur Del Canon

Witt Road

NM 585

water
tower

Rio Fernando de Taos

El Nogal
parking lot
begin Section 6-8

7546

7218

Route 64

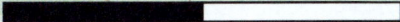

0   0.25   0.5 mi

S6-9: Taos Cow to Taos Plaza

1.4 miles. 31 feet ascent. 82 feet descent.

Having perhaps gotten some food from the Taos Cow, go out to Witt Road and walk toward the much larger road on your left, which is Kit Carson Road, also known as Route 64.

Take a left at Kit Carson Road, walking basically north/northwest, for 1.36 miles, all the way into Taos Plaza. You'll start seeing hotels and gift shops and whatnot as you approach Taos Plaza.

Once you're at Taos Plaza you'll be within a couple minutes' walk or less of several dozen restaurants, bars, hotels, motels, gift shops, ice cream shops, etc. Taos is fun. 0.55 miles down Route 64 from the Plaza is El Pueblo Lodge. I have stayed there many times, including after I first did the thru-hike in 2018.

Walk into Taos Plaza, past the Veteran's Memorial, and over to the steps of the gazebo. These steps mark the conclusion of your journey.

Congratulations. You have completed the Santa Fe to Taos Thru-Hike.

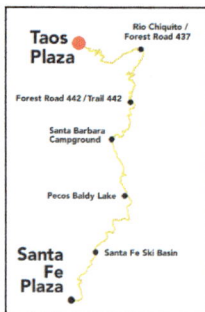

Taos Plaza.

Taos Plaza
end Section 6, 6-9

Route 68

Route 68

Kit Carson Road

Rio Fernando de Taos

The Taos Cow
begin Section 6-9

Witt Road

Kit Carson Road

0   0.25   0.5 m

7218

Alternate route: Intersection of 164 and 164B to Witt Road (avoiding Route 64 and El Nogal)

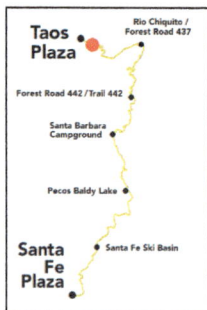

Walking on Route 64 is not ideal. It has almost no shoulder and the traffic through there moves fast. So I have tried to find a way around it. After scouting six different alternate routes, at least now I know I've found the best one. Maybe not a great alternative, but the best alternative for now.

Here it is: From the intersection of South Boundary (164), Ojitos Connector (164B), and the little unnamed shortcut, look west, away from the trail marker at the intersection. Head west, down Ojitos Connector (164B). The trail slopes down; you'll have a big view of Taos in front of you. You may be able to see the water tower a bit to the left of the trail in the distance as you walk.

Go 0.1 mile and look for a trail branching off to the right. You'll have veered a bit right as you walked the 0.1 mile, too. Take this right branch.

You'll walk another 0.1 miles, mostly north, on wide dry track. You'll be in full sun surrounded by dry junipers. There may be a lot of broken glass along the way. You may also notice quite a lot of animal tracks. The animals use this as a corridor (which is part of why all the broken glass is such a bad thing).

0.1 miles on, the trail will split in front of you. Go right, walking down for another 0.1 miles and then continuing on the faint path as the trail bends left, toward Highway 585. You'll be heading north for about 300 feet that includes this bend. You'll be getting very close to the road, then the trail will bend more tightly left at the very last bit.

Scramble over the dune/berm that's between you and the road, and you'll come out on to the shoulder of Route 585. Turn right, heading east, walking along the shoulder of 585 for about 0.2 miles until Witt Road is on your left, across the highway. Cross Route 585 and continue on Witt Road and the standard route of the thru-hike.

This is the walk along Route 64 that the alternate route described on this page avoids.

Julia Del Sur Del Canon

Acequia Madre Del Norte Del Canon

Route 585

water tower

Ojitos Trail (166)

alternate route

164B

7218

Rio Fernando de Taos

trail marker for
164 and 164B

unnamed trail

South Boundary Trail (164)

unmaintained trail

Route 64

Ojitos Trail (166)

El Nogal parking lot

Rio Fernando de Taos

0   0.125   0.25 mi

Planning

Pond just before the marmot area and just after Azul Trail. Section 3-2.

What to Know Before You Go

Answers to common questions about the thru-hike

Q: How long does it take to do the thru-hike?
A: It depends how fast you go.

If you can do 20 miles a day, it takes a week. (130 miles / 20 miles a day = 6.5 days). At a pace of 13 miles a day, you'd finish in ten days. If you can do ten miles a day, it would take two weeks. If you want to be leisurely, so you can have lots of time to contemplate the mountains and lakes, three weeks would be ideal. That would have you covering about six miles a day.

For all those distances, keep in mind that you'll be above 9,000 feet elevation most of the time. That's going to slow you down, especially if you're coming from sea level. Also take into account that you'll be doing 2,000 to 4,500 feet of elevation every day, depending on how much trail you cover. And you'll be carrying a full pack, which could be anywhere from 20 to 40 pounds depending on what you bring. All those factors will have a significant impact on how fast and how far you can go, or how far you'd want to go.

Q: Is there water on the route?
A: Yes! There is water every 3-4 miles for most of the route.

The thru-hike goes right by nine lakes: Lake Katherine, Stewart Lake (and Stewart Pond), Pecos Baldy Lake, Truchas Lakes, No Fish Lake, Los Esteros (a pond), La Cueva Lake, and Bernardin Lake. That's not counting Lake Johnson and Indian Lake, which are each about 1 mile off the route.

The route also goes along or crosses the Santa Fe River, Little Tesuque Creek, Big Tesuque Creek, Rio en Medio, Rio Nambe, Winsor Creek, Rito Oscuro Creek, Cave Creek, Panchuela Creek, Jack's Creek, the West Fork of Rio Santa Barbara, Rio Santa Barbara, the Middle Fork of Rio Santa Barbara, Indian Creek, Agua Piedra Creek, Rio del Pueblo, Rio Grande del Rancho, Rito de la Olla, Rio Chiquito, American/Bear Spring, and Rio Fernando de Taos. That does not include about two dozen rills (rills are tiny streams about two to three feet wide) and another dozen small unnamed creeks. The route of the thru-hike was expressly designed to maximize reliable water access.

The two longest stretches without water are:
- 9 miles without reliable water from the rills on Ojitos Maes trail to where Rio Grande del Rancho and Forest Road 439 intersect.
- 10 miles from FR 437 / Drake Canyon entrance to El Nogal, or 11.6 miles if you skipped the water at El Nogal (which is probably a good idea due to dog waste contamination) and continued on to Taos Cow at Anglada. However, if you made a 1-mile detour from the thru-hike route and got water from American/Bear Spring on the South Boundary Trail, you'd have a water source a mere 4.3 miles from the Drake Canyon entrance.

Both those distances are much shorter—and shadier—than the 13 miles on the Colorado Trail where you go through the Hayman Burn area.

Q: When is the best time to go?
A: Anytime from June until mid-October would work.

In terms of "best," probably August, but it depends on what you like. August is a great month to do the thru-hike because the weather is excellent and we're in mid-monsoon season so all the water sources will be in good shape. If you like seeing people, you'll see more of them in August than at any time of the year, though much of the thru-hike goes through places remote enough that you may not see more than a few people a day, if that.

July is also a great month. You'll see slightly fewer people in July than in August. September is the best month if you want a balance of optimal weather and fewer people. Mid-June forward is fine, too. You may see some lingering snow in the highest elevations in even mid-June, and if monsoon season is even a little bit late you might skip some of its afternoon showers. Early June is dicey because if we got a good snow pack, you might be picking your way over some icy old snow in spots.

Early October is lovely. Late October is workable. The foliage will be pretty and there will be far fewer people out. Late May could be fine if you're staying in the lower elevations, or if you're willing to bring a pair of Yaktrax to get yourself over icy spots. Any earlier than late May is questionable, but if we had an extremely light snow pack it'd be fine. May and June are fire season.

Q: What are trail conditions like?
A: Generally good, but be prepared for fallen trees.

The thru-hike goes through some very lightly traveled trail in spots. This dovetails with the issue of the Forest Service being grossly underfunded and results in a lot of trail that doesn't get maintained. We have several local non-profits that do trail maintenance, like the wonderful people at the New Mexico Volunteers for the Outdoors (NMVFO) and the Rocky Mountain Youth Corps, but they have to pick their projects carefully. We are only going to have more issues with treefall (aka "blowdown") as the trees recently killed by bark beetles or drought and heat fall and take their time to decay.

These are a few parts of the trail that get rough:

- About half of Skyline Trail between Stewart Pond and Cave Creek.
- Going up toward Ripley Point on Indian Creek Trail (some of this was cleared, but the last mile up gets rough).
- Between Spirit Lake and Skyline Trail on Winsor Trail.
- About two miles on Middle Fork Trail, coming down from the Santa Barbara Divide. The rough section starts a little bit past No Fish Lake.
- The trail up to Lake Johnson from Skyline Trail.

The thru-hike used to go along Skyline Trail between Horsethief Meadow and Rito Perro Trail, but I rerouted that due to the excessive blowdown in that area.

Q: What's the weather like?
A: Be ready for hail, wind, lightning, and temperature drops.

Mountain weather gets interesting. Ferocious hail storms are not uncommon up at any of the big mountain lakes (Katherine, Baldy, Truchas). These storms can leave the ground covered in several inches of hail. Think about this when you decide where to put your tent. Some shelter under trees is a good thing; having a tree fall on your tent is not a good thing.

Be mindful of lightning when you are crossing ridgelines. The Santa Barbara Divide, for example, should probably not be attempted if you've seen lightning and there are lightning-capable clouds around. If the weather looks dicey, consider overnighting at No Fish Lake if you're on the north side of the Divide, or find a protected spot off Skyline Trail if you're on the south side. Wait until conditions improve.

Weather is a major issue for the Tesuque Peak alternate route, too. And I expressly added the Spirit Lake alternate route so there's an option to avoid the saddle by Santa Fe Baldy that you'd have to go over to get to Lake Katherine. The Trailriders Wall, while fabulous, is also very exposed, though there is a little patch of trees about in the middle of it that you could shelter in during a storm. There are also trails in decent intervals along the Trailriders Wall that you could use to get down off of it if necessary.

In terms of clothing and sleeping bags and pads and tents, you need to be ready for a 20-degree temperature drop. Just in case. This can be fairly easily managed just by carrying a couple of extra oversized emergency blankets.

Q: Are there resupply points?
A: Yes. See page 138 for information about resupply.

Q: Can I take my dog?
A: If it can handle the distances you'll be covering.

See the gear list for more about what you need to know about taking your dog. But yes—there are quite a lot of dogs out on the trails in the Santa Fe National Forest, in the Pecos Wilderness, and in Carson National Forest.

Q: Do I need a permit to do the thru-hike?
A: No.

Q: Do I have to do the whole thru-hike all at once?
A: Nope.

Day hiking and doing the thru-hike in bits are encouraged. See the "thru-hike in weekends" section or the day hikes section of this book. You could even do a section a year. Or you could use part of the route as inspiration for your own treks. Do whatever you want.

Q: I'm worried about wild animals—should I be?

A: Be aware, but not afraid. But manage your dog.

There are black bears (the little bears, not the big brown grizzly bears) here. It is quite rare for them to bother people, but of course there are stories about it. I do use a bear hang, but that is in part because I am almost always out alone and I don't want any trouble. I also often have a dog with me, and the most likely scenario of me getting into trouble with a bear is the dog getting into a tangle with the bear and me trying to save the dog. I am tidy with my food on the trail, even putting dog treats in a plastic bag in my pocket rather than directly in my pocket. And I do carry grizzly bear mace.

There are mountain lions here, too. Every few years, a dog gets attacked by a mountain lion. Usually the dog lives. Oddly enough, I have only heard of this happening in the trails between Santa Fe Plaza and the Ski Basin. But do be aware that mountain lions are around, though it is highly, *highly* unlikely you will even see one. I've never seen one. I personally would not let my toddler run several hundred feet ahead of me on the trails around Santa Barbara Campground, for instance, but mostly because Rio Santa Barbara moves fast, not because of mountain lions.

Do be wary of the bulls. Cattle are allowed in the wilderness, and while cows are chill, sometimes bulls are not. They are not likely to bother you, but... respect them. Ranchers can legally shoot your dog if they interpret your dog's behavior as threatening their cattle.

Also respect bighorn sheep. Their territory typically starts around Pecos Baldy Lake and goes potentially all the way to Taos, but don't expect to see them north of Ripley Point, if that. The females may beg for food, especially at Truchas Lakes. Do not feed them. They may also try to get into your tent, so keep it zipped closed if you aren't near it. The male bighorns will defend what they interpret as their turf. They are likely to go after a dog if they feel threatened.

We do also have elk. Again: Manage your dog. It may be every dog's lifelong dream to chase a herd of elk, but that might not end well.

Q: Can I leave my car somewhere while I do the thru-hike?
A: Yes.

There is long-term parking available at the Santa Fe airport for $7 per day, though sometimes finding a parking spot there is a challenge. There is also the Santa Fe Community Convention Center Municipal Garage, which is about ten minutes walk from the Plaza at 119 South Federal Place. That has 489 spaces and two EV chargers. And there is the Water Street Municipal Lot at 100 East Water Street, only 0.1 miles from the Plaza. That is the only Santa Fe public lot that mentions full day rates of up to $12 per day on the Santa Fe website's parking page (SantaFeNM.gov/public-works/parking).

In Taos, there are "approximately 250 free parking spaces located at Town Hall, Taos Public Library, Bedford Street Lot, Kit Carson Park, Kit Carson Street Parking and Quesnel Street" according to the Town of Taos's website (TaosNM.gov). There is also a "paid" parking lot a block west of Taos Plaza, on the west side of the Our Lady of Guadalupe Parish. That lot has a few overnight parking spaces. It is marked as a paid lot, but the payment machine is broken, so you can park for free for now.

If you asked really, really nicely, the people at Sipapu might let you keep your car in their very large parking lot for a week or so.

If you are flying into the Albuquerque Sunport, you could leave your car there in long-term parking, then take the Road Runner (a train) up to Santa Fe. Then take the Blue Bus from the Road Runner South Capitol station to Santa Fe Plaza. The Sunport offers uncovered parking for $4.50 per day (Booking. apsunport.com/).

Q: Is there public transportation between Santa Fe and Taos, and to some of the trailheads?
A: Yes—the Blue Bus.

The Blue Bus is a small bus transit system that goes all over northern New Mexico and many areas of the thru-hike. It is free. The website NCRTD.org has a lot of information, including all the routes, timetables, and stops. I still recommend calling them and talking to a human, just to be 100% sure.

The Blue Bus "305 Taos Express", runs between Santa Fe and Taos on Saturdays and Sundays. You can pick it up at the Santa Fe Depot on Montezuma Avenue in Santa Fe, or at the Taos County Administration Building in Taos, plus several other spots along the way. It will get you from Santa Fe to Taos or vice versa in about two hours.

The Blue Bus also runs from downtown Santa Fe to the Ski Basin, and it has a stop about five miles away from Sipapu, at the "Rockwall" stop on the Peñasco line.

Q: How fit should I be to do the thru-hike?
A: Fit enough to hike for at least four hours, with modest inclines, with your full pack.

How fit you'll need to be depends on three things: 1) Are you doing the whole route straight through, or doing a section weekend? 2) Are you used to altitude? 3) Do you have flexibility in your schedule to change plans in case you can't go as far as you first thought you could?

To train for the thru-hike, I recommend you start two to three months before your thru-hike if you're doing it all at once. Find a steep hiking trail with less than optimal footing. Start hiking it several hours a week, adding more time as you can. When you're doing two hours a day fairly easily, add pack weight, about five pounds at a time. Don't have access to a good training trail? The big stair climbers available at some gyms are a good substitute. Nalgenes filled with water are excellent for weighing down a pack.

Recommended gear lists

For a day hike

MUST HAVE

- ☐ A fast pack with a filled 100 oz. water bladder.
- ☐ A shell for wind and/or rain ("shell" = jacket).
- ☐ Sunscreen (preferably 50 SPF with UVA/UVB protection).
- ☐ Digital map: Gaia paid, Strava, or CalTopo with your route and surrounding areas downloaded.
- ☐ Printed map. If you have hiked the route you're going out on recently, you can skip the map. However, you may run into people who don't know the area and don't have a map. Be nice and give your map to them.
- ☐ Electrolytes and/or gel chews.
- ☐ High-energy snack (trail mix, dried fruit, chocolate bar, jerky, etc.)

NICE TO HAVE

- ☐ Hiking poles.
- ☐ Hat (if it's cold, this belongs on the "must have" list).
- ☐ Sunglasses if you wear them.
- ☐ 2-3 tissues to clean your nose/glasses/sunglasses/camera.
- ☐ Headlamp (in case you end out longer than expected).
- ☐ Blister care.
- ☐ 2 extra-large emergency blankets, just in case.
- ☐ Garmin InReach Mini or similar device.
- ☐ Mini compass.
- ☐ Lip balm.
- ☐ Silk or wool neck gaiter.
- ☐ A bivvy bag. I like the S.O.L. (Survive Outdoors Longer) Emergency Bivvy XL. 84" x 60". 5.8 oz.
- ☐ Water treatment tablets or drops.

For a one- or two-night overnight

Everything listed above plus all this:

SLEEPING

- ☐ Tent (including stakes, footer, rain cover).
- ☐ Sleeping bag. Sleeping bag should be rated for at least 15 degrees below the lowest temperature you're expecting.
- ☐ Sleeping pad.
- ☐ Compression sack for sleeping bag.
- ☐ Nice to have: A short roll of Tenacious Tape for random gear repair.
- ☐ Nice to have: A tiny flashlight to hang from the inside top of your tent. Get one that uses the same batteries as your headlamp and other gear.
- ☐ Nice to have: A strap to lash the sleeping pad to the outside of your pack.

EATING

- ☐ Stove.
- ☐ Stove fuel and lighter/matches. If you bring extra fuel, you can heat some for bathing. Being able to clean up every day with even half of a Nalgene of warm water is nice. Also remember that the colder it gets and the higher you are, the more fuel you'll need.
- ☐ Backup lighter or matches.
- ☐ Pots, cups, long spoons.
- ☐ Stuff sack to hold all food-related things for a bear hang.
- ☐ Bear hang (about 60 feet of cord + a carabiner). Use cord that can double as shoelaces.
- ☐ Breakfast (I like instant oatmeal with shaved almonds and brown sugar).
- ☐ Coffee or tea (and maybe evening herbal tea).
- ☐ Snacks for daytime and lunch, like shaved almonds, dates, chocolate bars, gel chews, crackers, sunflower seeds, etc.
- ☐ Dinner (freeze-dried meals). Or, as you're only out one night, it's okay to bring semi-perishable food if you can keep it cool.
- ☐ Something fun to eat/drink. Dessert, a nip of whiskey.
- ☐ Wilderness Wash.
- ☐ Water treatment.
- ☐ Water treatment backup.
- ☐ Triple battery backup if your water treatment systems require power.
- ☐ 100 oz. water bladder.
- ☐ Nalgene bottle.
- ☐ A backup foldable water container. I like the Platypus Platy 2-Liter Ultralight Collapsible Backpacking Water Bottle.
- ☐ Nice to have: Backup mouthpiece for the bladder.

CLOTHES

These clothing suggestions assume you are not going to be out in sub-40 degree temps.

- ☐ Backpack (counting this as clothes because you will be wearing it).
- ☐ Boots you love, have worn recently, and can stay dry in in 4" of water.
- ☐ Light shirt.
- ☐ Heavy shirt.
- ☐ Down hoodie or jacket.
- ☐ Socks and backup socks.
- ☐ Long underwear / yoga pants (to sleep in, or as backup). Alpine weather changes fast. You must be ready for a cold snap, even in summer.
- ☐ Hiking pants *with zippable pockets*.
- ☐ Neck gaiter (if you'd wear it). Also makes a good sleeping mask.
- ☐ Underwear.
- ☐ A backup pair of hiking boot laces.
- ☐ Optional: Camp shoes. Ideally your camp shoes are also your river-crossing shoes.

PERSONAL CARE

- [ ] Toothbrush (broken in half to save weight and space).
- [ ] Tiny tin of toothpaste and floss only if you'd use it.
- [ ] Sunscreen.
- [ ] Lip balm.
- [ ] Small hand towel (cut in half) to wash the worst of the dust off with.
- [ ] Whatever personal care items you need to feel comfortable. Try to keep them to six ounces or less.
- [ ] Something to read or entertain yourself with.
- [ ] Pain killers and/or anti-inflammatories. Whatever you like: Advil, Aleve, etc. Also consider some of the salves/ointments/liniments available.
- [ ] Medicine for whatever you might get. Allergies? Heartburn? Insomnia? Prescribed medications? Also something for stomach issues, just in case.
- [ ] Foot blister care.
- [ ] Basic medical kit. The meds you want plus enough to treat a cut or a burn (including sunburn) or a twisted ankle. To treat a cut, you need to clean it thoroughly. Then apply antibiotic ointment, then protect it with a bandage that will stay in place. Same treatment for a burn. For a twisted ankle, bring a roll of medical tape. Medical tape is handy for lots of things, including keeping bandages in place. Consider bringing a large trauma bandage, especially in hunting season. A small water syringe for cleaning wounds and a good pair of tweezers are also useful. Never wash wounds, including open blisters, in untreated water.
- [ ] Ear plugs (optional, and only if you're a light sleeper and will use them).
- [ ] Two extra-large emergency blankets. Highly recommended. If someone gets hurt or sick, keeping them warm will help a lot. Also, if you have a surprise temperature drop, put an emergency blanket inside the bottom of your tent, underneath your sleeping pad. You will be much warmer. If you are still cold, put the second emergency blanket over your sleeping bag. You'll crinkle, but you'll be much warmer. For two extra ounces, emergency blankets are excellent insurance. Just get the oversized ones. The regular-sized blankets aren't big enough to really help. And even with the big ones, you'll want two if you end up actually needing them.
- [ ] Purell.
- [ ] Wilderness wash (also used for washing pots).
- [ ] Cat hole "shovel." Optional if you are confident you can find a properly shaped rock or piece of wood.
- [ ] Tissues if your nose runs or you want to clean your glasses or camera.
- [ ] Nice to have: A stuff sack that's fuzzy/soft on the inside so you can turn it inside out, put some clothes into it, and have a pillow.
- [ ] Nice to have: A small stuff sack attached to the top inside of your backpack, so you can access personal items, or whatever, fast.
- [ ] Nice to have in cold weather: Something to sit on. This will keep you warmer than you'd think. Even one square foot of closed-cell foam works. Or sit on your sleeping pad, inflated or uninflated. Just put a barrier between you and cold ground.

COMMUNICATIONS AND NAVIGATION

- ☐ Battery pack/source to recharge your phone.
- ☐ Your phone. (Dare you to not take it.)
- ☐ Headlamp with backup battery.
- ☐ Printed, fold-out map. Because things happen. Phones get lost or run out of power. Or maybe you'll want an extra map for some reason, like you have to split up your group. Or you run into someone who needs a map.
- ☐ GPS device or digital maps, pre-downloaded or available offline. **Be familiar with your navigation tools BEFORE you leave.**
- ☐ Mini compass.
- ☐ Garmin InReach Mini or similar device so you can text in an emergency, or to alleviate other people's anxiety about you being out in the wilderness. It's also nice to have a backup tracking device.
- ☐ A base camp contact. Tell someone reliable where you are going, your basic route, and when you'll be back. Have them looking out to hear from you when you return.
- ☐ All the various cables you'll need to charge things. So 1) phone cable 2) GPS device cable 3) headlamp cable 4) ...?
- ☐ Bear mace (a sort of communication device). Optional.
- ☐ Emergency whistle.

For a three-night or overnight or doing the complete thru-hike

Everything listed for the one-night overnight, plus:

- ☐ More food (and varied food). How much food depends on how many nights you'll be out and how much you tend to eat.
- ☐ More printed maps or downloaded route maps.
- ☐ More battery power. Or a reliable solar panel. Or both. To minimize battery usage:
  - Set your phone to low battery mode.
  - Switch your phone to airplane mode.
  - Reduce the brightness of your phone's screen.
- ☐ More personal care items—again, whatever you need to be comfortable. Expect blisters and bruises and soreness. Expect that you'll want to wash clothes.
- ☐ More gear repair. Like a sleeping pad repair kit.
- ☐ Hiking poles if you weren't already taking them.
- ☐ A multi-tool with a small knife, tweezers, scissors, and a phillips and flathead screwdriver.
- ☐ River shoes, or boots that can handle at least six inches of water. Especially when you're crossing Rio Santa Barbara into Indian Canyon.
- ☐ Optional: A notebook and a pencil to take notes, or write a journal entry or a from-the-trail letter. Or if you want to draw a few things, or to make personal maps as a way to document your days.
- ☐ Optional but recommended: This guidebook.

You may notice that the gear list for the full thru-hike isn't radically different from the one- or two-night gear list. Obviously, you'll need more food, fuel, and battery power. You may need more clothing for varied weather conditions. And most of the "nice to have" things for a short trip become "must haves" for a multi-night trip.

This is not as extensive a gear list as other thru-hikes have because the Santa Fe to Taos Thru-Hike is not 1,000+ miles long. If you do 10 miles a day, you'll be on the trail for two weeks. That's not long enough to need many of the things required to do one of the mega trail thru-hikes. You do not need any special gear to do the thru-hike. I do strongly encourage you to bring and use the best sun protection you can and to drink water with electrolytes.

Highly recommended: Go out for an overnight before you do a multi-night trip. A "gear test" night is the best thing you can do to have a good experience on a multi-night trip. It's also excellent physical training. Doing 12 miles and 3,000 feet elevation with a 30-lb pack is a different experience than doing it with a 10-lb day pack. After hauling a 30-lb pack around for even one day, you may decide you don't need a lot of stuff you thought you did. You may also decide to make a few strategic gear upgrades. A test overnight will tell you if that 2-person tent you thought would work will cut it with you and your 6'2" friend sharing it in a rainstorm. Look on eBay or any of the used-gear sites if you can't afford new stuff. Go for quality. Cheap gear can become a safety risk.

Another tip: For every overnight you do, capture a list of the things you had that you didn't need, and things you didn't have that you wanted. Or things you wished you had done before you left. This can be recorded as a voice memo on your phone as you're driving home.

Resupply Options

There are two resupply options, each close to Agua Piedra Campground at the end of Section 4-5/beginning of Section 4-6.

1) The Santa Fe to Taos Members' Resupply.
This is an outfitted 12' x 24' storage unit 0.2 miles off the route of the thru-hike in the very small village of Tres Ritos (Section 4-6). It is one of the storage units for the Tres Ritos Lodge, which is unfortunately currently closed.

If you are a member (see page 184 for information about membership), you can ship a box and other gear to yourself c/o The Santa Fe to Taos Thru-Hike, and we will take your box / gear to the storage unit and put it in a secure locker. We'll then send you the code both to the storage unit's front door and to your temporary locker so you can access your stuff when you go through Tres Ritos. The storage unit is 0.2 miles from the entrance to La Cueva Canyon.

Membership also includes access to the "wilderness store" goods in the storage unit, and to the basic services available for members in the storage unit. The services are *very* basic, but there is a power station to recharge your electronics, a table and two chairs, ample lights, and a huge ice chest with sodas and beer. There's also a mirror, a radio, and tasty water. As a member, you get to vote on what services and stuff are available. So if you want, say, a big whiteboard or a plastic inflatable palm tree, just vote for it. This a space for thru-hike members to have what they need and want.

The "wilderness store" is also stocked based on members' requests, and it has a selection of trail food, fuel, first aid and personal supplies, and gear repair. It also has replacement supplies like sleeping pads and socks—whatever members want. All store items are in locked lockers, but as a member you get the access codes to the lockers. So take what you need, log what you take, and pay for it via Venmo, PayPal, or Zelle. We do not keep cash in the unit.

2) Sipapu Ski and Summer Resort (https://www.Sipapu.ski/).

Sipapu is 2.3 miles northeast along Route 518 from Agua Piedra Campground (and the route of the thru-hike). Unfortunately, there is no public transportation to it and there is no off-road trail. You have to walk northwest on NM 518 to get to it. Most of that distance, there will be decent shoulder on the side of the road for you to walk on, but it is not ideal.

You can mail yourself a package to Sipapu (Sipapu Ski & Summer Resort, 5224 NM-518, Vadito, NM 87579) and they will hold it for you for free. Call ahead to confirm your package is there before you leave. (575) 587-2240.

Sipapu also rents cabins and rooms year round. They have a restaurant, a store, and a little gas station. If you want to rest for a day or two off-trail approximately half-way through the thru-hike, Sipapu is your best option. I have stayed at Sipapu in one of their suites. It wasn't fancy, but it was functional. They are okay with dirty hikers, even a group of dirty hikers. The kitchens are well-equipped. The water is hot. The heat works, though it's loud. In addition to the king-sized bed in my suite, there were four bunk beds and a wood stove. They accept dogs in some units.

If You're Taking a Dog

- Something for your dog to drink out of.
- The dog's food. Tip: Freeze-dried food cuts pack weight.
- Lend your dog a jacket or something to sleep on in the tent.
- A leash. Dogs are supposed to be leashed in both the Pecos Wilderness and Carson National Forest. This is not a strictly enforced rule, until you run into a Forest Ranger. Dogs go missing in these areas. They can get into tangles with wildlife in a split-second. A male bighorn sheep can easily kill even a big dog. So can elk, mountain lions, black bears, packs of coyotes, bulls, and, potentially, angry ranchers. Manage your dog.
- A bear bell attached to your dog's collar has a number of benefits:
  1) Your dog is less likely to get shot by a hunter.
  2) It gives animals more warning, so they can get away or not be as surprised by you.
  3) If your dog takes off, the bear bell makes it easier to find them.
  4) If your dog comes up on a group of people fast, they'll hear the

jingle first. This keeps people calmer (and more friendly) because they realize your dog isn't a wild animal running out of the bushes.

A Word About Altitude

The altitude is going to slow you down, even if you're fit. If you ignore it, and just push through, you could end up in need of medical care.

Altitude sickness has three levels of severity: Acute mountain sickness (AMS), High altitude pulmonary edema (HAPE), and High altitude cerebral edema (HACE). HACE is unlikely, but AMS is fairly common, and HAPE is possible.

Most likely, you'll just feel tired and maybe a little queasy. If you wear rings, you might notice them becoming tighter. The Cleveland Clinic's website says "Almost everyone who ascends quickly to 11,000 feet (3,352 meters) will develop AMS." The Tesuque Peak alternate route, Puerto Nambe and Lake Katherine, almost all the way from Rito Perro Field to No Fish Lake, and Ripley Point and Los Esteros are all 11,000 feet or higher.

Try to take it easy the first day or two. If you are coming from sea level, hang out around town for a day or two before you start your hike. Or cut whatever would be your typical mileage down by a third to a half for the first few days.

Also remember that the route has some considerable climbs. Are you used to doing 3,000 feet of elevation a day? How about 5,000?

The best way to adjust to the altitude is to give yourself time and drink water. A lot of water—like three liters a day more than you had been drinking.

Walking through the Jaroso Fire burn scar. 11,000 feet elevation. Section 2-9.

Itineraries

Pecos Baldy Lake. End of Section 2, beginning of Section 3.

The Thru-Hike by Miles per Day

The mileage, ascent, and descent measurements here are based on my recorded tracks and plotted routes in the Gaia Maps website app. They are not perfect. CalTopo's app gives me slightly different distances from the same GPX files. You may end up recording as much as 8% more or less than what's shown here as you walk, and even minor differences between individual tracks can add up to quite a lot over 130+ miles. Also note that the elevation changes are not down-to-the-foot precise.

4-8 Miles a Day without Alternate Routes

This is the shortest, easiest itinerary that gets you to the nicest spots possible while taking water access into account. It's a good itinerary if you are acclimating to altitude and perhaps not in particularly great shape. The last day is long because if you're that close to Taos Plaza, you'll probably want to go all the way to it (and because there aren't very good campsites between American Spring and Taos Plaza).

Day	Point to point	Section	Miles	Ascent	Descent
1	Santa Fe Plaza to Sierra del Norte Trailhead. No overnight; this is a day hike because the first good place to camp is at the Winsor / Juan intersection, which is more than 8 miles from Santa Fe Plaza.	S1-1 to end of S1-3	4.4	643	90
2	Sierra del Norte Trailhead to about 0.4 miles past the Winsor / Juan intersection. First overnight.	S1-4 to S1-6	5.1	1,152	1,333
3	To the field east of the Winsor / Borrego Trail intersection.	S1-6 to S1-8	4.0	1,301	138
4	To just short of Winsor Trailhead, about 350 ft past Rio en Medio (creek and trail) and 150 ft or so east of the trail.	S1-8 to S1-9	4.4	2,164	464
5	To just short of Puerto Nambe, either in the fields before the switchbacks or along the switchbacks up to Puerto Nambe.	S1-8 to S2-2	4.1	1,398	801
6	To far side of Lake Katherine. This short day gets you to the lake early, so you'll get a better campsite. If you take a detour to summit Santa Fe Baldy, then the day is 5.6 miles with 2,450 ft ascent, 1,500 ft descent.	S2-2 to S2-4	3.4	1,421	475

7	To campsites just short of Cave Creek / Skyline Trail intersection.	S2-4 to S2-5	6.4	585	2,554
8	To Dockweiler Field and rill.	S2-5 to S2-8	6.4	1,831	1,621
9	To Pecos Baldy Lake. If you add a summit hike to Pecos Baldy it's 6.9 miles with 2,710 feet of ascent and 1,333 feet of descent.	S2-8 to S3-1	4.4	1,616	230
10	To Truchas Lakes. Zip up Rio Quemado Trail to the view from the Truchas Peaks' ridgeline to make the day 6.1 miles, 1,785 feet ascent and 1,355 descent.	S3-1 to S3-3	5.2	1,269	852
11	To field just past the West Fork of Rio Santa Barbara.	S3-3 to S3-5	7.1	952	2,897
12	To 0.2 miles or so (wherever looks comfy) into Indian Canyon.	S3-5 to S4-1	6	850	1,804
13	To Los Esteros.	S4-1 to S4-4	5.4	3,007	816
14	To Indian Lake.	S4-4 to S4-5	6.2	1,018	2,644
15	To fields just short of Forest Road 442.	S4-5 to S4-9	7.5	2,281	1,534
16	To flat areas just out of view and just short of Forest Road 339 and Rio Grande del Rancho.	S4-9 to S5-2	8.5	1,242	1,974
17	To campsite just short of FR 438 by the Palociento Creek fish barrier.	S5-2 to S5-4	7.8	1,626	2,093
18	To fields by Rio Chiquito bridge. Skip Bernardin Lake to cut a mile, or overnight at Bernardin Lake if you want to split the day. It's 2.4 miles and 800 feet ascent from the fish gate to Bernardin Lake.	S5-4 to S5-7	8.9	1,714	1,758
19	To fields across from Rio Chiquito and opposite road at entrance to Drake Canyon.	S5-7 to S6-3	7.5	224	1,594
20	To American Spring.	S6-3 to S6-5	4.3	1,818	239
21	To Taos Plaza.	S6-5 to end	10.7	684	2,998

4-8 miles a day with alternate routes

This is as close to the "4-8 miles a day without alternate routes" itinerary as I could get it, but I've added in the alternate routes for Spirit Lake and Jicarita Peak. The Tesuque Peak alternate route requires dry camping one night. Tesuque Peak is not ideal for the shorter mileage of this itinerary.

Day	Point to point	Section	Miles	Ascent	Descent
1	Santa Fe Plaza to Sierra del Norte Trailhead. No overnight; this is a day hike because the first good place to camp is at the Winsor / Juan intersection, which is more than 8 miles from Santa Fe Plaza.	S1-1 to end of S1-3	4.4	643	90
2	Sierra del Norte Trailhead to about 0.4 miles past the Winsor / Juan intersection.	S1-4 to S1-6	5.1	1,152	1,333
3	To the field east of the Winsor / Borrego Trail intersection.	S1-6 to S1-8	4.0	1,301	138
4	To a bit short of Tesuque Peak, off of Forest Road 150. Dry camping. No campfires.	S1-8 to Alt route	7.1	3,271	320
5	To Spirit Lake.	Alt route	6.2	1,433	2,123
6	To campsites just short of Cave Creek / Skyline intersection.	Alt route to S2-5	6.4	585	2,554
7	To Dockweiler Field and rill.	S2-5 to S2-8	6.4	1,831	1,621
8	Pecos Baldy Lake. Summit Pecos Baldy if you want.	S2-8 to S3-1	4.4	1,616	230
9	To Truchas Lakes. Summit Truchas Peak if you want.	S3-1 to S3-3.	5.2	1,269	852
10	To the little ponds about 0.8 miles along East Fork Trail off Skyline.	Alt route	6.7	1,557	1,604
11	To Serpent Lake.	Alt route	6.2	1,116	1,184
12	To Los Esteros.	Alt route to S4-4	5.4	3,007	816
13	To Indian Lake.	S4-4 to S4-5	6.2	1,018	2,644
14	To fields just short of/south of Forest Road 442.	S4-5 to S4-9	7.5	2,281	1,534

15	To just short of Forest Road 339 and Rio Grande del Rancho.	S4-9 to S5-2	8.5	1,242	1,974
16	To campsite just short of Forest Road 438 by Palociento Creek fish barrier.	S5-2 to S5-4	7.8	1,626	2,093
17	To fields by Rio Chiquito bridge. Skip Bernardin Lake to cut a mile, or stay overnight at Bernardin Lake if you want to split the day. It's only 2.4 miles and 800 feet elevation from the fish gate to Bernardin Lake.	S5-4 to S5-7	8.9	1,714	1,758
18	To fields past Rio Chiquito, opposite road and Drake Canyon entrance.	S5-7 to S6-3	7.5	224	1,594
19	To American Spring.	S6-3 to S6-5	4.3	1,818	239
20	To Taos Plaza.	S6-5 to end	10.7	684	2,998

View from the fields just south of Forest Road 442 at the end of Section 4.

8-10 miles a day
without alternate routes

Day	Point to Point	Section	miles	ascent	descent
1	Santa Fe Plaza to about 0.5 miles past the intersection of Juan (399) and Winsor Trail (254).	S1-1 to S1-6	9.5	1,807	1,423
2	To campsite up and off Nambe Lake Trail from the Y. From the Y, go towards Nambe Lake for 0.2 miles. Campsite is about 200 feet to the right of the trail and the river.	S1-6 to S2-2	10.3	4,589	1,245
3	To Stewart Lake via Katherine.	S2-2 to S2-4	8.3	2,246	2,749
4	To Dockweiler field and rill.	S2-4 to S2-8	9.4	2,157	2,366
5	To Truchas Lakes.	S2-8 to S3-3	9.6	2,923	1,081
6	To campsite near merge of West Fork and Middle Fork of Rio Santa Barbara.	S3-3 to S3-5	10	1,301	3,839
7	To Los Esteros.	S3-5 to S4-4	8.5	3,498	1,696
8	To La Cueva Lake.	S4-4 to S4-7	8.8	1,965	2,961
9	To just short of FR 442, FR 439 and Rio Grande del Rancho.	S4-7 to S5-2	10.3	1,644	2,272
10	To Bernardin Lake.	S5-2 to S5-6	10.1	2,410	2,192
11	To any campsite near Buena Suerte Canyon on Forest Road 437.	S5-6 to S6-2	8.9	953	2,054
12	To fields around American Spring. Note that the spring is not on the standard route of the thru-hike.	S6-2 to Alt	9.4	1,937	1,263
13	To Taos Plaza.	S6-2 to end	10.6	650	2,944

8-10 miles a day with alternate routes

Including Tesuque Peak, Spirit Lake, and Jicarita Peak.

Day	Point to Point	Section	miles	ascent	descent
1	Santa Fe Plaza to about 0.5 miles past the intersection of Juan (399) and Winsor Trail (254).	S1-1 to S1-6	9.5	1,807	1,423
2	To northeast of Tesuque Creek and Forest Road 150 (aka "Aspen Vista") intersection.	S1-6 to Alt rt	7.5	3,328	294
3	To Spirit Lake.	Alt rt	9.8	2,804	2,442
4	To fields by creek, west and off trail, just past Cave Creek / Dockweiler Trail intersection.	Alt rt + S2-4 to S2-6	8.9	805	3,183
5	To Pecos Baldy Lake.	S2-6 to S3-1	7.9	3,404	379
6	To Middle Fork Trail / Middle Fork Rio Santa Barbara off Skyline.	S1-1 to S3-3 + Alt rt	10.9	2,313	2,149
7	To Serpent Lake.	Alt rt	7.8	1,796	1,685
8	To just short of Agua Piedra Creek.	Alt rt + S4-4 to S4-7	9.6	1,249	3,358
9	To just short of Forest Road 442.	S4-7 to S4-9	8.5	2,304	1,711
10	To Forest Trail 142, next to Rio Grande del Rancho, after Forest Road 440 split.	S4-9 to S5-3	10.5	1,654	2,089
11	To Bernardin Lake.	S5-3 to S5-6	8.9	2,065	2,120
12	To any campsite near Buena Suerte Canyon on Forest Road 437.	S5-6 to S6-2	8.9	953	2,054
13	To fields around American Spring. "Alternate" because the spring is not on the official route.	S6-2 to Alt	9.4	1,937	1,263
14	To Taos Plaza.	S6-2 to end	10.6	650	2,944

10-12 miles a day
without alternate routes

Day	Point to Point	Section	miles	ascent	descent
1	SF Plaza to 1/2 mile or so before the Jawbone / Winsor Trail junction.	S1-1 to S1-6	10.4	2,093	1,434
2	To the fields off trail just short of Puerto Nambe.	S1-6 to S2-2	10.7	4,175	1,177
3	To campsite off Cave Creek Trail near the caves.	S2-2 to S2-6	11.4	2,129	3,954
4	To Pecos Baldy Lake.	S2-6 to S3-1	9.0	3,412	845
5	To field just past West Fork Trail / West Fork Rio Santa Barbara.	S3-1 to S3-5	12.2	2,209	3,780
6	To Los Esteros.	S3-5 to S4-4	11.5	3,821	2,585
7	To fields just short of Forest Road 442.	S4-4 to S4-9	11.5	2,370	3,293
8	To Trail 124 / Rio Grande del Rancho just past FR 439A / FR 440 split.	S4-9 to S5-3	10.5	1,765	2,206
9	To Bernardin Lake.	S5-3 to S5-6	9.0	2,129	2,223
10	To fields on far side of Rio Chiquito, opposite entrance to Drake Canyon.	S5-6 to S6-3	13.7	1,076	3,097
11	To Taos Plaza.	S6-3 to end	13.0	2,109	2,843

10-12 miles a day with alternate routes

Day	Point to Point	Section	miles	ascent	descent
1	Santa Fe Plaza to 1/2 mile or so before Jawbone / Winsor Trail junction.	S1-1 to S1-6	10.4	2,093	1,434
2	To a bit short of Tesuque Peak, off of Forest Road 150. Dry camping.	S1-8 to Alt	9.9	4,208	388
3	To campsites just short of Cave Creek / Skyline Trail intersection via Spirit Lake.	S2-2 to S2-5	11.4	2,086	3,755

4	To Pecos Baldy Lake.	S2-5 to S3-1	10.9	3,477	1,841
5	To East Fork Trail and the ponds off Skyline Trail.	S3-1 to Alt	11.9	2,837	2,469
6	To Los Esteros.	Alt to S4-4	10.6	1,761	2,419
7	To fields just short of Forest Road 442.	S4-4 to S4-9	11.5	2,370	3,293
8	To Trail 124 / Rio Grande del Rancho just past FR 439A / FR 440 split.	S4-9 to S5-3	10.5	1,765	2,206
9	To Bernardin Lake.	S5-3 to S5-6	9.0	2,129	2,223
10	To fields on far side of Rio Chiquito, opposite entrance to Drake Canyon.	S5-6 to S6-3	13.7	1,076	3,097
11	To Taos Plaza.	S6-3 to end	13.0	2,109	2,843

Rito Perro Field, Section 2-8.

La Cueva Lake, Section 4-7.

12-14 miles a day
without alternate routes

Day	Point to Point	Section	miles	ascent	descent
1	Santa Fe Plaza to field east of Winsor / Borrego intersection and north of Tesuque creek.	S1-1 to S1-7	13.4	3,051	1,535
2	To far side of Lake Katherine.	S1-7 to S2-4	11.6	4,801	1,574
3	To Rito Perro Field.	S2-4 to S2-8	13.8	2,748	4,263
4	To Pecos Baldy Lake.	S2-5 to S3-1	10.9	3,477	1,841
5	To No Fish Lake.	S3-1 to S3-4	12.1	3,286	2,083
6	To pond off Forest Road 1877. (1.1 miles off the "official" route.)	S3-4 to S4-2 + Alt	12.5	2,782	4,229

7	To La Cueva Lake.	S4-2 to S4-8	13.9	3,973	3,817
8	To Forest Trail 124 / Rio Grande del Rancho just past Forest Road 439A and Forest Road 440 split.	S4-8 to S5-3	11.6	2,018	2,321
9	To field just southwest of Rio Chiquito bridge. Skip Bernardin Lake to cut a mile.	S5-3 to S5-7	15.7	3,085	3,847
10	To fields near American Spring.	S5-7 to S6-3	11.8	2,032	1,818
11	To Taos Plaza.	S6-3 to end	10.6	650	2,944

12-14 miles a day with alternate routes (Founder's Favorite)

Day	Point to Point	Section	miles	ascent	descent
1	Santa Fe Plaza to field east of Winsor / Borrego intersection and north of Tesuque creek.	S1-1 to S1-7	13.4	3,051	1,535
2	To Spirit Lake.	S1-7 to Alt	13.2	4,706	2,446
3	To Rito Perro Field.	Alt to S2-8	12.8	2,696	3,295
4	To Pecos Baldy Lake.	S2-8 to S3-1	10.9	3,477	1,841
5	To East Fork Trail and ponds off Skyline Trail.	S3-1 to Alt	11.9	2,837	2,469
6	To little creek about 0.9 miles short of Agua Piedra Creek.	Alt to S4-4	13.4	3,171	5,313
7	To Forest Road 442 / Rio Grande del Rancho intersection.	S4-4 to S5-2	16.6	3,540	3,671
8	To Bernardin Lake.	S5-2 to S5-6	9.9	2,400	2,162
9	To fields on far side of Rio Chiquito from FR 437 and the entrance to Drake Canyon.	S5-6 to S6-3	13.8	1,058	3,103
10	To Taos Plaza.	S6-3 to end	13.2	2,150	2,873

14-16 miles a day
without alternate routes

Day	Point to Point	Section	miles	ascent	descent
1	Santa Fe Plaza to little creek 0.5 miles short of the Norski parking lot on Winsor Trail.	S1-1 to S1-9	16.4	4,574	1,753
2	To campsites just short of the Cave Creek / Skyline Trail intersection.	S1-9 to S2-5	14.6	3,876	3,914
3	To Truchas Lakes.	S2-5 to S3-3	16.0	4,739	2,681
4	To Bull Field.	S3-3 to S4-1	13.9	2,480	4,736
5	To fields just short of Forest Road 442.	S4-1 to S4-9	15.6	4,820	4,099
6	To campsite just short of Connector / FR 438 intersection.	S4-9 to S5-4	16.7	2,820	4,080
7	To fields on far side of Rio Chiquito from FR 437 and the entrance to Drake Canyon.	S5-4 to S6-3	15.9	1,873	3,231
8	To Taos Plaza.	S6-3 to end	13.2	2,150	2,873

14-16 miles a day with alternate routes

Day	Point to Point	Section	miles	ascent	descent
1	Santa Fe Plaza to Big Tesuque Campground.	S1-1 to Alt	16.1	4,359	1,691
2	To campsites just short of Cave Creek / Skyline Trail intersection.	Alt to S2-5	15.7	3,918	3,800
3	To Truchas Lakes.	S2-5 to S3-3	16.0	4,767	2,694
4	To Los Esteros.	S3-3, Alt, to S4-4	15.7	3,001	3,704
5	To fields just short of FR 442. Next campsite near water would have you going 18 miles.	S4-1 to S4-9	11.5	2,490	3,353
6	To campsite just short of Connector / FR 438 intersection.	S4-9 to S5-4	16.7	2,820	4,080

| 7 | To fields on far side of Rio Chiquito from FR 437 and the entrance to Drake Canyon. | S5-4 to S6-3 | 15.9 | 1,873 | 3,231 |
| 8 | To Taos Plaza. | S6-3 to end | 13.2 | 2,150 | 2,873 |

Approaching Bull Field, Section 4-1.

16-18 miles a day without alternate routes

Day	Point to point	Section	miles	ascent	descent
1	Santa Fe Plaza to just short of Winsor Trailhead at the Ski Basin. Small field off the east side of the trail, north of Rio en Medio.	S1-1 to S1-9	17.7	5,240	1,997
2	To the campsites by Panchuela Creek just past Cave Creek / Dockweiler intersection.	S1-9 to S2-7	17.6	3,743	5,558

3	To No Fish Lake.	S2-7 to S3-4	16.3	5,335	2,330
4	To little creek about 0.9 miles short of Agua Piedra Creek.	3-4 to 4-4	17.9	4,256	6,013
5	To Forest Trail 124 / Rio Grande del Rancho just past Forest Road 439A and Forest Road 440 split.	S4-4 to S5-3	18.0	4,053	3,811
6	To Buena Suerte Canyon / Forest Road 437.	S5-3 to S6-2	17.8	2,984	4,223
7	To Taos Plaza.	S6-2 to end	18.0	2,222	3,870

16-18 miles a day with alternate routes

Day	Point to point	Section	miles	ascent	descent
1	Santa Fe Plaza to Big Tesuque Campground.	S1-1 to Alt	16.1	4,359	1,691
2	To campsite by the caves off Cave Creek Trail.	Alt to S2-6	17.5	3,979	4,787
3	To Truchas Lakes. Zip up Rio Quemado Trail to the view from the Truchas Peaks' ridgeline if you crave even more distance.	S2-6 to S3-3	14.2	4,690	1,692
4	To the little creek about 0.9 miles short of Agua Piedra Creek.	S3-3 to S4-4	18.3	3,063	5,269
5	To Forest Trail 124 / Rio Grande del Rancho just past Forest Road 439A and Forest Road 440 split.	S4-4 to S5-3	18.0	4,053	3,811
6	To Buena Suerte Canyon along Forest Road 437.	S5-3 to S6-2	17.8	2,984	4,223
7	To Taos Plaza.	S6-2 to end	18.0	2,222	3,870

18-20 miles a day
without alternate routes

Day	Point to point	Section	miles	ascent	descent
1	SF Plaza to campsite off Nambe Lake Trail from the Y. From the Y, go up Nambe Lake Trail ~0.2 miles. Campsite right of the trail and the river.	S1-1 to S2-2	20.1	6,280	2,558
2	To Rito Perro Field.	S2-2 to S2-8	18.9	4,711	5,192
3	To campsite near merge of West Fork and Middle Fork of Rio Santa Barbara.	S2-8 to S3-5	18.8	3,916	4,872
4	To fields just south of FR 442.	S3-5 to S4-9	20.0	5,983	4,991
5	To Bernardin Lake.	S5-3 to S5-6	19.3	3,641	4,171
6	To fields on far side of Rio Chiquito from FR 437 and the entrance to Drake Canyon.	S5-6 to S6-3	13.7	1,032	3,057
7	To Taos Plaza.	S6-3 to end	13.2	2,150	2,873

18-20 miles a day with alternate routes

Day	Point to point	Section	miles	ascent	descent
1	Santa Fe Plaza to trail off FR 150 (Aspen Vista) along Tesuque Creek.	S1-1 to Alt	17.1	5,150	1,723
2	To campsites by Panchuela Creek past Cave Creek / Dockweiler intersection.	Alt to S2-7	18.7	3,616	5,597
3	To ponds off East Fork Trail (off Skyline).	S2-7 to Alt	19.6	6,210	2,816
4	To La Cueva Lake.	Alt to 4-7	19.5	3,727	5,385
5	To Bernardin Lake.	S5-3 to S5-6	20.4	4,116	4,545
6	To fields on far side of Rio Chiquito from FR 437 and the entrance to Drake Canyon.	S5-6 to S6-3	13.7	1,032	3,057
7	To Taos Plaza.	S6-3 to end	13.2	2,150	2,873

The Thru-Hike
in a Series of Weekends

SECTION 1: Santa Fe Plaza to Winsor Trailhead at the Santa Fe Ski Basin

2 days; 1 night. 19.5 miles. Approximately 10 miles and 2,000-3,400 feet of ascent per day.

Start: Park at the Sandoval Municipal Garage (https://santafenm.gov/public-works/parking), 216 West San Francisco Street. The garage is open daily, 7 a.m. to 11 p.m. Rates are $12 per day. The website says: "trailers or bike racks are not allowed at the Sandoval Municipal Garage."

From the Sandoval Municipal Garage, walk 0.2 miles east along West San Francisco Street (towards the Cathedral) to the far corner of Santa Fe Plaza. Look for a three-foot-high grey granite marker on the southeast corner of the Plaza. That's the end marker for the Old Santa Fe Trail, and the official starting point for the Santa Fe to Taos Thru-Hike.

Overview: Follow the individual section directions for Section 1-1 through to the end of Section 1-5 for the first day. The second day you'll do Sections 1-6, 1-7, 1-8, and 1-9.

Section 1 is 19.5 miles, so if you're going to complete it in a weekend, you'll need to do basically ten miles a day. The best place to camp that's approximately 10 miles from the Santa Fe Plaza is about a half mile past the Juan (399) and Winsor (254) Trail junction. It's in Section 1-6. You'll climb 2,093 feet and go down 1,434 feet to get to that point. The next day you'll climb 3,400 feet over the ten miles you'll go to get to Winsor Trailhead at the Santa Fe Ski Basin. You'll start at 7,000 feet elevation at the Plaza and be at about 10,300 feet elevation at Winsor Trailhead.

You can also, of course, camp a bit beyond that spot half a mile from the Juan / Winsor intersection. This part of Winsor, and all the way up it to just past where it intersects with Borrego, is mostly flat with lots of fields and nice little out-of-the-way spots to put a tent. It is all along Tesuque Creek, too, so there's ample water. Do be aware of the mountain bikers, and try to get off trail far enough for some privacy and quiet.

Getting back to your car at the Sandoval Municipal Garage: Either place a car at the Ski Basin / Winsor Trailhead parking lot ahead of time, get a ride from someone you know, or take the Blue Bus down via its "255 Mountain Trail" route. More info at NCRTD.org/255-mountain-trail-route/. The Blue Bus is free. You can pick it up at the "NM475 @ Ski Santa Fe Upper Lot" stop. The closest stop to the Sandoval Parking Lot is the "Alameda @ Galisteo" stop. It's about two blocks away from the Sandoval parking garage.

It will take about 45 minutes to get from the Ski Basin to downtown Santa Fe.

The bus leaves three times a day on weekdays and six times a day on weekends. Double-check the schedule and the stops on the NCRTD website.

The view looking east after you have just turned on to East Alameda (about a block past the Loretto Chapel). Section 1-1.

SECTION 2: Winsor Trailhead at Santa Fe Ski Basin to Pecos Baldy Lake

The end of this section—Pecos Baldy Lake—is remote, which makes doing Section 2 on its own a little trickier. Section 2 is also longer than Section 1, making things trickier still. Most people will want to do this section in two weekends or in a long weekend. But if you're up for two very long days, it can still be done in a weekend.

In one weekend
2 days; 1 night. 26.2 miles. Approximately 17 miles and 3,500 feet of elevation per day.

Start: Place a car at Jack's Creek Horse Camp in the Pecos Wilderness, so you have transport home at the end of your hike. Leave from (i.e., start your hike from) the Santa Fe Ski Basin.

Overview: Leave from Winsor Trailhead at the Ski Basin, then go to Lake Katherine, Stewart Lake, along Skyline Trail to Cave Creek Trail, then head down Cave Creek to just short of Panchuela Campground, where you'll camp in the narrow fields next to Panchuela Creek about 0.2 miles south/southeast from the intersection of Cave Creek Trail and Dockweiler Trail.

The next morning you'll do the climb up Dockweiler Trail, continue on Dockweiler for a while, then pass through the camping area around Jack's Creek the creek, continue on past Jack's Creek all the way to Pecos Baldy Lake, then turn around and come back down Jack's Creek Trail all the way into Jack's Creek Horsecamp... where you will pick up your car.

It is 31.3 miles and 6,972 feet of elevation all in. The most precise halfway point is fairly close to Panchuela Campground, in the aforementioned fields next to Panchuela Creek about 0.2 miles south/southeast from the intersection of Cave Creek Trail and Dockweiler Trail. That said, if you have the energy to do the Dockweiler climb and get yourself to, say, Dockweiler Field or Rito Perro Field for your overnight, that would work, too. The climb up Dockweiler is no small thing, though. Consider resting before you do it, especially after having already logged 17 miles and 3,500 feet of elevation "just" to get the fields near the Dockweiler / Cave Creek split.

The intersection of Cave Creek Trail (288) and Dockweiler Trail (259). End of Section 2-6; beginning of Section 2-7.

In two weekends
This is the same route as doing it in one weekend.

Weekend one: Winsor Trailhead at the Santa Fe Ski Basin to Panchuela Campground.
17 miles or so. Approximately 7-11 miles per day. Up to 2,700 ft of elevation on day 1; 850 ft on day 2.

Overview: From Winsor Trailhead to either Lake Katherine or Stewart Lake or Spirit Lake (you pick), overnighting at the lake of your choice, then cruising along Skyline Trail and then down Cave Creek Trail, to pick up your car at Panchuela Campground on the end of Day 2.

Start: Place a car at Panchuela Campground in the Pecos Wilderness so you have a way to get home at the end of your hike. You'll have to pay $2 per day for parking at Panchuela Campground. Bring a pen/pencil to fill out the parking form. Leave from the Santa Fe Ski Basin.

Day 1: From Winsor Trailhead at the Ski Basin, follow the directions laid out in the Section 2 section-by-section directions to get to the lake of your choice. Go to Lake Katherine for a big dramatic view. Go to Stewart Lake if you want to push a little further. Go to Spirit Lake if you like solitude.

Day 2: Lake of your choice to Panchuela Campground. See the Section 2 subsection pages for how to get from the lake of your choice to Skyline Trail, then down Cave Creek Trail, then out to Panchuela Campground.

Weekend two: Panchuela Campground to Pecos Baldy Lake to Jack's Creek Horse Camp.
16 miles or so. 8-9 miles per day. 3,600 feet elevation day 1; 140 feet elevation and 2,700 feet descent day 2.

Overview: From Panchuela Campground, go up Dockweiler Trail (259), then pick up Jack's Creek Trail (257) and take it to Pecos Baldy Lake. Overnight at Pecos Baldy Lake, then on day 2 take Jack's Creek Trail then Beatty's Trail (25), heading south, into Jack's Creek Horsecamp. Walk on the road or take the shortcut to get back to your car at Panchuela Campground.

Start: You don't have to place a car for this. You can walk back from Jack's Creek Horse Camp to Panchuela, either via the road or by a shortcut that will save you about two miles of walking along the road.

Day 1: From Panchuela Campground, walk in to the junction of Cave Creek Trail and Dockweiler Trail. Follow the directions for S2-7, S2-8, and S2-9 to get to Pecos Baldy Lake. This will be about 8.3 miles with 3,602 ft elevation. While this looks straightforward on paper, this is a big day. You'll start at 8,800 ft elevation and finish at 11,500 ft. The first half of this is also quite remote. You may not see anyone until you reach Jack's Creek camping area.

Note that "Jack's Creek camping area" is not "Jack's Creek Campground." The Campground has facilities and a road. The "camping area" (my name for it) is 4.5 miles into the Pecos Wilderness.

Consider splitting day 1 into two days, stopping for the first night at Rito Perro Field or Dockweiler Field, then continuing on to Pecos Baldy Lake the next day. The lake is a nice place to spend time, and it's good to get there early in the day to get a good campsite. Use the extra time to summit East Pecos Baldy or zip over to get a look at the Trailrider's Wall.

Where to camp: Pecos Baldy Lake. There are campsites all around the lake basin, especially on the northeast and south sides. If it's a clear night, get out at look at the stars, especially in the middle of the night.

Day 2: Pecos Baldy Lake to Jack's Creek Horse Camp. 7.2 miles, 140 feet elevation, 2,747 feet descent. Go back out on Jack's Creek Trail, through the burn again, and to the north end of where Jack's Creek Trail and Dockweiler Trail intersect. Continue on Jack's Creek / Dockweiler until you get into Jack's Creek camping area, then cross Jack's Creek (the creek), leaving Dockweiler but still on Jack's Creek. Over the next few miles you'll come out of the woods and go through a couple of enormous fields, with the iconic Round Mountain on your left for a while. The trail will drop a wee bit and run into Beatty's Trail. Take Beatty's Trail southwest, then do the long switchbacks down into Jack's Creek Horse Camp.

Getting back to your car: If you left your car at Panchuela Campground, you can walk back to it pretty easily from Jack's Creek Horse Camp. Pecos River Trail (397) connects the two trailheads. It's 1.4 miles with 147 feet of elevation and 596 feet of descent. Or walk 3.7 miles along the road.

©Gaia GPS, ©OpenStreetMap contributors.

SECTION 3: Pecos Baldy Lake to Santa Barbara Campground

3 days; 2 nights. 26.7 miles. Averages 9 miles, but the distances are very uneven. 1,350 to 2,700 ft elevation per day.

Overview: This will require a long weekend unless you are super fit. I have included a simple itinerary for it as a regular two-day weekend, but I like it more as at least a three day trip. It is possibly the nicest slice of the thru-hike.

Start at Jack's Creek Horse Camp, then go up to Pecos Baldy Lake and over the Trailriders Wall to Truchas Lakes. From there you'll go over the Santa Barbara Divide and make the very long way down into Santa Barbara Campground, mostly along Rio Santa Barbara the whole way.

You can also take the alternate route, skipping the Santa Barbara Divide to instead follow the ridgeline along Skyline Trail. Get off the ridgeline either from Middle Fork or East Fork Trail if you want to come into Santa Barbara from the south (like the standard route). Or you can continue even further along the ridgeline, summiting Jicarita Peak, which will have you coming down into the north side of Santa Barbara Campground via Indian Canyon.

Start: Place a car at the free parking lots at Santa Barbara Campground. Leave from the parking lot at Jack's Creek Horse Camp ($2 per day). Bring a pen for the parking form.

Day 1: Jack's Creek Horse Camp to Pecos Baldy Lake. 7.2 miles, 2,759 ft elevation, 134 feet descent. From the paid parking lot at Jack's Creek Horse Camp, take Beatty's Trail (25) up the switchbacks and then north until it meets Jack's Creek Trail (257). Take the left, heading gradually up through big fields, eventually with Round Mountain on your right. The trail goes back into the woods and soon comes to Jack's Creek the creek. Cross Jack's Creek to pick up Dockweiler Trail (259) while also continuing on Jack's Creek Trail to the right and northwest. Follow the instructions for Section 2-9 to get to Pecos Baldy Lake.

Overnight 1: Pecos Baldy Lake.

Day 2: Pecos Baldy Lake to Truchas Lakes. 5.3 miles, 1,358 ft ascent, 910 ft descent. Follow the directions for Sections 3-1 and 3-2. This is a short day, but it is so beautiful. Savor it. If you really want extra distance and the weather is good, take Rio Quemado Trail (153) from Truchas Lakes and check out the Rio Quemado Falls area on the other side of Truchas Peaks. It's only 1. 3 miles from Truchas Lakes. Or even overnight there.

Overnight 2: Truchas Lakes. Zip your tent to keep the bighorn sheep out.

Day 3: Truchas Lakes to Santa Barbara Campground. 12.9 miles. 1,662 feet elevation, 4,676 feet descent. Follow the directions for Section 3-3 to 3-6.

SECTION 3 IN ONE WEEKEND

Day 1: Jack's Creek Horse Camp to Truchas Lakes. 12.4 miles, 4,112 feet elevation, 1,062 feet descent. Camp at Truchas Lakes.

Day 2: Truchas Lakes to Santa Barbara Campground. 12.9 miles. 1,662 feet elevation, 4,676 feet descent.

SECTION 3 WITH ALTERNATE ROUTES

4 days; 3 nights. Up to 30 miles. Approximately 8 miles and 1,000-2,000 feet of elevation per day.

All of the alternate routes start just short of the Santa Barbara Divide, at the intersection of Skyline Trail (251) and Beatty's Trail (25). The "official" route of the thru-hike takes Beatty's Trail over the Santa Barbara Divide, where Beatty's becomes West Fork Trail (25).

Your options for the alternate routes include: 1) Going 3.1 miles further from the Beatty's/Skyline split to take Middle Fork Trail (24) off the ridgeline. 2) Going 4.4 miles further from the Beatty's/Skyline split to take East Fork Trail (24) off the ridgeline from Divide Trail (36)... because Skyline Trail branches off to the right and down along the way, and you have to be on Divide Trail from there to stay on the ridgeline. 3) Going the entire 13.4 miles from the Beatty's/

Skyline split to summit Jicarita Peak and then rejoining the official route of the thru-hike at the intersection of Divide Trail (36) and Indian Creek Trail (27).

You have two things to manage for in this area: weather and water. Both are critical. You will be on a ridgeline, at 12,600 ft elevation. Watch for thunderstorm activity and get off the ridgeline at the first sign of one. There are several places to get off the ridgeline; please see the directions for these alternate routes earlier in the book.

The other issue is water. At first glance, it looks like there's no water on the ridgeline, but there are actually three places to get water: 1) along Middle Fork Trail, about a mile off the ridgeline, 2) along East Fork Trail, again about a mile off the ridgeline, and 3) along Serpent Lake Trail about 0.2 miles off the ridgeline (about 1.5 miles south of Jicarita Peak).

Your best bet may be to take your fourth night along Middle Fork Trail, either at the rills one mile off the ridgeline or lower down, wherever you like. Or you can continue on and stay at Serpent Lake. Then the last morning summit Jicarita Peak in the morning (good idea) and take the rest of the day to come down and then down some more into Indian Canyon and the north side of Santa Barbara Campground.

Approaching the Trailriders Wall. Truchas Peaks in the distance. Section 3-1.

SECTION 4: Santa Barbara Campground to Forest Road 442

2 days; 1 night. 18.6 miles. Averages 9 miles. 1,350 to 2,700 ft elevation per day.

Overview: This is up Indian Canyon, past Los Esteros (a pond), down into Agua Piedra Campground, along Route 518, up La Cueva Canyon, through La Cueva Field and past La Cueva Lake up to Forest Road 442. It's basically 3,000 ft up, 3,000 feet down, then another 2,500 feet up.

Start: Place one car at Santa Barbara Campground's free parking lots and another along Forest Road 442 and Trail 442. This is the hardest car placement of the thru-hike, because you'll need two four-wheel-drive, high-carriage vehicles to get to that spot along FR 442. You need two because it's two to drive in, then one to drive out with the driver of the vehicle you just placed. (Note that I am not using the word "car" here.)

You should also come to this FR 442 / Trail 442 point from the west side. Get off Route 518 and on to FR 442 at "US Hill." FR 442 east of the FR 442 / Trail 442 intersection is okay, but really only if you're going east/north on FR 442. If you drove to the FR 442 / Trail 442 point from the east side, via 439 and then 442 (i.e., the opposite direction), you'd have to go up a steep, sharp turn and get up over a very rocky little semi-cliff on the south side of Rio Grande del Rancho. I wouldn't try it in a Subaru. Do not get stuck out here. AAA will not come to get you. AC Towing & Transport Services ((575) 758-1111; ACTowingOnline.com) in Taos might be able to help.

Given all the issues around getting a car placed at FR 442 / Trail 442, **it might be best to just place (park) a car at Agua Piedra Campground and then hike back to Agua Piedra after you've gotten yourself to FR 442 / Trail 442 and completed Section 4.** If you liked going up Ojitos Maes Trail well enough, just come back down it and walk back to Agua Piedra. It's only 5.5 miles from FR 442 / Trail 442 to the Agua Piedra Bridge.

Get information about Agua Piedra reservations and services here: https://bit.ly/agua-piedra-reservations-and-services.

Parking at Agua Piedra also opens up the possibility of getting a ride, as Agua Piedra is way more accessible than FR 442. ShuttleTaos.com drives people from trailhead to trailhead. I've used them in the past. In late 2024 they quoted me $155 for four people plus $15 for each additional person for a pickup at Agua Piedra Campground and a drive back to Santa Barbara Campground. Not cheap, but it's a way to do this section with just one car.

There is public transportation service to Agua Piedra Campground via the Blue Bus... sort of. The Rockwall stop on the 330 Peñasco route "provides fare-free service Monday through Friday". Rockwall is at the intersection of NM 518 and NM 75. It is a 5-mile walk along NM 518 from Sipapu and a 7.1-mile walk along NM 518 from Agua Piedra to get to the Rockwall stop, but the Blue Bus will take you to Taos, and for free. Visit https://www.ncrtd.org/all-routes/330-penasco/ for the route schedule.

Day 1: Santa Barbara Campground to Indian Lake. 11.9 miles, 4,026 feet of elevation, 3,340 feet of descent. Follow the directions for S4-1 to S4-5.

Alternative Day 1: Skip Indian Lake and camp anywhere near Agua Piedra Creek before you get to the big field before Agua Piedra Campground. Approximately 7-10 miles, 3,000 feet elevation and 3,000 feet descent.

Camp at: Indian Lake or anywhere near Agua Piedra Creek.

Day 2: Indian Lake to Forest Road 442. 7.7 miles, 2,331 feet elevation, 1,495 feet descent. Follow the directions for Sections S4-5 to S4-9.

SECTION 5: Forest Road 442 / Trail 442 to Rio Chiquito Bridge / Forest Road 437

In one weekend. 26 miles.

Overview: You'll walk along FR 442 for 8.4 miles, briefly passing through a burn scar. There is limited access to water, though there are a couple of seeps along the way until you reach Rio Grande del Rancho. You'll walk along 439A and the rio briefly, then climb up FR 440, take a left, and get to the entrance to the Corridor about two miles later. You'll wend your way through the Corridor, come out at FR 438, walk up to Bernardin Lake, then walk out along Forest Roads 438 and 478 to Rio Chiquito Bridge.

Start: This section has the same issues with placing a car at Forest Road 442 / Trail 442 as in Section 4. See my recommendation in Section 4 about placing a car at Agua Piedra instead and just adding 5.5 miles to your trip.

If you've got access to two good, high-carriage, four-wheel-drive vehicles, start by placing one of them at Forest Road 442 / Trail 442. Place the second one in the vicinity of the Rio Chiquito bridge, preferably a little out of sight. There is a campsite right near the bridge, north and west of it, less than a tenth of a mile away. You could also park a car about half a mile short of the bridge on FR 478. This is a bit dicey, as it is possible someone might take an "interest" in your car. Don't leave any valuables in it.

Day 1: From FR 442 / Trail 124 to just a ways down on Trail 124 after it splits off from FR 439A. 9.7 miles, 1,600 feet elevation and 2,078 feet descent. See the directions for Section 5-1 to 5-3.

Camp at: A bit along Trail 124 near the split of FR 440 and FR 439A.

Day 2: A bit along Trail 124 near the split of FR 440 and FR 439A to the Rito Chiquito bridge. 14.7 miles, 2,449 feet elevation and 3,434 descent. See the directions for Section 5-3 to 5-7.

This makes for a long second day. If you're concerned about it, **consider adding a night at Bernardin Lake.**

I've split it this way because:
- There is no great place to camp between the little ways down Trail 124 and about a mile into the Connector, which is the first water source after you leave Rio Grande del Rancho.
- Getting you to that next water source would add four miles to your first day, which is about as unequal a split as the suggested route, which gives you a long second day.
- If you've parked a car at Agua Piedra, your day 1 with this plan is 15 miles and 2,500 feet elevation, which is a pretty hearty day already.
- 14.7 miles on day 2 is long, but it's mostly on forest roads, thus easier.

SECTION 6: Rio Chiquito Bridge / Forest Road 437 to Taos Plaza

In one easy weekend. 20 miles.

Overview: This is the easiest section of the thru-hike. Walk along FR 437 for 7.3 miles, camp opposite Drake Canyon, and then the next day climb Drake Canyon Loop trail, come down Ojitos Trail, and then stroll into Taos Plaza.

Start: Place a car near Rio Chiquito Bridge, possibly just a bit up FR 478 from the bridge and off the road a little. Fewer people will see it there. Or hire ShuttleTaos.com to drop you off at the bridge. FR 437 isn't too bad to drive on, but it does have rough spots. It's fine for, say, a Subaru. Don't attempt it with anything that can't handle a few deep mud puddles or a stretch of very rocky road.

Day 1: Rio Chiquito Bridge to the far side of Rio Chiquito across from Drake Canyon. 7.3 miles, 223 feet elevation, 1,425 descent. See sections 6-1 to 6-3 for directions.

Camp at: The far side of Rio Chiquito from the road. The Rio is shallow enough here to get across in good boots. There are several small narrow fields on the opposite side. This keeps you far enough away from the road to not be seen and to get some peace and privacy, though you will probably hear a few RVers or ATVs go by.

Day 2: Entrance to Drake Canyon to Taos Plaza. 12.8 miles, 2,088 feet elevation, 2,826 descent. See directions for Sections 6-3 to 6-9. Make sure you load up on water before you leave Rio Chiquito. Drake Canyon and Ojitos Trail are the longest stretch without water on the thru-hike. It's 10 miles from Rio Chiquito to El Nogal, but I don't recommend drinking the water at El Nogal unless you walk upriver past where most of the dogs go. Your next water source is at the Taos Cow, where they keep a water dispenser on the counter. There is water at American Spring, on South Boundary Trail, but it's not very appetizing.

The gazebo at Taos Plaza. The end of the Santa Fe to Taos Thru-Hike.

25 Day Hikes Along the Route

VERY EASY

Easy enough to bring small children.

1) The Plaza to Enchanted Small Falls

This is a simple out-and-back walk along sidewalks until you get to the Falls. It could take up to an hour or more with a curious child. There are benches and picnic tables along the way.

See the directions in Section 1-1. Enchanted Small Falls are shown on the map.

Enchanted Small Falls, Section 1-1.

2) Arroyo Polay to Chasing Dreams

An out-and-back walk that can be done in 15 minutes. Park at the Arroyo Polay trailhead off Cerro Gordo Road. Follow the directions for Section 1-3. There's a photograph of Chasing Dreams (which is an abandoned convertible facing "upstream" in Arroyo Polay) with the section directions.

3) The Interpretive Trail along Route 518 near Agua Piedra Campground

A 30-40 minute out-and-back walk, even for little kids. There are several benches along the way. Some of it is paved. See the directions in Section 4-6.

4) The El Nogal Nature Trail in Taos

Park at the El Nogal parking lot / trailhead. Follow the path that goes upstream, next to the little creek. The path is shown on the map for Section 6-7. Don't play in the water until you are past where most of the dogs go.

5) Aspen Vista parking lot to wherever you want to turn around (near the Santa Fe Ski Basin)

Park at the Aspen Vista parking lot and walk toward the mountain. You'll see a gate and a dirt road, plus signs about managing dogs and other trail advice. Just walk up the road, which is Forest Service Road 150, more popularly known as Aspen Vista.

There is a little creek (Big Tesuque Creek) about half an hour's walk up the road, but there are some nice views before that. And there are the teepees. Walk in about 10 minutes, and just as you are coming up the first tiny little hill, look for a trail on the right. You'll be able to see the first of three teepees from that point. This trail is extremely popular during fall foliage.

EASY

One- to two-hour walks with some tiny slopes/hills for adults or big kids.

6) Patrick Smith Park to Cerro Gordo Park

Another out-and-back walk, this time from park to park, with a lovely bit of shade and coolness along the Santa Fe River. There are two very narrow "bridges" (thick planks, really) to cross, so a little balance or some help is recommended. Takes maybe 40 minutes if you don't stop. If you have the time, bring water gear (like river shoes, shorts and a t-shirt) for yourself or kids and spend some time on the tire swing that hangs over a wide, shallow part of the Santa Fe "River". Directions and a map are in Section 1-2.

7) Arroyo Polay to Sierra del Norte and back

A trailhead-to-trailhead out-and-back walk on the Dale Ball Trails system, which is well-marked and well-maintained. Keep an eye out for mountain bikes. Wear sunscreen and a hat in summer, or go early or late in the day. See the directions for Section 1-3.

8) The Plaza to Patrick Smith Park

Take the walk to Enchanted Small Falls a little further. See the directions in Section 1-1. You could make a nice loop of this walk if you continued on East Alameda just past Patrick Smith Park, then picked up Canyon Road and let it take you in about a 180-degree turn so that you were walking back towards the Plaza on Canyon Road. Stop at the Santa Fe Teahouse and Bistro at East Palace and Canyon Road if you want a rest along the way.

9) Unnamed trailhead off Hyde Park Road to Junction D / Little Tesuque Creek

A mostly shaded, creekside walk that takes 45 minutes or so. See the directions in Section 1-4, but know that you'll be going backwards, from Hyde Park Road towards Junction D, instead of what's described in the directions.

Park just off Hyde Park Road; you'll see other cars parked alongside the road about a quarter mile after you've passed "Nun's Corner" (also called "Texas Corner"), which is about half a mile past 10,000 Waves.

10) Taos Plaza to Taos Cow

1.4 miles out and back along Kit Carson Road. See the directions (reversed) in Section S6-9. Taos Cow (their Anglada location) is open seven days a week from 7:30 am to 5 pm. They make great ice cream and tasty sandwiches.

MEDIUM

About two hours with some hills, going deeper into the woods.

11) Agua Piedra Campground parking lot to Indian Lake

See the directions in Section 4-5. It's about 1.8 miles with 1,000 feet of elevation gain to get from the parking lot by the horse corral at Agua Piedra Campground to Indian Lake. The trail to Indian Lake is 19C. It's marked.

12) Sierra del Norte to Little Tesuque Creek

An out-and-back "hike" because there is some up and down to this. Nice views of the Santa Fe hills and then a brief look at Little Tesuque Creek when you turn around at Junction D of the Dale Ball Trails System. You'll be on the Dale Ball Trails the whole way, which is good: They're well-maintained and well-marked. Don't leave valuables in your car when you park at the Sierra del Norte Trailhead parking lot. Directions in Section 1-4.

13) Unnamed trailhead near Juan Trail (399) to Winsor Trail (254) / Big Tesuque Creek

Same departure point and parking for day hike #9. Follow the directions in Section 1-5. Goes through the lovely but steep Juan Canyon. Also includes a bit of a climb up before you get to Juan Canyon. Nice views, though.

14) Winsor / Borrego / Bear Wallow Loop

A nice loop with a fair amount of up and down, in mostly shade, with about a quarter of the way along Big Tesuque Creek. Sometimes heavily used by mountain bikers, especially on weekends, especially on the section along Winsor Trail and Tesuque Creek.

Take Hyde Park Road up to Borrego Trail (150) Trailhead. There is a parking lot on the left if you're driving up from Santa Fe. On busy days the parking lot fills and you'll have to park on the side of the road. The directions and map for Section 1-7 will help, but not completely. You'll take Borrego Trail (150) out from the parking lot, down into the woods. 0.4 miles along the trail there's a split where you can go left, on to Bear Wallow Trail (182), or go right and stay on Borrego. As you're doing a loop, it doesn't really matter which way you go.

Both trails will bring you to Winsor Trail (254) and Tesuque Creek. If you think of the loop like it's a triangle, Winsor Trail and Tesuque Creek make the last third and far side of the triangle from the trailhead/parking lot.

The trail is well-maintained and marked, but bring backup navigation or this book just to be sure. This is a long enough hike (4 miles, 1,000 feet ascent and descent) that you ought to carry water or a fastpack. Keep your dog under control, as there is wildlife about.

15) Panchuela parking lot to Panchuela crossing, little field, and fishing trail

1.7 miles out and back with about 500 feet of ascent and descent (so 3.4 miles all in). Along Panchuela Creek, mostly in shade. See the directions in Section 2-6. You'll pass the split for Cave Creek Trail and Dockweiler Trail about halfway to the turnaround point. Stay on Cave Creek Trail. The turn-around point is where Cave Creek Trail crosses Panchuela Creek. The creek is crossable here if you've got good boots or your balance is good enough to get across the rocks set out in the stream. Or if you don't mind wet feet.

There's good fishing up from this point if you take the much less traveled trail that continues straight, heading directly upriver along Panchuela Creek, on the right/east side of the creek. For hikers/walkers, just hang out by the nice spot by the creek then walk back.

HARD

Up to 15 miles into deep woods. Bring appropriate gear and backup navigation.

16) La Cueva Loop

10 miles and 2,500 feet of elevation all in from Agua Piedra day use parking, along the Route 518 interpretive trail, up La Cueva Canyon (see the directions in Section 4-6 to 4-9) through the lovely fields along La Cueva Canyon Trail, down La Cueva Canyon Trail past the Flechado Trick Tank, bringing you back to La Cueva Field. Walk back down La Cueva Canyon, back along Route 518 and the interpretive trail, and finally back to your car. Afterwards, consider a meal at the not-too-far-away Sugar Nymphs Cafe in Peñasco.

17) Lake Katherine

The most "iconic" hike near Santa Fe? Maybe. And it's only about 7 miles out and back. What will get you is the elevation: 2,700 feet ascent and 1,200 feet descent... and that's just getting to the lake. You'll also be hiking at 10,000 to 11,600 feet elevation. See the directions in Sections 2-1 to 2-3. There's good fishing at Lake Katherine. Be prepared for hail.

18) Indian Canyon to Ripley Point from Santa Barbara Campground

Nice hike if you don't want to see a lot of people. Directions and maps are in Section 4-1 to 4-3. Go a little further to Los Esteros if you want to visit a nice little pond or if you need water. About 10 miles and 3,500 feet of ascent to Ripley Point and back. Great view of Jicarita Peak.

19) Cowles to Stewart Lake

From the Cowles parking and fishing area north of Pecos, take Winsor Ridge Trail up until you reach Skyline Trail. See the directions in Section 2-4 to get you from that point to Stewart Lake. About 12 miles and 2,500 feet of elevation round trip. Stunning during fall foliage, but good anytime.

20) Jack's Creek Horse Camp to Pecos Baldy Lake

Directions in Section 2-8 and 2-9 and in the "Thru-hike in a Series of Week-ends" part of this guidebook for Section 2. About 14 miles out and back. 2,800 ft of ascent. Add another 2.4 miles and 1,100 feet of ascent to summit East Pecos Baldy.

Stewart Lake, Pecos Wilderness. Section 2-4.

VERY HARD

Not recommended unless you are fit. Do not attempt unless you are ad-justed to the altitude. If you can complete any one of these, you can do the thru-hike at 10-12 miles a day.

21) Dockweiler / Jack's Creek Loop

This is "Weekend 2" of Section 2 if you do Section 2 in two weekends. 16 miles round trip from Panchuela Campground. See directions on page 159.

22) Ojitos Trail to top of Drake Canyon

An up-and-back hike from El Nogal in Taos. You'll be doing the reverse of what's described in the guidebook. See the directions and maps for Sections 6-5, 6-6, and 6-7. Limited water unless you get some from American Spring on South Boundary Trail. About 15 miles round trip if you go all the way to American Spring, with about 3,300 feet of ascent and descent.

23) Tesuque Peak Loop

From Big Tesuque Campground, up FR 150 / Aspen Vista to Tesuque Peak. Then over Deception, Lake and Penitente Peaks, down into Puerto Nambe on Skyline Trail, west on Winsor Trail, then down to the Ski Basin. From the Ski Basin, get over to the southeast parking lot of the Ski Basin. On the southeast side of that lot, pick up a trail that takes you past Bear Cave to Alamos Vista Trail. Take Alamos Vista Trail to come down to almost the edge of the Aspen Vista parking area, where you can then take Aspen Vista "road" / FR 150 to pick up Tesuque Creek Trail back to Big Tesuque Campground.

See the directions in Section 1 for the Tesuque Peak Alternate Route, then do the reverse route for Sections 2-3, 2-2, and 2-1. Bring a GPS device for the part between the Santa Fe Ski Basin facilities and Alamos Vista. 17.5 miles with 5,250 feet of ascent and descent. You can trim this down a little if you come down Raven's Ridge, skipping Puerto Nambe and a big chunk of Winsor Trail.

24) Santa Barbara to Santa Barbara Divide

An epic out-and-back hike. You'll be doing the reverse route from what's described in the directions for Section 3-6, 3-5, and 3-4. About 21 miles and 5,100 feet of ascent and descent.

25) Lake Katherine / Spirit Lake Loop

Starting from Winsor Trailhead at the Ski Basin, take Winsor Trail to Puerto Nambe, then go left up Skyline Trail (for Lake Katherine) or right to stay on Winsor and go to Spirit Lake. If you go to Katherine first, you'll be following the standard route of the thru-hike and coming down from Katherine on Skyline Trail, where you can then take a right on to Winsor Trail and head up to Spirit Lake from there.

From Spirit, continue on Winsor to bring yourself back to Puerto Nambe, then back out to the Ski Basin Trailhead via Winsor. See the directions in Sections 2-1 to 2-4 to get yourself to Lake Katherine and then down Winsor to Skyline Trail. Then do the reverse route as described in the Alternate route for Section 2 for Spirit Lake to get yourself back to Puerto Nambe. Note that the trail conditions between Spirit Lake and Skyline Trail are poor; expect to get slowed down by blowdown. 16 miles, 4,500 feet of ascent and descent.

Lake Katherine, Pecos Wilderness. End of S2-3, beginning of S2-4.

Elevation Profiles

Get GPX files of the full route or of subsections at https://SantaFeToTaos.org/gpx-files/

Full route: Santa Fe Plaza to Taos Plaza (132.5 miles per my recorded tracks with the Gaia GPS app)

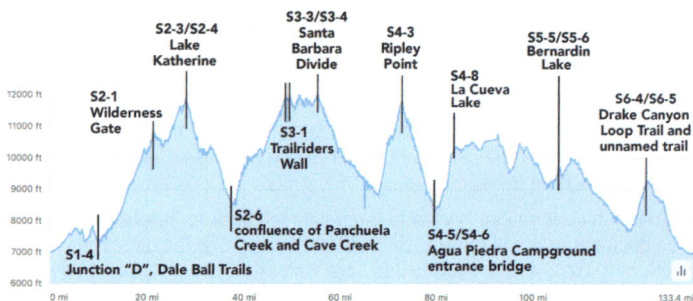

Section 1: Santa Fe Plaza to Santa Fe Ski Basin (20.1 miles)

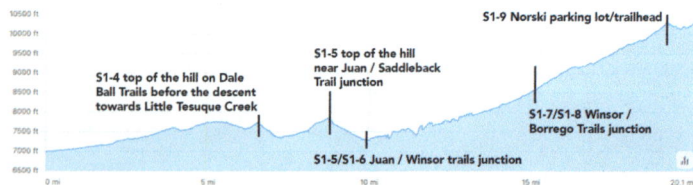

Section 2: Santa Fe Ski Basin to Pecos Baldy Lake (26.4 miles)

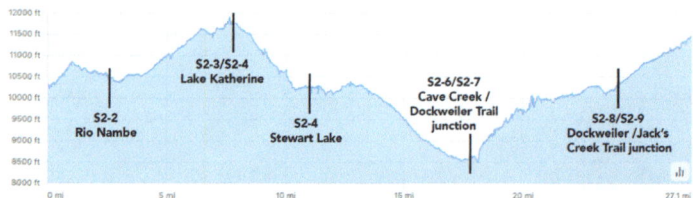

172

Section 3: Pecos Baldy Lake to Santa Barbara Campground (19.6 miles)

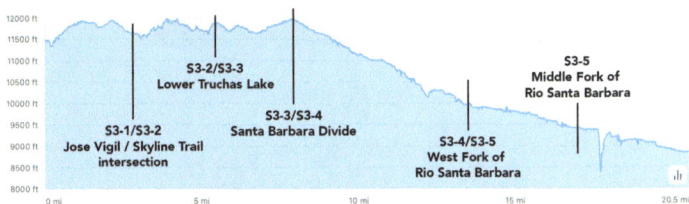

S3-1/S3-2
Jose Vigil / Skyline Trail intersection

S3-2/S3-3
Lower Truchas Lake

S3-3/S3-4
Santa Barbara Divide

S3-4/S3-5
West Fork of
Rio Santa Barbara

S3-5
Middle Fork of
Rio Santa Barbara

Section 4: Santa Barbara Campground to Forest Road 442 (18.6 miles)

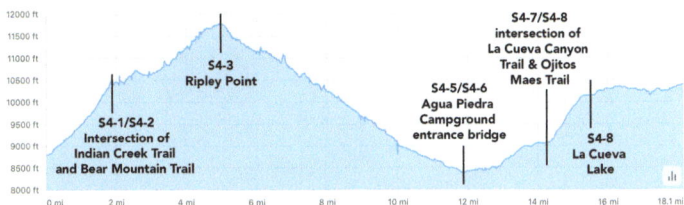

S4-1/S4-2
Intersection of
Indian Creek Trail
and Bear Mountain Trail

S4-3
Ripley Point

S4-5/S4-6
Agua Piedra
Campground
entrance bridge

S4-7/S4-8
intersection of
La Cueva Canyon
Trail & Ojitos
Maes Trail

S4-8
La Cueva
Lake

Section 5: Forest Road 442 to Rio Chiquito / Forest Road 437 (26.0 miles)

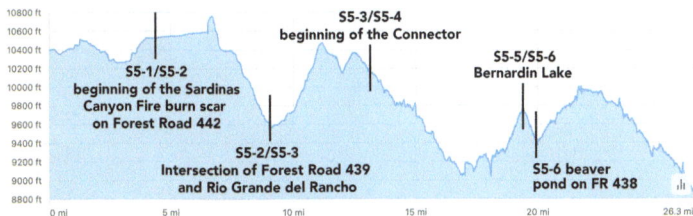

S5-1/S5-2
beginning of the Sardinas
Canyon Fire burn scar
on Forest Road 442

S5-2/S5-3
Intersection of Forest Road 439
and Rio Grande del Rancho

S5-3/S5-4
beginning of the Connector

S5-5/S5-6
Bernardin Lake

S5-6 beaver
pond on FR 438

Section 6: Rio Chiquito bridge / Forest Road 437 to Taos Plaza (20.0 miles)

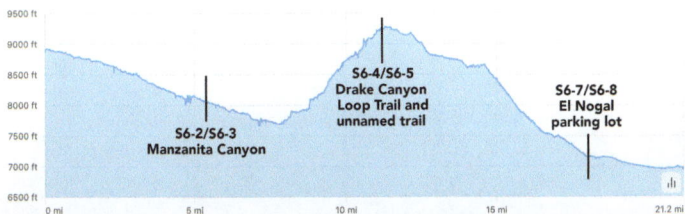

S6-2/S6-3
Manzanita Canyon

S6-4/S6-5
Drake Canyon
Loop Trail and
unnamed trail

S6-7/S6-8
El Nogal
parking lot

Santa Fe, Taos, and The High Road

Santa Fe: Lodging, Dining, Things to Do

LODGING

Closest "budget" hotel to the Plaza: El Sendero Inn
Four-minute walk from the Plaza. Has a Chinese restaurant. Roughly $110 per night in off-season (February); $210 per night peak season (August). https://www.choicehotels.com/new-mexico/santa-fe/ascend-hotels/nm268. 311 Old Santa Fe Trail, Santa Fe, NM, 87501, (505) 982-1851.

Closest large hotel to the Plaza: La Fonda on the Plaza
Southeast corner of the Plaza. Has a restaurant and shops. Roughly $175 per night in off season; $500 per night peak season. LaFondaSantaFe.com. 100 E San Francisco Street, Santa Fe, NM 87501, (505) 982-5511.

More upscale: Hotel Saint Francis
Three-minute walk from the Plaza. Has a restaurant. Roughly $235 per night off season; $275 per night peak season. HotelStFrancis.com. 210 Don Gaspar Ave, Santa Fe, NM 87501, (505) 983-5700.

DINING

The Shed. Two-minute walk from the Plaza. Classic northern New Mexican. Nice, big, usually busy, surprisingly affordable. 113 1/2 E Palace Ave, Santa Fe, NM 87501, (505) 982-9030. SFShed.com

Plaza Cafe. West side of the Plaza. Diner with northern New Mexican. 54 Lincoln Ave, Santa Fe, NM 87501, (505) 982-1664. PlazaCafeDowntown.com.

Del Charro. Five-minute walk from the Plaza. Bar and grill. Affordable, nice enough but not fancy. Open late. 101 W Alameda St, Santa Fe, NM 87501, (505) 954-0320. DelCharro.com.

San Francisco Street Bar and Grill. Southwest corner of the Plaza, second floor up the stairs. Pub/diner-esque food and drinks. 50 E San Francisco St, Santa Fe, NM 87501, (505) 982-2644. EatSanFranBarGrill.com.

THINGS TO DO / PLACES TO GO

10,000 Waves. Luxe spa and hot tubs. Worth the splurge. Hyde Park Road.
Santa Fe Railyard. Nice park plus the Farmer's Market, movie theater, REI, a few cool galleries and, on the far side, The Sage Inn and Whole Foods.
Train ride on the SkyRailway.com.
The Saint Francis Cathedral. Often with performances.
IAIA Museum. Opposite the street from the Cathedral.
Doodlets. Gift shop and toy store.
Georgia O'Keeffe Museum. Quintessential Santa Fe museum experience.
The Lensic. Book talks, music, dance, streamed live opera, and more.
Music on the Plaza. Some summer nights.
Travel Bug and **Collected Works.** Bookstores.

Taos: Lodging, Dining, Things to Do

LODGING

El Pueblo Lodge
14-minute walk from Taos Plaza. I've stayed here several times, including the first time I did the thru-hike. Has a pool and a good breakfast. Rooms have little kitchens; some have fireplaces. Takes dogs. Roughly $140 per night in off season (March); $160 per night peak season (August). https://ElPuebloLodge.com. 412 Paseo Del Pueblo Norte, Taos, NM 87571. (800) 433-9612.

The Historic Taos Inn
A four-minute walk from Taos Plaza. Ranges from under $150 per night during off season to as much as $280 per night on a weekend in peak season. TaosInn.com, 125 Paseo Del Pueblo Norte, Taos, NM 87571, (855) 961-1143.

Hotel Willa
Seven-minute walk from Taos Plaza. A new hotel. Has a pool and other amenities. Leans upscale. $300-$400 a night. Suites (no rooms). Dog-friendly. 233 Paseo del Pueblo Sur, Taos, NM 87571. email: info@hotelwilla.com.

Upscale: El Monte Sagrado
Nice splurge if you want to contrast being a dirty forest child with rolling into a luxe spa experience. Directly on the route of the thru-hike. They have breakfast, super-nice dinner, a big bar, a pool, on-site massage and spa, and yoga. They take dogs and have fireplaces in some rooms. 13-min walk from the Plaza. Roughly $190 per night off season; $420 per night peak season. ElMonteSagrado.com. 317 Kit Carson Rd, Taos, NM 87571, (575) 758-3502.

DINING / DRINKING

Manzanita Market. Directly off Taos Plaza. 8:30 am to 3 pm. Closed Sundays. Sandwiches, soups, salads, smoothies, and coffee/soda.

The Alley Cantina. One-minute walk from the Plaza. More bar than bar and grill, but a good place to wander into after a very long walk. Affordable. Open late. 121 Teresina Ln, 87571. (575) 758-2121. AlleyCantina.com.

Taos Mesa Brewing Taos Tap Room, aka "The Taos Brewery."
Want a beer after you finish the thru-hike? This is the go-to place to do that. Four-minute walk from the Plaza. Also has good food. 201 Paseo Del Pueblo Sur, 87571, (575) 758-1900. TaosMesaBrewing.com.

La Cueva Cafe. Affordable, tasty northern New Mexican. Nice staff. Outside seating. 135 Paseo Del Pueblo Sur, 87571, (575) 758-7001. LaCuevaCafe.com.

THINGS TO DO / PLACES TO GO

Kit Carson Park. May be renamed, but a nice place to hang out regardless of what it's called. Has music events. **Bent Street Shops.** Wander. Eat. Pick up a gift for the folks at home. **Couse-Sharp Historic Site** or **Kit Carson Museum** if you don't have a car. **Taos Pueblo** if you do.

Lodging and Dining and Things to Do along The High Road

LODGING

Hacienda de Chimayó
Lovely, quiet hotel with seven suites/rooms that include private baths and fireplaces. Closed Mondays. $90 to $120 a night. No dogs. No children under ten years old. RanchoDeChimayo.com/hacienda. 297 Juan Medina Rd, Chimayó, NM 87522. (505) 351-2222.

On the patio at Sugar Nymphs Cafe.

Casa Escondida
A bed and breakfast very close to Chimayó. Takes dogs. Nine rooms. Up to queen-sized beds. Roughly $135+ per night in off season; $220 per night peak season. *You must stay at least two nights in peak season*. CasaEscondida.com. 64 Co Rd 100, Chimayó, NM 87522, (505) 351-4805.

DINING

Sugar Nymphs Cafe. Delicious and affordable. Dine in or takeout. Closed Tuesdays. 15046 NM-75, Peñasco, NM 87553, (575) 587-0311. SugarNymphs.com.

Rancho de Chimayó. Classic, classy, award-winning northern New Mexican. Big expansive ranch-style spread, and right by Santuario de Chimayó, Hacienda de Chimayó (listed above), and Ortega's and Trujillo's Weaving Shops. All that plus this being pretty close to halfway between Taos and Santa Fe makes Chimayó an ideal place to stop if you want to break up the drive or just linger a little. 300 Juan Medina Rd, Chimayó, NM 87522, (505) 351-4444. RanchoDeChimayo.com.

Tesuque Village Market. Good food on the way out of Santa Fe. The real draw here is the atmosphere and the possibility of seeing a celebrity. There is a small grocery store here. 138 Tesuque Village Road, Santa Fe, NM 87506 (505) 988-8848. TesuqueVillageMarket.com.

THINGS TO DO / PLACES TO GO

Sipapu. Skiing in the winter. Fishing and hiking and a good place to stop or stay for the night in the summer.

Many trailheads. Excellent hiking from Trampas Medio Campground. Take Forest Road 207 off County Road 76. Also consider **Santa Cruz Lake** and **Nambe Lake Falls Recreation Area**.

Flora and Fauna You Might Meet Along the Way

I've included a few simple descriptions of animals and plants you may see or want information about. If you want dramatically better descriptions, photographs, species reports, and more, go to the New Mexico Department of Fish and Game's "Species Search" page: https://bison-m.org/SuperSearch.aspx.

Bear. Black bears, not brown bears (aka grizzly bears). We used to have grizzly bears in the Pecos, but we killed the last one in 1923. While there are still black bears around, there aren't a lot of them. Do use a bear hang and don't keep food in your tent. But, please: Don't worry about the bears. I have been hiking in these woods for 20 years and have seen *one* bear. I do still carry bear mace, just in case, but also because it can be useful against more than bears. I bring bear mace when I'm out solo, or out for more than three nights. Grizzly bear mace is best because it has a longer range (40 ft) and has 2% capsaicin. It is heavy: You'll add 15 oz to your pack weight if you bring the full-size, 10.2 oz Counter Assault Bear Deterrent Spray. Skip the human-grade pepper spray; it's not strong enough and won't reach far enough.

Beaver. The beavers are awesome. Any creature that can take a trickle of a stream and make it into a wet area the size of a football field has my support. You'll see beaver sign around Forest Road 438 and Rio Chiquito in Carson National Forest.

Bighorn sheep. You probably will see a few bighorn sheep, especially around Truchas Lakes. The females are not aggressive and may beg for food. Do not feed them. The males can be aggressive. As mentioned elsewhere in this book, the males will defend what they perceive as their turf. They will go after a dog or even a human if they feel threatened. Manage your dog.

Bighorn sheep may try to get into tents. They crave salt—so much so that they'll try to get it from sweaty backpack straps. Keep your tent zipped.

Bobcat. These are cool-looking and nothing to worry about. They don't get much bigger than 30 lbs.

Cows. Will there be a day when we can have "wilderness" without cows? I hope so.

Coyotes. You're likely to hear them, even if you never see them. Some

Bighorn ewes begging for food.

are pretty big. Yet another reason to keep your dog under control, but don't worry about them bothering a human.

Deer. Mule deer are common. There's not too much to say about them beyond a) Don't try to feed them b) Control your dog and c) In hunting season, where there are deer, there will be hunters.

Elk. Elk were extirpated (hunted to extinction, like we did to the grizzly bears) in New Mexico by 1909, but we managed to bring them back, reintroducing herds starting in 1911.

The range for elk near the thru-hike route is generally from about Stewart Lake north. Unfortunately, I see far fewer of them than I did a decade ago. But it is possible you'll see one, or even a herd of them. Having elk around means there are elk hunters around. If you're out in the fall, it's a real good idea for both you and your dog to wear bright colors.

Marmot. Marmots are like large, vocal gophers that live at high altitudes. We don't have a lot of them, but there are some along Skyline Trail, south of Truchas Lakes. They will "bark" a warning sign at you. I did have a marmot near Wheeler Peak walk right up to me, clearly expecting to be fed. I haven't seen the marmots on the thru-hike do this yet. If they start, do not feed them.

Mountain lion. It is highly, *highly* unlikely you will encounter a mountain lion, but they are around. Every three years or so, a dog gets attacked by a mountain lion in the hills just north of Santa Fe. If you encounter a mountain lion (again, extremely unlikely), and get attacked (even more extremely unlikely), the best course of action is to fight back.

Mountain lions are not afraid of people, so you're going to have to be super-aggressive. Kick, hit, yell for all you're worth. But if your dog's life was on the line, you would probably do that anyway. All that said, really: Seeing a mountain lion is spectacularly unlikely. If you do see one, please tell me about it, because I have never been lucky enough to see one. Despite how rare sightings are, keep your dog close and under control, and maybe even on a leash.

Rabbit. We have two types of rabbits: Jackrabbits and cottontails. Jackrabbits are much larger and faster. They tend to stay in the foothills. Cottontails also stick to the lower elevations.

Salamander. Many of the alpine lakes either have salamanders or trout. The salamanders look like axolotls at first glance, but they are actually neotenic tiger salamanders. The "neotenic" aspect is interesting; these salamanders never leave their larval stage, in that they never lose their gills and grow lungs. But they do become sexually mature and can reproduce.

BIRDS

Blue grouse. About the same size and shape as chickens, but with a distinctly more camouflaged look. You will probably spook at least a couple of them while you're out.

Clarkson's jay. These look like blue jays in terms of size and shape, but they're gray and white. If you stand still with food in your hand, like a nut or a cracker, they may land on your hand to grab a snack.

Raven. Western ravens are more tolerant of humans than eastern ones, so you're likely to see a few. Ravens are larger than crows and have more hooked beaks.

Clarkson's jay, also begging.

Woodpeckers. You will almost certainly hear or see a few woodpeckers. They've got ample food with all the bark beetles. There are three kinds: the Red-Headed woodpecker (the whole head is red), Lewis's Woodpecker (the area around its beak is red and it has a pink breast) and the Acorn Woodpecker (the back of its head is red).

TREES

Cottonwood, including Rio Grande, narrowleaf and Fremont. These are the huge deciduous trees that grow along streams and washes. Rio Grande and Fremont cottonwoods have wider, almost triangle-shaped leaves.

Douglas-fir. Identifiable by the "mouse tails" or flag-like pieces sticking out between the scales of the cones. Their twigs and needles used to be a coffee substitute. Grow between 6,500 and 9,500 ft elevation.

Gambel oak (aka shrub oak). These are small or mid-sized trees, almost always growing in close stands between 5,000 and 8,000 feet elevation. Their acorns are edible for wildlife. These may not

tolerate rising temperatures well.

Pinyon pine. These evergreens are one of the key elements in "pinyon-juniper" habitat, which is the dry, sparse forest with mid-sized trees around 5,000 to 7,000 feet elevation. Pinyon trees produce the coveted and edible pinyon seeds and have short, stiff needles.

Ponderosa pine. These are the very large, 40+ foot tall pines with often perfectly straight trunks, long needles, and 5+ inch cones. When the Spanish arrived around 1540, they logged ponderosas for ship masts.

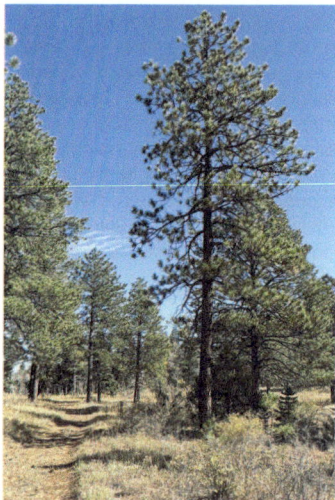
Ponderosa pine.

One-seed juniper. These grow in the same areas as the pinyons, and are also small to medium shrubby-looking evergreen trees. Female junipers have small, dark blue, dusty-looking berries. Junipers have flexible, shorter "needles" that look more like scales. Their roots can be up to 200 ft long—the second longest in the world.

Spruce, including Engelmann spruce, and White spruce. These make up the largest net volume, biomass, and basal area per acre on forest land by forest type in the Santa Fe National Forest. Blue spruce you'll recognize as looking like a Christmas tree. Engelmann spruce are much larger, growing up to 100 feet high or more, and tend to be at high elevations or in wet canyons. Spruce-fir refers more to the type of forest, much like "pinyon-juniper" refers to the lower elevation forests in this area.

Quaking aspen. These are the iconic deciduous trees with round leaves and white and black bark. Aspen groves are considered one organism because each tree is a genetic replicant of the others.

White fir. Can be as tall as 135 feet, with gray bark that is brown underneath. They have flat needles one to three inches long. Their cones are two to four inches long and fairly smooth and tube-shaped.

PLANTS & WILD-FLOWERS

Balloon flower. Purple blooms about 1 to 1.5 inches wide, with five petals growing on one- to two-foot-high plants. Likes hot and dry soil up to 10,000 ft elevation. Often grows in or on the edge of fields.

Blue flag iris. These grow in damp spots in fields, even above 10,000 feet elevation. They bloom in early to mid-June.

Firecracker penstemon. Fire-engine red tubular blooms on multiple spikes coming from a cluster of basal leaves. Grows in hot, dry soils from 6,500 to 9,500 ft elevation. One

of over a hundred types of penstemons that grow in New Mexico.

Indian paintbrush. Bright red, 9- to 18-inch wildflower that grows in dry areas at pretty much any elevation. The flowers look almost like modified leaves.

Kinnikinnick. A densely growing evergreen groundcover with rounded shiny leaves about 1/2 inch long. Has white flowers that turn into red berries that wildlife eat. Grows from 7,000-12,000 feet elevation.

Parry's mountain gentian. Purplish-blue, goblet-shaped blooms with white centers on plants 3 to 16 inches tall. Typically has three or so blooms at a time per plant. Blooms from July to September. Grows at 8,500-12,000 feet.

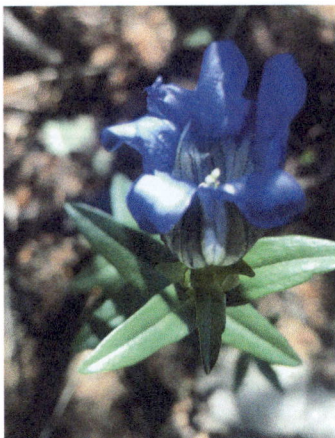

Parry's Mountain Gentian.

Purple verbena. Low growing, almost groundcover, light purple flowers in rounded clusters about one to four inches wide in hot, dry areas. Common around the Dale Ball Trails area in Santa Fe.

Sacred datura. 4- to 6-inch white, trumpet-like blooms that grow out of vine-like, 2- to 3-foot high mounds of leaves in dry areas, usually at or below 7,500 ft.

White yarrow. 1-3 foot tall perennial herb, with fern-like leaves and rounded clusters of 20-30 tiny white blooms with even smaller yellow stigmas. A yellow version is grown extensively in xeric gardens. Grows up to 12,000 ft elevation.

Woods rose. Bright pink flowers about two inches wide with yellow centers. Grows from one to six feet tall, but rarely more than four or five feet, often in the understory below tall trees. Flowers become red hips in fall; leaves turn rust-red. Typically grows in thickets at 5,500 to 10,000 feet elevation.

Yerba mansa. A six- to ten-inch perennial herb that grows in wet soil or on the edge of bogs up to 10,000 feet elevation. Will have about a half dozen white flowers that appear from March to September coming out of a tight cluster of basal leaves.

Yerba mansa.

Trout

There are four types of trout here: German browns, brook trout, rainbow trout, and Rio Grande cutthroats. The native cutthroats are the fish we want to protect the most. Their markings vary, and they can interbreed with other trout, but look for their pink or rose-colored belly, bottom fins, or sides. They also have an increasing number of spots closer to their tails. Do not keep a cutthroat if you catch one. It's taken a lot of work to keep them off the endangered species list. All of the other types, especially German browns, are okay to keep and eat. German browns tend to not be as rose-colored and have larger and more dispersed brown spots. German browns also tend to push out the native cutthroats, so trimming their numbers a little is fine.

You'll have both lake fishing and creek fishing along the route of the thru-hike. Lake Katherine and Lake Stewart are big draws for fishers, as is Lake Johnson (if you're okay with climbing over the fallen trees to get to it). Spirit Lake, Nambe Lake, Stewart Pond, Pecos Baldy Lake, Truchas Lakes, No Fish Lake, Indian Lake, La Cueva Lake, and Bernardin Lake have no fish. Any of the lakes that do have trout have them because they are stocked. You can find out where fish have been stocked at the NM Game and Fish Department: https://wildlife.dgf.nm.gov/fishing/weekly-report/.

You will need a fishing license. It's $25 annually. Get it online: https://www.takemefishing.org/new-mexico/fishing/fishing-license/.

The lakes are great, but streams are good, too. Larger rivers like the Pecos and Rio del Pueblo are fairly heavily fished. Rio Santa Barbara also gets fished a lot, but not quite as heavily. Even if you can't hike, you can drive close enough to all three of those rivers to find a fishing spot. Rio Chiquito also has a number of great spots that are close to where you can bring a car. Even Rio Fernando de Taos, which runs through El Nogal, has good fishing. Just go upriver from the dog activity.

If you can hike in a little, the smaller creeks like Panchuela Creek, Rio Grande del Rancho (aka "Little Rio Grande"), Winsor Creek, Rio de la Olla, Cave Creek, and Aqua Piedra Creek are good. The fish may be smaller, like six to eight inches, but they're quite plentiful. You have an especially nice opportunity to fish the upper branches of Rio Santa Barbara as you go through Section 3, and you could take a detour in the early part of Section 3 to fish the upper parts of the Pecos and its tributaries. Still, don't underestimate the smaller streams. I have seen nine-inch trout in some of the pools along Big Tesuque Creek. Even the Santa Fe River has trout, especially in the pools along the Corridor (S1-2).

As backpackers, we have an extra edge, because the little high-country streams don't get fished a lot. It doesn't take much more than a line, a dry fly, a hook, and some stealth to catch a fish.

I've walked into several trout fishing stores and asked to be set up to fish with just the most minimalistic basics and a budget of about $50. For tippet (line), I've been given Rio Products "Fluoroflex Strong" 4x, 7.3 lbs and Berkley Trilene XL Smooth Casting 4 lb. The experts also gave me Aquel floatant by Loon Outdoors. Put a few drops on your

14-inch trout in an alpine lake. Pecos Wilderness.

fingertips and smudge the fly with it so it's less likely to sink. For flies I was given a few Parachute Adams, two Beadhead San Juan Worms, a grasshopper and a few other things, all with super-tiny barbs on 14- or 16-size hooks.

If you bring a rod, make it short, like 6', and no more than 10'. 2-3 weight is good for a 6' rod; 4-5 weight works for a 10'. Tenkara rods are easy to fish with, collapse into 16-20 inches, and weigh only a few ounces. You can spend hundreds on one, or get a nice start with a $42 SeaQuest Tenkara Rod kit. Apparently the 6'9" Goture Red Fox practically has a fan club. Or just jerry-rig a long stick as a pole.

Casting can be tough along the brushy little streams, so some fishers adopt a "bow and arrow" style where they carefully hold and pull the hook, like a slingshot, then aim it to where they want the fly to go. Just don't hook yourself.

The Santa Fe to Taos Thru-Hike as an Organization

The mission of the Santa Fe to Taos Thru-Hike is to:

1. Raise awareness that the thru-hike exists; that people can hike from Santa Fe Plaza to Taos Plaza.
2. Get people excited enough about the thru-hike to consider doing it themselves, and to give them confidence that they can do it.
3. Give them enough information and resources so they can have a great time on the thru-hike.
4. Give people a positive experience of the wilderness so they will care enough about it to take ongoing, meaningful action to preserve it.

The Santa Fe to Taos Thru-Hike is a 501(c)(3) organization. Tax ID 93-3897864. To learn more about the thru-hike, go to SantaFeToTaos.org.

If you are interested in guided day hikes, overnights, and the full route, sign up for the newsletter: https://SantaFeToTaos.org/newsletter/.

As of this writing, the thru-hike is almost entirely self-funded. Please consider donating: SantaFeToTaos.org/donate/.

Become a Member

Members get access to the Tres Ritos resupply services and "wilderness store". Go to SantaFeToTaos.org/membership/ to learn more.

About the Author

Pam Neely has lived in Santa Fe for over 20 years. She began work on the thru-hike in 2015 and completed it all the way through for the first time in 2018. Since then she has refined the route many times. Even now, she is still exploring alternate routes between Santa Fe and Taos.

Acknowledgements

Huge thanks to all the supporters of this guidebook and of the thru-hike. Special thanks to:

- My husband, Robert Hoffman, who has listened to me talk about the thru-hike for possibly a thousand hours, including the time I woke him up in the middle of the night to tell him about the Sangre de Cristo Pea Clam Zoological Area. He's the handsome guy in the logo, too.
- My mother, Roselle Neely, for introducing me to the adventure of exploring forest roads, and for her financial support of this project. My father, James W. Neely Jr., for telling me I was good with maps.
- Minor Gordon for his years-long support and interest in this project. And for being a beta reader.

- **All the beta readers**: Bruce Katlin, Missy Lee, Andrew Peterson, Matt Bagwell, Cheyanne Warren, Kelsie Donleycott, and Paul Geimer. Your feedback helped enormously. **Thank you!**
- Francisco "Cisco" Guevara, Loren Bell, and Brad Higdon of Taos.
- Randy Randall, Tourism Director of Santa Fe, for supporting the project and offering to co-market it.
- James W. Neely III, for serving as a board member and being such a great brother.
- John White and Doug Scott for their correspondence and extensive experience in the field. I am grateful to have found fellow explorers.

Lower Truchas Lake, Pecos Wilderness, 2019.

Index

You Don't Need a Campfire

This is a map of the Luna Fire, which started October 17th, 2020. The Forest Service has determined the fire was caused by "an improperly built and/or extinguished campfire in a general forest area about one mile from the east end of the Rita de la Olla Trail."

It burned 10,142 acres.

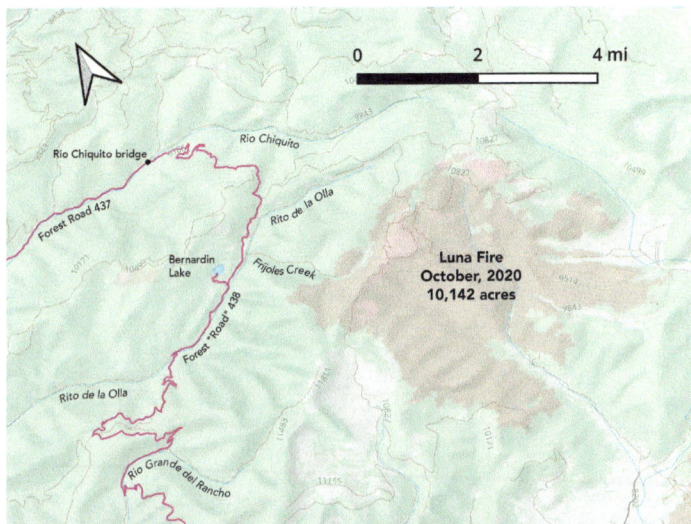

A small part of those 10,142 acres was where my dog Riley and I came through the first time we did the thru-hike in 2018. It was where I thrashed through a grove of hemlock trees, trying to stay on what the map showed as a trail. The hemlocks were thick; their branches cut into my hands and face. For a moment, I didn't think we'd make it through. Then Riley took off, and I tore myself out of the hemlocks and ran after him, terrified I'd lose him.

He brought me directly to Frijoles Creek, to someone's fishing spot along the Chile Waters there, marked with blue trail tape. Just beyond that, I noticed what looked like a gap in the trees. When I walked closer to it, I found the trail I was looking for.

That all burned in the Luna Fire.

Santa Fe and Carson National Forest Service personnel find hundreds of campfires still burning every year. Put yours out.

If you must have a campfire at all, keep it small. Use wood small enough to break with your hands. Put the fire out before you go to sleep. Put the fire out by pouring at least two liters of water on it, then stir the water and the embers with a stick, making what is called "campfire soup."

BV - #0041 - 061025 - C163 - 178/114/11 - PB - 9780989868211 - Gloss Lamination